UNSLUT

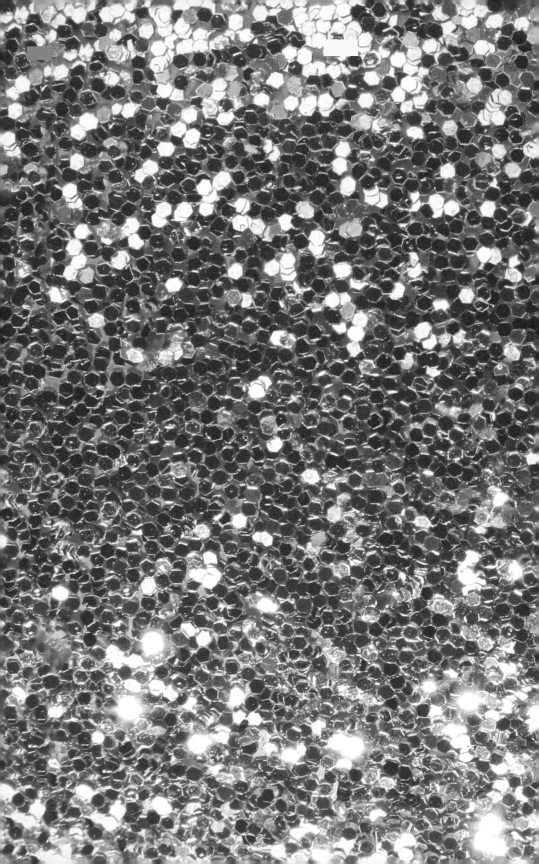

EMILY LINDIN

UNSLUT

A DIARY AND A MEMOIR

ZEST BOOKS

SAN FRANCISCO

CONTENTS

Connect with Zest!

- zestbooks.net/blog
- zestbooks.net/contests
- twitter.com/zestbooks
- facebook.com/BooksWithATwist

35 Stillman Street, Suite 121, San Francisco, CA 94107 | www.zestbooks.net

Manufactured in the U.S.A. | 4500565221 | DOC 10 9 8 7 6 5 4 3 2 1

FOREWORD

BY AMANDA HESS

A couple of years ago, I started noticing a curious refrain repeated again and again in stories about American teenagers. When two high school football players were convicted of sexually assaulting a girl in Steubenville, Ohio, the judge advised teenagers to be careful "how you record things on the social media so prevalent today." When a group of Virginia high school boys gleefully spread naked pictures of their female classmates through an Instagram "sexting ring," local cops warned the girls about the dangers of logging online. "Social media is destroying our lives," one sixteen-year-old girl sighed to *Vanity Fair* in 2013. Girls as young as eleven were competing to look sexy online, then branding other girls "sluts" for doing the same. "We're seeing depression, anxiety, feelings of isolation," a California youth counselor said of the young women she worked with. The culprits, she said, were Facebook, Instagram, and Ask.fm.

Something about this explanation didn't feel quite right to me. I had braved the middle school hallway at a time before texting. It was hellish then, too. Many of the teen terrors that were now being pinned on the Internet—sexual assault, bullying, and the pursuit of the perfect body—had been fixtures of the analog girl world I had inhabited. Now that I was all grown up, it felt as if my fellow adults were suffering from a kind of collective cultural amnesia. Maybe we had all repressed our most disturbing middle school memories. Or maybe it was just comforting to blame new gadgets for problems that had been plaguing us for generations. It's easier to confiscate a girl's iPhone than to cleanse society of sexism. And anyway, there had been no Twitter or Tumblr back when we were that age. Grown-ups had detailed records of what our teen lives had really been like.

Then I found Emily Lindin's blog. In 2013, twenty-seven-year-old Emily had dusted off her old middle school diary and started republishing the entries, verbatim and in chronological order, on a Tumblr called The UnSlut Project. Soon after, I discovered it and read it all in one sitting. In eleven-year-old Emily's world, Leonardo DiCaprio was the designated tween heartthrob. Limp Bizkit was the toast of *Total Request Live*. Tween boys gelled their hair into an inflexible shell that culminated in a ridge of spikes just above the forehead, and this was considered attractive. Hey: it was the late '90s. Except now, it was all online.

Clicking through Emily's Tumblr for the first time felt like exploiting a glitch in the space-time continuum. Here was a girl who chatted with friends on her *Clueless*-themed landline phone, slept in a bedroom plastered with Hanson posters, and could only access the Internet through a glacial dial-up modem that linked up to a free trial version of America Online. But her drama was thoroughly modern. Her sixth-grade "boyfriend" fed her whiskey and forced himself on her while his friend looked on. Her classmates decided that made her a bad girl. Unsourced rumors spread through notes and whispers. Boys told her to show them her boobs. Girls told her to kill herself. In her diary, Emily was naïve, precocious, a little nerdy, and totally sexually inexperienced. At school, she was the class "slut."

With each entry, Emily revealed another social antecedent for problems that we now like to think of as "online" issues. Before sexting, boys drew naked pictures of their female classmates on sheets of paper and passed them around. Before Facebook stalking, kids secretly eavesdropped on each other through three-way phone calls. Before texting, awkward middle schoolers enlisted friends to courier their love notes across the hall. Before cyberbullying, kids smiled in person then wheeled around and smeared each other with Machiavellian precision. Before Instagram, girls knew they were valued above all for the way they looked. Before Steubenville, boys figured out how to turn sexual assault into a team activity, goading one another into groping girls and directing one another's unwanted advances.

Watching Emily and her peers fumble through adolescence at the dawn of the social web, it's clear that our sexual bullying problem didn't originate online. The Internet just helped kick it to the next level. As soon as Emily logged onto AOL Instant Messenger for the first time, an anonymous user calling herself DieEmilyLindin casually messaged: "Hi Emily. Why haven't you killed yourself yet, you stupid slut?" But before AIM, Emily had been advised to commit suicide via a handwritten note. And before we started calling this stuff "the dark side of social media" or "the danger of the Internet," we called it drama, or dating, or just being a girl. In one entry, Emily watches *The Basketball Diaries*, a 1995 teen drama film starring—who else?—Leonardo DiCaprio, and says of herself: "I almost wish I had a screwed up life so I could be cool and record all of my thoughts." I feel so grateful to eleven-year-old Emily, who recorded all of her thoughts in her diary even though she couldn't recognize at the time just how screwed up her circumstances really were. And I'm in awe of adult Emily, who now has the tenacity to revisit these most intimate and painful experiences, and the wisdom to show us a new way of using the Internet—to fight back.

INTRODUCTION

BY EMILY LINDIN

In April 2013, I read a news story about a seventeen-year-old girl named Rehtaeh Parsons from Halifax, Nova Scotia. She had been allegedly gang-raped by her classmates, who took photos of the attack and spread them around her school and community. She was targeted as a "slut" as a result, and suffered constant bullying in school and online. Over the next year and a half, she transferred schools multiple times to try to escape her reputation. Unable to cope with the emotional trauma, she began using drugs and alcohol. After a year and a half, she made the decision to end her own life.

As tragic and terrifying as it was, Rehtaeh's wasn't the first story like this that I'd heard. Girls throughout the United States and Canada—Amanda Todd, Audrie Pott, Phoebe Prince, Felicia Garcia, to name a few of the many—have made the decision to commit suicide after relentless sexual bullying. Sometimes they are targeted after being the victim of sexual assault at the hands of their classmates. Sometimes the bullying follows their decision to engage in consensual sexual activity. Sometimes it's because of the way they dress. Sometimes it's because they developed breasts earlier than other girls. And sometimes, it's for absolutely no discernible reason at all—not that there's ever a justifiable reason for sexual bullying.

Sexual bullying doesn't always result in suicide. But it is a particularly devastating type of bullying for a young girl to endure regardless of how she reacts to it. That's because unlike victims of most other types of bullying, victims of sexual bullying usually can't turn to the adults in their life for support. A girl might fear that her parents, teachers, or community leaders will worsen the situation by accusing her of bringing the bullying upon herself by "asking for it" through her dress or behavior. And in many cases, her fears will be well-founded. The idea that girls are to blame for the abuse they receive is prevalent in the United States and Canada—and in many other countries we like to think of as relatively progressive when it comes to female sexuality and issues of women's equality—and it is cause for international concern. On an individual scale among teenagers and preteens, I refer to it as sexual bullying. On a larger, societal scale, the term "'slut' shaming" has become commonplace over the last few years. Ideas about what constitutes "slut" shaming vary: I define it as the implication that a girl or woman should feel inferior or guilty because of her sexual behavior, whether real or perceived.

My own interest in sexual bullying comes from personal experience. At the age of eleven, I was labeled the school "slut" by my classmates. For the next few years of my life, I was bullied incessantly at school, after school, and online. As you'll read, it started after my then-boyfriend "Zach" and I "went to third base." For us, that meant he put his hands down my pants in a clumsy imitation of what we had seen in movies like *Fear* (1996)—but that iconic roller coaster scene between Mark Wahlberg and Reese Witherspoon was nothing like our awkward, hardly sexual interaction as two eleven-year-olds in a friend's basement after school. Immediately after that afternoon, Zach and his friends spread rumors about me, and soon, it felt like everyone in our town knew about my reputation as a "slut." I also witnessed sexual bullying happen to my friends, sometimes even instigating or participating in the bullying myself. (One common misconception about bullying is that there are always defined bullies and victims. But it's becoming clearer and clearer that most of us, at different points in our lives, will play different roles in different bullying situations.) In the pages that follow, you'll read about how I struggled to navigate the constantly changing social scene of my middle school, alternately betraying friends and suffering betrayal, all with the stigma of living with the label "slut." At the time, I didn't feel comfortable confiding in my parents or in the other adults in my life.

But I kept a diary. Writing became a way for me to process my experiences. I wrote down conversations I had with classmates in exact detail—and printed out pages and pages of online conversations—so I could analyze what had happened and plan for future interactions. I wrote poetry because it made me feel like a serious, artsy person and because I wanted to believe that my feelings were reflective of some larger human experience. I wrote in a voice that alternated between that of the person I imagined I should be and that of the scared, selfish, curious girl I probably was. When each spiral-bound notebook was filled, I stashed it next to the last one in the bookcase in the back corner of my bedroom. I always knew the diaries were there; they'd catch my eye when I was visiting my parents during college vacation or, after graduating, from my new home across the country. But it wasn't until nearly fifteen years later, armed with what I hoped was enough emotional distance, that I piled the notebooks beside me on my childhood bed and opened the first one, dated 1997.

A few months later, I launched The UnSlut Project. I simply typed up those diary entries and posted them online as a way to contribute to the growing conversation surrounding "slut" shaming and its consequences. Soon, girls and women from all over the world started getting in touch with me, wanting to share their various experiences with "slut" shaming. Quickly, The UnSlut Project grew into an online community of shared stories, where girls who are currently suffering can find comfort in knowing they're not alone. At first, I was nervous about the idea of sharing such a personal experience in such a public forum. I didn't want to subject my family or the people mentioned in my diary to any pain or humiliation. My purpose was not to call anyone out for behavior that originally took place over a decade ago. For that reason, I launched the project under the pen name Emily Lindin and changed the names of my classmates and teachers, as well as all identifying information about them.

UnSlut: A Diary and a Memoir presents my diary, word for word, alongside the commentary of my current perspective. As a diary, it offers a limited narrative. What I wrote here is the truth, but it is my truth; the lives of my classmates, friends, and family are only represented through the filter of what I chose to write down as a preteen girl. It would not be fair to them to assume that this story is the entire story. Now, as a woman in my late twenties, I've tried to provide necessary context from the perspective I wish I had had back when I was keeping this diary, in the form of commentary accompanying each diary entry. I've greatly expanded this commentary from the version I first posted online as a blog, adding more details, perspective, and insight into what I chose not to include in the diary as a preteen. But even now, it cannot do justice to the life experiences of the people whose stories are woven into mine.

In publishing this diary, I don't claim to speak for all girls who suffer from sexual bullying. I come from a background of privilege: I was born to white, affluent parents and attended a prestigious public school in New England. It was in large part due to these privileges that I was able to overcome the emotional burden of my reputation, by focusing on academic work and enrolling in extracurricular activities that allowed me to define myself as something other than a "slut." That's why The UnSlut Project, as a growing online community (www.unslutproject.com), focuses on encouraging all women to come forward and share their stories, whether they have been victims, witnesses, or instigators of sexual bullying. If you or someone in your life can relate to these experiences, or if you want to learn more about the larger issues of "slut" shaming, sexual assault, and self-harm, be sure to check out the Resources section at the back of this book.

My story is not unique. It's not an exaggeration to say that throughout recorded history, across many religions and cultures, girls have continuously been shamed and scorned for their sexuality, which is often seen as inappropriate at best and evil at worst. I just happened to cope with this reputation by writing about it in detail in my diary. I hope this diary can serve as a useful primary source for adults who are struggling to understand the experience of a girl who is sexually bullied, as well as a source of inspiration for girls who are currently suffering. I also hope that reading my diary will inspire conversations among people of all nationalities and backgrounds who might never have considered the issue of "slut" shaming at all and that soon, the word "slut" won't even make sense as an insult.

CAST OF CHARACTERS

(ALL NAMES HAVE BEEN CHANGED)

ME

Emily: I was among the tallest and most physically developed of my female classmates. For much of middle school, I wore braces on my teeth and spent about an hour each morning carefully styling my bangs (which I had cut to hide the smattering of zits on my forehead). I had a reputation as the school "slut."

THE POPULAR GIRLS[1]

Catherine: I didn't have a close relationship with Catherine, but I knew I wanted her to like me. She was quick to laugh, whether pleasantly or cruelly, so her face was often slightly red.

Emma: People in our class generally found Emma to be funny and cute, but at the time I always had the sense that she had something of a malicious streak—she talked about people behind their backs, for example.

Hailey: I'm sure Hailey had a lot going on, but I only remember her as bolstering the "popular" girls' group by giggling at everyone else's jokes and rolling her eyes when appropriate.

Hannah: Hannah was thin, blonde, and, in my opinion as a middle school student, excessively cool. I always assumed that whichever boy I had a crush on would prefer to date Hannah over me.

Jenna: Jenna, like me, was the target of "slut" shaming in middle school. She, too, had developed physically before most of the other girls. We never bullied each other directly, but our relationship vacillated between one of supportive friendship and one of cool indifference.

1. Being a "popular" girl was not, by any means, a permanent status at my school. Your popularity depended on the overlap of many factors, including which girls admired you; which boys had a crush on you; your perceived confidence among your peers; and complete, utter, inexplicable chance. As far as I can tell, it didn't necessarily have to do with being typically pretty or having rich parents, as many movies about preteens and teenagers in the 1990s would have you believe.

Kaylee: I saw Kaylee as competition for boys' attention, so our friendship was always tenuous. I envied her lean, athletic body and the way she managed to flirt with boys at parties and then play soccer with them at recess the next day.

Lisa: I was never close friends with Lisa, but I always wanted to impress her. She came from a wealthy family and even as a preteen, she had mastered the art of appearing not to care what others thought of her.

Steph: Steph and I became best friends when our families moved to town before the start of fifth grade. We bonded immediately as the "new girls," but by the middle of sixth grade, I saw Steph as leading the sexual bullying against me and ruining my social life.

THE LESS POPULAR GIRLS

Erin: Erin was tiny and full of energy. I never considered her one of my best friends, but we were often caught up in the same drama. She had an older brother who protected her by threatening to beat up anyone who bullied her.

Gina: I thought of Gina as a good friend, but I also took her friendship for granted and I often ignored her feelings. She didn't have much self-confidence and she often went along with whatever I said I wanted to do.

Laura: Laura was beautiful and kind, and she got along with most people, including the "popular" girls. She and I often had crushes on the same boys, but I trusted her.

Maggie: Loyal and agreeable, Maggie was often unknowingly caught up in drama she had no interest in. She was the oldest of four siblings, but I often thought of her as a little sister, partly because she was physically much smaller than I was.

Melanie: I don't remember exactly how we became friends, but Melanie's patient support was one of the reasons I survived middle school. Despite living with unhappy, troubled parents, Melanie was precocious and quite wise for her age. She is still one of my best friends and favorite people.

Michelle: Michelle's was one of a handful of Jewish families in our town. Despite her loyalty, I never valued her friendship. She was slightly socially awkward and was treated poorly by most of our peers.

Shauna: I became friends with Shauna through Melanie, since they had lived on the same street their whole lives. I rarely spent time with Shauna one-on-one, but I loved hanging out at her house because her mother was hardly ever home and she had an awesome trampoline.

Stacy: I considered Stacy one of my closest friends, but I saw her as being less mature than I was and I often lost patience with her. Beyond that, I sexually bullied her and joined in when others made fun of her.

THE POPULAR BOYS[1]

Hunter: Hunter was handsome, confident, and physically more mature than most of the other boys in our class. I never had an interest in dating him because I found him intimidating.

Jacob: Jacob was small for his age but he carried himself with the nonchalant swagger that was typical of his "skater boy" persona. Most of the girls in my class found him physically attractive, but what really drew me to him was his thoughtful manner of conversation. I guess he was probably a good listener, but it's possible he was just really good at maintaining eye contact.

Matt: I saw Matt as the mastermind behind the conflicts in my social life. He was cruel in a charming way that made him magnetic and pop-

1. I have no idea what made boys "popular." Being funny? Good at sports? All the "popular" boys at my school had a lot of self-confidence, but it's hard to say whether that came from being popular or whether they were popular because they were self-confident.

ular, kind of like a young Daniel Tosh. He also had access to alcohol, cigarettes, and drugs—or at least he wanted people to believe he did—so I thought of him as impossibly cool and mysterious.

Ryan: I never knew Ryan very well, but he was often peripherally involved in sexually bullying me. He was soft-spoken and cynical, and he never seemed to take anything very seriously.

Tyler: Tyler's family had moved to town from England, so despite not really having an accent himself, he had an exotic appeal to me. He was one of the few boys I thought of as my intellectual equal, so I desperately wanted his approval.

Zach: Zach was the first boy I kissed. Our on-and-off relationship and the rumors he spread about me were the cause of most of my stress in middle school. I always blamed Zach for encouraging others to label me a "slut."

THE LESS POPULAR BOYS

Daniel: I never thought of Daniel in a romantic way, but he was always making sexual jokes and had a knack for steering group conversations toward my sexuality. I could never tell if he thought of me as a friend or if he just got a kick out of making me uncomfortable.

James: Perhaps in part because he had two older sisters, James was uniquely empathetic when I was being sexually bullied. Despite the rare occasions when he participated in "slut" shaming me, I still trusted him and valued our friendship. He is someone who I hope will recognize himself in this diary; I'm not sure he ever knew how much I cared about him or our friendship.

Louis: With bright orange hair and covered in freckles, Louis was an adept class clown. He also made a point of being brutally honest, a quality I admired in him, but that meant he often said things that were plain mean.

Mark: Mark was serious and intense. I don't believe his behavior was intentionally threatening toward me, but for some reason I didn't feel empowered to dictate the terms of our physical relationship when we were dating.

Nathan: I thought of Nathan as beautiful, mysterious, and wise. I loved getting attention from him, but I never felt comfortable around him, even when we were dating. We lost touch when he went to a private school, but years later he came back into my life when, in a strange coincidence, he started dating my college roommate. They dated until we were all well into our twenties and I got to know Nathan as a hilarious and smart adult.

Scott: Scott was agreeable in a way that, to many of his middle school peers, must have made him seem like a "follower" or a "poser." I felt bad for Scott because people dismissed him as goofy and unimportant, but at the same time, I dismissed him myself.

Steven: I dated Steven throughout high school, and our relationship was partly responsible for undoing my reputation as a "slut." As the youngest of six brothers, Steven was incredibly easy-going and well liked by pretty much everyone. He won "Most Likely to Be Approved by Your Parents" in our high school yearbook; in contrast, I won "Most Argumentative." We stayed close friends throughout college but lost touch when I moved across the country.

THE OLDER KIDS

Aaron: During sixth grade, Aaron's friendship meant a lot to me because he was the only eighth-grade boy who defended me against bullies and who seemed to like me for my personality, despite my reputation. We lost touch when he went to a private high school the next year, and soon after he came out as gay.

Alicia: I first met Alicia through my sister, who was two years ahead of me in school and one year ahead of Alicia. Alicia had beautiful long hair and a laid-back attitude that made her irresistible to the boys we both liked. We lived just down the street from each other, which made it awkward when she decided she didn't want to be my friend anymore.

Amanda Collins: For much of my middle school career, "Amanda Collins"—never just "Amanda"—represented everything I was afraid of. She had a reputation as a "slut" before I did, and I always thought of her as a sexual threat to my relationship with Zach. I never got to know her outside that context.

Andrew: As the oldest boy of the only African-American family in our town, Andrew was somewhat revered by Chris Walker and his other peers who were drawn to what they understood to be "black culture." His younger sister was in my class and, like most of my classmates, disliked me, but I was never sure how Andrew felt about me. Sometimes he intervened when Chris Walker sexually harassed me, but not all the time.

Chris Walker: I don't know anything about Chris Walker's home life, but whatever he was going through imbued him with a violent temper and a creepy disposition. I saw him as dangerous—not in a way someone might find sexy or attractive, but in a way that was truly scary.

'll get married and go to
honeymoon, unless you w
ere else, like Disney Wo
think Europe would be
? we'll travel the wor
money, but we bothe
of course, and then we'll
s and have three kids nar
~~████~~, and ~~████~~ ~~████~~
~~████~~, but of
go by his middle name s
~~████~~, with no midd
e name really sounds goo
~~████~~, ~~████~~ being spelled
that way is just so muc

SIXTH GRADE[1]

1. My town had two elementary schools and only one middle school, so sixth grade was a time of social upheaval. All of a sudden, our class size doubled, and we were introduced to a whole slew of new potential friends (and potential enemies). I had just moved to this town, an upper-middle-class, almost completely white suburb of Boston, from a regular-middle-class, also almost completely white suburb of Boston the year before. The main difference between the two towns, as far as I could tell at age eleven, was that people in my old town did not pronounce the letter r and that people in my new town made fun of me when I slipped up and spoke that way by accident.

NOVEMBER 21, 1997

There was a dance tonight! Word had gotten around that Lisa liked Matt, even though she was still going out with Tyler, technically.[1] When the first slow song came on, Lisa and Matt were dancing together, and his hands weren't on her waist, they were on her hips, even though they're both dating other people.[2]

Then everyone was like, "Oh, Zach and Emily, dance together!"[3]

He put his hands on my shoulders and I put my hands around his neck and we just kind of swayed. Finally, he tentatively placed his hands on my waist and I sucked in my stomach the whole time. It was exhausting. We kept swaying and talked a little bit, but didn't look at each other. When the song was over, he ran away.

Later, we were all standing around outside the gym. I was talking to Kaylee and she turned to Zach and I heard her whisper, "Kiss her!" Then Kaylee sat down on a bench, leaving Zach standing next to me, looking pretty uncomfortable. He grabbed my shoulders, turned me to face him, leaned over, and pressed his lips against mine quickly. His lips weren't really pursed enough. They were wet.[4]

He turned to Kaylee and said, "There! Did you see?"

She looked up from her Coke. "Huh?"

He sighed and went into the gym. I licked the part of my lips where he had kissed me. It tasted like sour apple because he had been eating an Airhead.[5] Toward the end of the dance, Stephanie and I were showing off dancing and I know I looked good.

1. Lisa was never one of my close friends—I don't think I ever went over to her house—but we often sat at the same lunch table and I remember feeling like she was someone I should be trying to impress. Matt was probably the most popular boy in our class and exerted an inordinate amount of control over his friends and, seemingly, everyone else I cared about. I didn't care very much about Tyler at this point, but I would later.

2. Given what dancing typically looked like when I was in middle school—awkward mutual swaying at a safe arm's distance away from each other—this whole hands-on-hips-instead-of-waist thing was *especially* scandalous.

3. Zach was my new boyfriend. He played drums in the middle school band and I "played" the flute—although I never got very good because I spent most of rehearsal spinning around in my front-row chair to catch a glimpse of Zach as he stared off into space in the back row, waiting for his chance to smash the cymbals. After months of yearning for him, I had finally caught his attention, and this was our first dance as an official couple.

4. So much of what we did—dancing, kissing—was at the behest of our classmates. I'm not convinced any of us actually enjoyed the romantic activities themselves—we just felt pressured to put on a show for people who, for some reason, seemed to care.

5. If you don't know what an Airhead is, you can safely consider yourself gastronomically superior to those of us who grew up gnawing on these rubbery sugar-sticks.

Zach told me so, too. He said, "You're good."[1]

Once we had stopped dancing, Zach said, "Emily." He bent his head down to the ground and I copied him. He laughed and covered his face with his hands and said, "God, I don't know how to ask you this." I smiled. I knew what he was going to ask me. He was going to ask me if I wanted to go to second base. I know because we had been discussing the possibility for like, a week.[2] But Steph grabbed my arm and pulled me away, so Zach never got to ask me.

Before I knew it, the dance was over and Steph, Nathan, Zach, and I were hanging around in the hall while the chaperones cleaned up. Nathan was like, "You guys gotta kiss."

And we were like, "I know."[3]

Zach said, "We can't do it right here—there are all these people around! Let's go outside."

There was a big group of our friends hanging around the door outside. There is a little corner right when you come out of the door, and that's where we stood. Zach was chewing on something, I think a sour apple Airhead. He finished chewing it, leaned forward, and kissed me. At first, both our mouths were closed, and I thought that was all it was going to be. But then his tongue slid into my mouth and I opened my mouth and our tongues kind of twisted around together. His tongue tasted like sour apple.[4]

Another person's tongue feels incredibly weird when you touch it with your own. I don't remember where either of our hands were, but I know he did not touch my ass or either of my boobs. It was Zach who ended the kiss by giving me a wet, pucker-up

1. I really *wasn't* good at dancing. At all. I'm still pretty terrible, and if I'm being honest, I blame my lack of improvement on the false confidence Zach's compliment gave me all those years ago.

2. The "bases" metaphor for sexual activity varies by region. For us, it worked like this: first base = French kissing; second base = hands on breasts (with the possible variations "over the shirt" or "under the shirt"); sloppy second = mouth on breasts; third base = hands on genitals; sloppy third = oral sex; home run or all the way = intercourse. I know. *I'm* not the one who made this stuff up.

3. Thank goodness this type of communal investment in whether or not two people kiss doesn't extend beyond middle school. It probably stems from everyone feeling curious and nervous about sexuality all of a sudden; pressuring other people to kiss was a way for us to experiment and learn vicariously.

4. He really needed to lay off those Airheads.

kiss on the corner of the mouth and saying, "Bye."

I lost him in a group of people, but I heard him say, "I did! Ask her. Emily, didn't I?" His best friend Matt looked doubtingly toward me. I nodded. Zach grinned triumphantly.[1]

That dance was even better than the last one, where Zach kissed me on the cheek. You see, then we were just little fifth-graders and kissing on the cheek was all we knew how to do. Or wanted to do, for that matter.

But now we're in sixth grade, and we can French-kiss, maybe even go to second, and perhaps third base. But not sex. Definitely not sex, not until I am at least fourteen. Matt has had sex. He has also fingered a tenth-grader—that's why I'm so worried about Lisa liking him.[2]

I can't wait until the next dance, if Zach and I are still going out. I hope we will be.

NOVEMBER 23, 1997

It's cool how when you kiss someone, everything works out so perfectly. Your mouths open at precisely the right time and you both lean toward each other just the right amount. And your open lips fit together like puzzle pieces. It's strange to think how Zach's mouth fit together with mine. He *wanted* to kiss me.

Before I had my first kiss, I was thinking that I would remember exactly what happened, each movement of our tongues, every turn of the head. But when the time actually came, I couldn't remember anything. And then he ended it with a sloppy peck on the corner of my mouth that got all crusty

1. So I guess we fulfilled our social obligation!

2. In hindsight, this might have been completely untrue. I don't know of any fifteen-year-old girls who would get involved sexually with an eleven-year-old boy. But the idea that he might make up something like that in order to impress his friends speaks to how different it is for boys and girls when it comes to sexual rumors.

not long after. It normally would be disgusting to have crusty spit next to your mouth, but it wasn't, because it was someone else's spit. And that someone else was Zach.[1]

You know how on TV shows and movies sometimes when people are kissing, they pull away and say, "You're suffocating me!"?[2] Well, the truth is, you can breathe while you're kissing someone. Through your nose.

Now that I think of it, I am quite curious as to where Zach's hands were during the kiss. Maybe on my waist, maybe on the back of my neck, but more than likely just hanging there stupidly at his sides. And I'd like to remember where my hands were, too. I hope not doing anything embarrassing while my mind was concentrating on more important things.[3]

DECEMBER 2, 1997

Today at lunch, I was sitting next to Zach and the rest of the group was kind of crowded around the area. Steph was absent again. Nathan was acting weird, pretending to be gay with Zach. Everyone was cracking up.[4] Zach kept leaning closer to me, and I got the shivers. I can't imagine what it would be like to not be going out with him, to not know that he likes me more than any other girl.

Jacob whispered something softly to Zach, and he had to repeat it: "Slap Emily's ass when she stands up." I pretended not to have heard, but I gave Jacob a suspicious look and he smiled sheepishly.

Zach whispered back to him, "No... not in school." I wonder if he would have slapped my ass when I stood up if we weren't in school.[5]

1. Still disgusting.

2. No, I don't know! What TV shows and movies was I referring to? I really can't remember, but it sounds like they were about sexual assault rather than consensual make-out sessions.

3. *What should I do with my hands?* is a question that confounds me to this day. If someone happens to figure out what I should be doing with my hands—just in general—I hope they'll let me know.

4. One thing about my middle school self that really embarrasses me is my passive, unquestioned homophobia. We laughed when two boys feigned physical intimacy together, since it seemed beyond the realm of possibility that either of them might actually *be* gay.

5. Right? A better answer would have been, "No... Emily's body is not an object that exists for my entertainment as her boyfriend, let alone for *your* entertainment as a bystander."

In Gym class, I learned from Hannah that she and Hunter were in a fight because Hunter had told Matt that Hannah looks good naked. Except he has never seen her naked. Obviously Matt told everyone, and now everyone thinks Hannah is a slut.[1] She kept commenting on how cute Jacob is—he is cute—and asked me to ask him out for her after Gym.

I did, and he said, "Yeah… I dunno."

Matt is having a birthday party two weekends from now.[2] He is inviting his girlfriend Lisa… yeah, that happened… his friends, and his friends' girlfriends. Except for me, because he hates me.[3]

Lisa said he was going to invite me, but I kind of blew it. Today, a guy came in to talk to us about the dangers of smoking. He had had his voice box removed. Afterward, Matt came up to my locker and said, "What's wrong? You look sad."

I shrugged and asked him, "Are you going to quit smoking?"

He glared at me for a long time before answering, "I never started." I looked at him like I doubted that, and he snapped, "Shut the fuck up, Emily."

Crap.[4]

DECEMBER 8, 1997

Yesterday I was walking to my bus and I saw Aaron. He is in eighth grade and is friends with Zach, and I guess he thinks he's friends with me, too, because when I saw him he put out his hand for me to give him a high five. When I slapped it, he held onto my hand, even though we were moving in different directions, so I thought my arm would break off.

People say Aaron goes out with girls just to

1. Crazy how that works, huh? Your boyfriend lies about having seen you naked, and *you* get labeled a slut.

2. If this seems like a long time out to plan a party, consider that this was before social media (so no Facebook invites) and we all lived with our parents, so we had to work around their schedules.

3. I never knew why, but from the moment I started dating his best friend, Matt made it abundantly clear that he hated me. He might have been jealous that Zach wanted to spend time with me instead of with him. Or our personalities might have just clashed in some way I wasn't really aware of.

4. Matt was going through some intense emotional struggles. The year before—just before I'd moved to this town, in fact—his father had been murdered by a notorious white-collar gangster. It was perceived by most of the adults in our town as a gruesome stain on our affluent area's otherwise peaceful outward appearance; nobody ever spoke of it, as far as I knew. If anything, Matt and his siblings were treated with suspicion, as if the circumstances surrounding their father's death had marked them as embarrassing at best and dangerous at worst. All this was unbeknownst to me in sixth grade. I could only grapple with Matt's actions on my own limited terms.

get somewhere and then dumps them. It's not like I'd ever dump Zach to go out with Aaron anyway, though.

Today I saw Aaron talking to Zach and I wanted a reason to go over there. I just asked Aaron some dumb question, but he grabbed my hand and started playing with my fingers. Steph popped up out of nowhere and was like, "You'd better stop that—her boyfriend's right there." I didn't see how Zach reacted.

At least I know that if Zach dumps me and I want to hook up, I can go to Aaron and he'll sleep with me if I want him to. Which I don't. Because I am not a slut.[1]

DECEMBER 10, 1997

Today at lunch, I heard a loud crash, like a chair clattering to the ground. I looked to where it came from and saw Zach on his knees, punching this random kid named Alex, who was lying on the ground. My first thought was that he might be embarrassed for me to see him fight, so I turned away and covered my face.[2]

But eventually I got curious and turned back to see what was happening: Ms. Covey was standing next to Zach with her hand on his shoulder. His shirt collar was all stretched out, almost off his shoulder, and he was glaring down at Alex. Then he, Ms. Covey, and Alex left the lunchroom, and things went back to normal.

I heard from Jacob that Zach had gotten suspended, so I went to the principal's office to see if I could find him before he was sent home. He was

1. I'm pretty sure sleeping with Aaron was never a real possibility in my mind. It's as if I wrote that in the persona of a girl much more experienced and confident than I was, as if I were speaking to someone I wanted to impress rather than writing in my (thankfully) nonjudgmental diary. Then I guess I was so embarrassed to have even written out that first thought—that I might have sex with Aaron to feel better about myself—that I felt compelled to vehemently deny it.

2. He *should* have been embarrassed for me to see him fight. But if he was fighting in public, the opposite was probably true: he most likely wanted me to watch. In our school, for boys and girls alike, saying you wanted to fight someone was just as much of a bullying tactic as actually fighting them. Since the former had no disciplinary consequences, there were many challenges and threats of physical fighting, but few actual fights. When they did happen, they were all anyone talked about for days.

sitting outside the office, looking bored.

"Do you know why I got in a fight with Alex?" he asked me. I didn't. "Alex called you a man, so I kicked him and he fell on the floor, and I beat the shit out of him."

So Zach beat someone up because they called me a man. Awesome...??[1]

Zach called today after school and we talked on the phone and watched the same shows on TV together. At one point I asked him, "Do you think I'm a slut?"

He said, "No. A slut will go anywhere with anyone, and the only person you've gone anywhere with is me. For instance, Amanda Collins is a slut." I didn't know that. "She went to third base with Aaron in the hall at school!" By the way, that is true.

Another thing that came up was Matt's party, the one I'm not invited to. I said, "Don't kiss anyone else while you're there."

"I won't."

"Don't touch anyone else, either. Don't lay a finger on another girl, okay?"

He laughed at me and said, "Okay, Crazy."

I love him![2] I love him for the person he is, not what he looks like, and I know that for a fact because he isn't even that cute.[3] It's weird that he'll be suspended from school tomorrow.

I'll have no reason to walk the long way to class, hoping to see him at his locker. I kind of like it that he beat up Alex in my defense. It's like he got suspended fighting for me.[4]

1. Not really. Since calling me a "man" would imply that Zach was gay for kissing me, this fight was probably more about Zach defending his own heterosexuality than about protecting me. And why did Zach feel the need to tell me the reason for the fight? It's almost as if he was trying to remind me that other boys didn't find me attractive, so I'd feel lucky that he did.

2. This direct leap from Zach calling me "Crazy" to a declaration of love for him strikes me as odd. People still call me crazy sometimes, but I don't find it so endearing. That's because calling a girl crazy is a really common way for a guy to dismiss her legitimate feelings without taking responsibility for his role in the problem. "Crazy" could really mean "annoyed that he cheated on her" or "frustrated at his lack of commitment."

3. Well, at least I was trying to be objective about the whole thing.

4. I certainly didn't shy away from the melodrama. Whether or not what was happening was actually dramatic, I seemed to want to represent it that way in my diary.

DECEMBER 15, 1997

I learned from people in school today that Matt's party really sucked.[1] Only a few people went, and Lisa assured me that Zach didn't kiss any of them. But the next night, there was a seventh-grade party. Zach and Matt were the only sixth-graders invited.

At the beginning of my last class of the day, Tyler came over and said, "Amanda Collins is looking for you." I went to the classroom door, and there was Amanda, a seventh-grader, and another girl, standing at an open locker.

Amanda asked me, "Are you Zach's girlfriend?" I nodded. She gave her friend a should-I-tell-her? look and then smiled at me degradingly and said, "Oh… well, I was with him at the party this weekend."[2]

On the bus on the way home, Andrew was like, "He told me not to tell you, but Zach's going to dump you. Matt told me to tell you that you're dumped." I didn't believe him at all, because it was suspicious that Andrew was suddenly extremely interested in sixth-grade gossip when he is a popular eighth-grader with more important things to think about. Also, he finished by saying, "You'd better call him and dump him before he gets around to actually dumping you."[3]

When I got home from practice tonight, my mom told me that Zach had called. Maybe he called to talk. Or maybe he called to dump me. I didn't call him back but I'll ask him about it tomorrow in school.

I hope he doesn't dump me—I can't imagine not going out with him anymore. I take him for granted

1. Although, who's to say that info was reliable?

2. There weren't two girls named Amanda Collins in the seventh grade. This is the same Amanda Collins whom, a few days earlier, Zach had pointed to as the most obvious example of a slut.

3. Yeah, that *is* suspicious! Here's one thing that definitely gets better as you get older: it's no longer socially acceptable for breakups to occur through the grapevine like this.

so much. I don't really appreciate him or do my part in the relationship all the time.[1]

On an unrelated note, Steph told me that she saw "I HATE EMILY" written on a desk in Math class, but she erased it. Someone else had written "EMILY'S BOOBS ARE FAKE" on another desk. I saw that one.[2]

DECEMBER 16, 1997

Today everyone was like, "Zach made out with Amanda Collins."

Even Steph told me, "Emily, Zach is going to dump you."

But when I confronted him about what happened at the party, Zach got all angry. He was like, "If I made out with Amanda Collins, I must have been totally shitfaced, because I do not remember doing that." I pretended like I believed him.[3]

My next class was English, and Zach has class in the same classroom right after me. At the end of the class, when most people were in the hall and some dorks had already entered their next class, I was still in the English room, packing up my stuff.[4] "Are you mad at me?" Zach's voice startled me. I hadn't even noticed he was there!

"No." I put my folder away and walked out of the room.

Before I was out the door, I heard him meekly call after me, "See you..." "and I missed the "later," because I was gone.

He must have thought I was awfully rude for not answering him, and I felt bad later, but he had cheated on me! I'm sure of it now because Kaylee ran up

1. I wonder what I thought "doing my part in the relationship" might look like. Calling him on the phone more often? Initiating our kisses? Sharing sour apple Airheads? Also, what even constituted a "relationship" for us?

2. This seems like a good time to mention that at this age, I had developed breasts. They certainly didn't look *fake* though, since most days I wore an unflattering, heavy-duty sports bra that smashed them down into one big, flattened uni-boob.

3. I'm not sure which would be more shocking: if he had called that girl a "slut," kissed her, and then denied it; or if, at age eleven, he actually had gotten so drunk that he blacked out. Getting "shitfaced" was one of those things I imagined all the cool kids were doing without me, but I'm not sure anyone actually was.

4. If only I had befriended those "dorks" who had the audacity to move so quickly between classes! I can definitely understand their objective of limiting their time spent in the hallways, where they might have had the misfortune of interacting with my friends and me.

to me when I was at my locker later in the afternoon and said, "Oh my god! I just saw Zach walking down the hall with his arm around Amanda Collins!"[1]

Zach called me today while Steph was over. She's always over.[2] He asked me why I was mad at him and I said because he was cheating on me. He insisted that it was just a friendly hug.

I said, "You never hug me."

He said, "Well, that's different."

"How so?"

"I dunno…" "he stammered, and then he really randomly snapped at me, "Well, why don't you dump me?"

I got nervous. "You sound like you want me to."

He said, "Shut up, Emily. Just don't talk to me anymore." There was a silence, but only a short one, because he said, "I didn't make out with Amanda Collins."

Tyler always asks me half-jokingly if I am going to dump Zach and I always say no. It is so obvious Tyler likes me: he writes me notes all the time and flirts with me so badly. I suppose if Zach were to ever dump me, I might consider going out with Tyler. He's kind of a loser. Not a total loser, though.[3]

DECEMBER 18, 1997

Today Zach broke my heart. Before Homeroom, Matt handed me a letter in an envelope.[4] I opened it in Homeroom and it said:

Dear Emily,

    I'd like you to know you are officially dumped. I hope you cry.[5] C'mon, two months is a long time to be going out,

1. It's as if we were all walking around, actively searching for things to make a big deal about. Rumors don't just start *themselves*, people.

2. Steph really was always over. We lived just a few doors down from each other and had both moved to town during the previous school year. Steph smoked cigarettes, spoke with a strong Boston accent, and seemed to know a lot about sex.

3. I clearly maintained some idea of a social hierarchy in my mind, although it's unclear exactly what one had to do to move between the levels. If Tyler was, at this point, "kind of a loser" in my opinion, what horrible offense would he have had to commit to be demoted to "total loser"?

4. Even in a time before text messages, having a friend deliver a letter in an envelope was still a ridiculously dramatic way to communicate with someone.

5. Now *that* seems unnecessary.

you'd think you'd be able to trust me. I should have listened to Matt on this one. If you want another chance, I might consider going out with you again, but now I want to leave you with three parting words: GO FUCK YOURSELF!

HAHAHAHAHA

Zach

I felt like my throat had been ripped open and my voice box had been torn out. I felt tears in my eyes, but the "I hope you cry" part made me more than ever determined not to.[1]

There was a substitute teacher for almost every class today and normally that would have been awesome, but now I was too depressed to enjoy it.[2]

I gave the note to Steph to read and Ms. Walsh took it away from her. Because of the swears, Zach has a detention on Monday after school.[3]

In the locker room after Gym class, I started to cry. But it was so weird. I wasn't really crying—like, tears weren't coming out of my eyes, but I was shaking pretty hard and making involuntary sobbing sounds. It hurt. I couldn't believe Zach would do such a thing. It was only the day before that he had knelt next to my chair at lunch and whispered in my ear.

Every girl sympathized with me and said they hated Zach. I was sad though, and I couldn't claim I hated him. What made it even worse is that Emma came up to me and said, "Zach says he never liked you."[4] How could he say that? Now that he is gone, I realize how much I love him.[5]

1. The most confusing part of this otherwise cruel note is the indication that if I wanted another chance, he "might consider" going out with me again. Not only did Zach assume my self-esteem was so low that I would likely ask him to take *me* back after receiving a note like this (an assumption that, admittedly, was probably true), he also admitted that he wasn't necessarily ready to say good-bye once and for all. If he was going to leave this little window open for a future relationship, why write the note at all?

2. Having a substitute teacher usually meant that all we had to do in class was watch a movie from the 1970s (or '80s, if we were lucky!) about a subject tangentially related to whatever we had been studying that week. For instance, one substitute played the second half of *Apollo 13* in a science class. Substitutes rarely cared enough to insist that we pay attention, so we were able to attend to whatever drama was unfolding in our lives with minimal adult intervention.

3. Assuming Ms. Walsh was at all invested in trying to ensure her students didn't grow up to be complete assholes, a more effective disciplinary measure might have been to discuss with Zach the damaging repercussions of writing a note so obviously intended to hurt someone. But who knows? Maybe after that detention, he never swore again.

4. What the heck, Emma? Chicks over dicks wasn't a thing yet, I guess.

5. Well, *that* seems like a bizarre conclusion to draw after an unusually cruel breakup letter.

When I got home from school, I just threw myself on my bed and cried till my face hurt.

DECEMBER 19, 1997

1. Coming off the previous entry from the night before, this emotional transition seems startlingly rapid.

Today was great![1] At the very beginning of the day, Hunter came up to me and held out a folded piece of paper and said, "This is a note… from guess who." He was being sarcastic.

I said, "I don't want it," and pushed past him.

A little bit later, Hannah came up to me and asked, "Did you see the letter Zach wrote you?"

I shook my head. "Is it mean?"

"No!" she said. "It's really nice."

After first block, when I was walking to Social Studies, Hannah gave me the note—she had acquired it somehow—and said, "Read it, it's good."

I went into the bathroom and read it in a stall. I had to bite my lip to keep from yelling something stupid in my state of pure joy. It was like floating—it's weird to be that happy.[2] I couldn't keep the grin off my face during Social Studies and people were giving me weird looks. Here is what the note said. I have read it like, a million times—I practically have it memorized:

2. What's even weirder is this drastic emotional shift, from crying until my face hurt because of a note Zach had someone else give to me just the day before to feeling so happy it was as if I were floating… *because of a note Zach had someone else give to me.* That kind of volatility has got to be exhausting.

> Dear Emily,
>
> It's one in the morning and I'm tired but I'm writing this note because I have to apologize but I have to say two words: I'm sorry. I shouldn't have went off at you. I just didn't know what I was doing. I take back everything I said and I don't mind if you hate me because of this incident. I'm really sorry it had to end like this. I just wish we could start over and forget about this, but I can understand if you don't

forgive me. I can't believe I wrote that to you and I don't care if you hate me for the rest of the time I know you. I hope you forgive me and I'm really sorry.

Sincerely,

Zach

Kaylee asked Zach out for me without my permission, and he said he'd tell her by the end of the day.[1] Then when I was walking to my bus after school, she ran up to me and yelled, "Emily! He says he'll go out with you!"

Right after school, Emma called me and she had Zach on the other line. She had to flash back and forth between us.[2] She told me that Zach said that he really missed me and that he wanted to go out with me again, but if we broke up he was afraid it would ruin our friendship.[3]

He called me after that and we talked about everything like nothing had changed—it was great. He called later tonight, too, and we watched TV together and it was so fun. I realized how much I love him and how much I need him.

He's really perfect. I can't believe he actually wrote me that second letter. According to *Seventeen* magazine, it's hardly ever that a boy says, "I'm sorry" and admits he was wrong. It's probably even rarer that a boy as egotistical and full of himself as Zach is says that. But knowing that makes his apologizing even more sweet.[4]

DECEMBER 28, 1997

We are on Christmas vacation until January 5th. Regularly that would kick ass, but I am grounded

1. So now I had played into what Zach predicted I'd do in his first note—and he was "considering" taking me back, like he said he might. How humiliating. And another thing: this second note wasn't even that *nice*.

2. We were on our parents' landlines using call waiting, so we had to "flash" back and forth between conversations. Some of us were lucky enough to have landlines with a "conference call" option, so we could set up fancy three-way conversations.

3. Well, yeah, if the breakup involved another "GO FUCK YOURSELF! HAHAHAHAHA," I'd say that might ruin our friendship.

4. Everything I need to know I learned from reading *Seventeen* magazine. Except, apparently, that it's impossible for someone to be "really perfect" while also being obviously "egotistical and full of himself." Back before it was possible to do a quick Internet search, *Seventeen* was my go-to source for fashion guidance, personality quizzes, and romantic wisdom. My parents never would have allowed my sister and me to subscribe to it, so we bought issues from the convenience store with our babysitting money and read them cover-to-cover before cutting them up to make collage art of our favorite words and images. I was often grounded, and the one positive thing I can say about it is that it really allowed me to develop my magazine-collage-making skills.

so it sucks. In fact, I am grounded until February 11th. My parents must really hate me; I hardly do anything wrong, like maybe I'll go over someone's house and forget to call and tell my parents where I am, and they'll ground me for a month. Literally—no exaggeration. Scary, huh? When I'm a parent, I will not ever be like that.[1]

DECEMBER 29, 1997

Today at about 2:15, I was sitting at my computer when the phone rang. It was Matt, calling from a strange number I didn't recognize. He said, "Hi, Emily?"

I said in an obviously disappointed voice, "Hi, Matt."

He said simply, "Zach doesn't like you anymore, so fuck off." Then he hung up.

I felt… depressed, but not as much as I would have expected.[2] The phone rang again like, two seconds later, and I answered it again without looking at the number. It sounded like Matt's voice that said, "Is Emily there?"

So I snapped, "Why do you keep calling me?"

He said, "What? I didn't call you. This is Zach."

I didn't answer. He continued, "Hi, what's up?" It had to be Matt, but what was he doing? He asked, "So, are you and Zach still going out?"

I said, "No."

He asked, "So, um, when did you guys break up?"

I said, "Just now, Matt called."

He said away from the receiver, "Matt, she thinks it's you!" I hung up on them.[3]

Two seconds later, the phone rang again. I didn't

1. My parents really did ground me almost constantly. I think it was just as much about trying to keep me safe as it was about punishing me; this was before cell phones, so it was really hard for them to track me down if I lied about where I was going (which I did quite often).

2. Probably because I was getting used to all this nonsense.

3. First of all, sorry this conversation is so confusing. Second of all, regardless of who was actually on the phone, what a terribly mean sequence of things to do to someone: First, write her a GO FUCK YOURSELF! breakup note. Then the next day, apologize and let her ask you to take her back. Accept her request. Be nice for a night. The next day, have a friend call her to tell her you're breaking up with her again. Then call her again and pretend to be someone else to confirm that she understands you've broken up with her, *just in case* she misunderstood.

answer it. Right now, I don't know how I feel. Zach has definitely played a huge role in my life. Definitely. It's so hard to grasp that I'll never be able to hold him again.[1] Why does he hang around with Matt? How come I still love Zach, even after everything he's done?

JANUARY 4, 1998

It's been a week since Zach dumped me and I think I'm over him. I'm surprised at myself for ever thinking I loved him. A boyfriend, as far as I'm concerned, should be three things:

1) Nice. If he weren't, he would be a complete waste of time.

2) Cute. If not, I couldn't fantasize about his cute face because it wouldn't be cute.

3) Popular. Because if he were not popular, to go out with him would make me disliked by everyone else.[2]

Zach was only one of those three things: popular.[3] He wasn't nice, that's for sure. He'd go out with me, then dump me to see if he could go out with someone else, and when they said no, he'd go out with me again. He was kind of using me as backup; Plan B, in case Plan A failed. And stupid me, I agreed to go out with him because my obsession didn't allow me to see what a loser he was.[4]

And he wasn't even that cute. He could do this thing with his eyes, this little squinty thing that made me fall head over heels in love with him. But his teeth were a mess and his head was kind of misshapen.

I think I could do better. I can find someone who

1. I'm pretty sure I got that line from a Mariah Carey song lyric. It's not like I ever "held him" in the first place, unless you count our awkward slow dancing.

2. That's another thing I learned from *Seventeen*: how to make and live by listicles.

3. Well, then he really didn't have much going for him, because *popular* is a word that pretty much disappears from your vocabulary once you graduate high school—unless you're talking about a TV show, or a restaurant with a chef from a TV show. But this listicle offers some insight into what determined popularity at my school: apparently, it was at least in part dependent on the popularity of your boyfriend or girlfriend. I think if I were to revise this list today, I'd keep "nice" and "cute"—but I'd replace "popular" with "intellectually curious" or something along those lines.

4. Well put! If only I could have seared this conviction into my mind and armed myself with it when I had to face him again.

appreciates me and who falls head over heels in love with me.

I don't feel well so I'm not going to school tomorrow.[1] I'll ask Steph to bring my homework to me. And I'll also ask her to stand up for me if Zach or Matt starts making fun of me. She probably will. Jenna might. Hannah probably won't. Emma maybe will and maybe won't, but most likely will.[2]

Right now I am promising myself, swearing to myself, that I WILL NOT go out with Zach if he asks me again, which he might or might not.[3] He's confusing like that—very unpredictable.

Matt, I think, has some kind of emotional disabilities. He doesn't care whose feelings he hurts, whose heart he tramples on, or whose life he ruins. But he must. He is human. How can he act so cruel? Doesn't he ever feel guilty or sorry?

JANUARY 7, 1998

Yesterday Zach didn't say one word to me. We didn't interact in any way. Then today I found out he's going out with Amanda Collins. Zach had told me that he hated her and that he thought she was a slut.[4] I was furious. I also felt sick to my stomach.

In study hall today, Tyler was in my classroom, doing make-up work or something. He asked if we could trade binders and write each other notes on them. I wrote him a stupid one, about how green is a gay color—he was wearing green.[5] In the middle of writing it, I heard Tyler's friend Ryan whisper, "Don't write that!" Only without much emphasis on the exclamation point because Ryan is pretty much always monotone.[6]

1. I wonder if I actually felt physically ill, if it was a psychosomatic effect of stress, or if I was referring to feeling not "well" enough emotionally to face my peers.

2. That's a good way to take stock of which people in your life are real friends: your level of confidence that they'll stick up for you if the person who just broke your heart starts making fun of you.

3. Spoiler alert: I didn't keep my promise to myself. I think I must have known, even as I wrote this, that I wasn't going to. That's a pretty common predicament in emotionally abusive relationships, even among adults. Emotional abuse in teenagers' romantic relationships is often dismissed as harmless immaturity, but it can have devastating immediate effects. It can also set patterns—for both parties involved—that lead to problematic relationships in adulthood.

4. I probably should have noticed that, for Zach, the line between deeming a girl a "slut" and going out with her was easily crossed.

5. How any color could possibly be "gay" is beyond me, but at the time, "gay" was considered such a horrible insult among my peers that I was clearly just grasping for ways to employ it.

6. I don't remember much else about Ryan, except that he used very little vocal inflection. That made him seem really cool to me, since it implied he didn't really care about anything.

Tyler whispered back, "Why not?"

Ryan said, "Because she'll show it to all her friends."

When we switched binders back, I read his note:

Emily,

You're the weirdest kid I know. There are lots of weird people in my life, but you're the weirdest. Just kidding. You're cool… I guess? I have no clue what to write. Oh, I just remembered something I can write. Will you go out with me? I really, really… no I don't. I had just no clue what to write. Pretty pointless note.

Tyler

So… think he likes me? The thing is, I kind of like him, too.[1]

This is the perfect opportunity to get revenge on Zach. Maybe Zach doesn't like Amanda Collins. Maybe he's just going out with her to make me jealous. Well, I can make him jealous, too.[2]

JANUARY 9, 1998

Today I found out some awful news: Hannah likes Zach! She asked him out, and he said he'd tell her after lunch, but he didn't. Emma keeps telling him to say yes.[3] I hope so badly he says no.

What is wrong with me? I still get jealous. Why would Hannah do that? Why does she like Zach when she knows I still like him? But… why the hell do I still like him?

JANUARY 11, 1998

Today is Sunday. Steph called and said she needed to come over to borrow my science book for

1. Tyler was a little bit like me in that his family had recently moved to town and that he was, clearly, interested in timidly exploring the art of flirtation. He was instantly popular because, having moved to our town in Massachusetts from England, he seemed kind of fancy and exotic. We had a friendship outside of school because we had been on the municipal swim team together (before I became painfully aware of the shape of my body and quit). Tyler's mother was the coach and he was one of the best swimmers. During practices, he would swim in the first lane with the other fast swimmers, and when he was done with his required laps, he would swim under all the lane lines to where I was dutifully plodding along in the slowest lane and pop up in front of my face, causing me to gasp and choke on the pool water. It wasn't the smoothest or safest attempt at flirting, but I remember it almost twenty years later, so… that's something, I guess.

2. What a shame that I mainly saw my flirtation with Tyler as a way to hurt someone else.

3. Thanks, *Emma*.

homework. I said sure, and would she call Hannah to see if she's going out with Zach yet? When Steph came to get my book, she nodded and said, "She is."

My stomach knotted up. I felt awful, like nothing was real.

I am so confused. I had almost convinced myself that I could live without Zach, so why do I feel so depressed when he goes out with another girl? I guess I really do like him, just sometimes I don't like the things he does.

And Hannah… oh, I am so mad at her! What a bitch. She knows I like him! Why would she pick him to go out with when she could have any boy in the sixth grade? I hope I can get through school tomorrow without crying in the bathroom.[1]

JANUARY 12, 1998

Today it was confirmed by everyone else that Hannah and Zach were, in fact, going out. I didn't see them interact in any way during the day, but Zach and I didn't interact either.

I told everyone I am going out with some random boy from summer camp named Adam, and they bought it. Only Steph knows the truth, and she won't tell.[2]

JANUARY 14, 1998

Today after school, some of us went to Curb Café. A bunch of popular seventh-grade guys came in and Zach was with them. Unfortunately, Hannah was with us, too.

Kaylee and Hunter have been flirting, so Kaylee wanted me to do this "compatibility test" for the two

1. Reading back now, I also hope I ended up getting through school the next day without crying in the bathroom. Either way, I didn't write about it.

2. I can't remember if Adam was completely fabricated, or if he existed and just wasn't interested in dating me. Probably the former, given the extravagance of my imagination. I remember writing notes to myself on my school binders in messy handwriting and pretending they were from him, with the hope that this forged "evidence" of our relationship would prove that I didn't care about Zach anymore.

of them. It just has to do with lining up your names, giving each letter a numerical value, and crossing off letters in a methodical way until you end up with a number from 1 to 100%. That's how compatible you are.

It's the dumbest thing in the world.[1]

I did it for Kaylee and Hunter and they came out to just 32% compatible.

Zach popped up over my shoulder and said, "Oh, I know how to do that test. Emily and I are 91%." I was shocked that he had taken the time to figure that out. Then he continued, "But if you put the other person's name first, it totally changes it. Like me and Emily the other way are only 72% or something."

I corrected him: "73%."

He looked at me funny. "How do you know?"

"Because I figured it out." There was an awkward silence, and I could feel him looking at me.

But when I finally looked up and our eyes met, Hannah ruined it by announcing, "Zach and I are 97%!" I just shrugged.[2]

JANUARY 15, 1998

When I went to pick up Steph today so we could walk to the bus stop together, she came out the front door of her house and asked, "Are you sad?"

I answered, "I don't know. Why?"

"Because when I tell you this, you're going to be so happy. Last night, Zach called Hannah and he dumped her. He said it was because yesterday at Curb Café, he realized he liked you more!"

At first it seemed too good to be true and I

1. Yet not dumb enough that I wouldn't try it. And then write about it.

2. This compatibility test was one of my tried-and-true flirtation devices for the majority of my middle school career. The results meant nothing, of course, but it could give you a little kick to discover that your crush on someone was backed up by *numbers*. It didn't matter how compatible you ended up being; just the fact that you took the time to figure it out indicated an interest. And if that interest wasn't returned, you could always back out of it by claiming to have done the test as a joke. I think Tyler pulled that on me once. Brilliant.

couldn't believe her. But when we got to school, people were betting money on whether or not I would go back out with him. Steph said it was very important to keep him in suspense, so every time someone asked me, I just said, "Maybe," trying to sound cryptic.

Emma came up to me and said, "Please don't go back out with him. I bet ten dollars you wouldn't."[1]

Hunter came over to our table at lunch and said, "Please, please, please go back out with Zach."

I took advantage of the situation and answered, "Only if you go out with Jenna." Jenna is embarrassingly obsessed with Hunter.

Hunter was like, "Maybe... more yes than no." He kept pestering me, but with Hannah sitting across from me with tears in her eyes, I didn't know what to do. All through the afternoon, I thought about it.

Okay, I knew I would end up saying yes, I just didn't know when or how. Strangely enough, Hannah was hanging around with me during Gym class and shared with me her plan to go out with Ryan.

After school, Zach called. He asked, "Are you mad at me?"

"No. Why do you always think I'm mad at you?"

"You always seem like it. Weren't you mad at me at Curb Café?"[2]

"Yes, because you were going out with Hannah."

"Well, I dumped her because I like you." At that point, my heart fluttered kind of uncontrollably. I didn't answer. He continued, "Will you go out with me?"

Before answering, I explained to him my theory

1. What sixth-grader has ten dollars to bet on the relationship, or lack of relationship, between two classmates? I am struck by how communal—and, apparently, commercial—the whole dating process was.

2. You mean when we discovered we were exactly 73% compatible, according to science?

about him using me as a backup plan. He denied it, of course. Then he said one of the sweetest things I've ever heard him say. "You know what? You're so well-rounded. You're not only pretty or only popular or only smart, you're everything, equally. You're like, perfect."[1]

I said, "Thanks, that was nice," stupidly.

We talked for another hour or so about everything. I guess we're going out again.

JANUARY 23, 1998

The sixth-grade dance was postponed because of the weather. Zach got like, five teeth pulled, and his face is all swollen.[2] So I wouldn't be able to French-kiss him anyway. He looks pretty weird.

While I was walking to lunch today, I ran into Aaron. He said, "Did you and Zach fuck?"[3]

I was like, "No! Who told you that?"

He said, "Matt." I asked Matt why he would say that and he denied it. But he was obviously lying.

On the way back from lunch I saw Aaron again and he said, "Matt just told me that you had sex with Zach!"

I wonder why Matt is having so much fun with this theory. Maybe Zach told him to! Oh, that would be great! That would mean Zach really likes me, or is proud of me or something.[4] But it's more likely that Matt is just full of shit.

JANUARY 26, 1998

Today when I got home from school, Matt called. I said immediately, "Zach dumped me, right?" "Well… yeah."[5]

1. "Well-rounded"! I always say, the best compliments sound like they're lifted from a college admissions letter. Way to go, Zach.

2. This was probably to make room in his mouth in preparation for getting braces.

3. *Fuck* was a word I was definitely not accustomed to hearing. Aaron's use of it might not have shocked me—after all, he was in the *eighth* grade—but I tended to use much less direct ways of talking about sex, like "going all the way."

4. No. No, it wouldn't. I was caught in a trap that is, unfortunately, quite common for girls: believing that my worth as a person was dependent upon what others perceived as my sexuality.

5. This is getting absurd.

"Why does he always do this?"

"Are you sad?"

"No," I quickly answered. "I just don't understand him."

Matt giggled and said, "You know tomorrow he'll just say he likes you again. Lisa does that to me, too.[1] In school I'll be like, 'Are we going out?' and she'll say we're not, but then she'll call me and say she wants to."

We ended up talking a lot about that—Lisa and Zach and how weird they are—and then I said, "All right well… bye."

"NO!" he cried. It surprised me.

So we kept talking about other things, like how girls don't eat so boys will think they're thin. It was weird—we never ran out of things to talk about.[2]

Then my mom came in and told me to get off the phone because I'm grounded from it, as always.

A little while later, Matt called back. He said, "Call Zach."

"I don't even want to…" I told him. "Trust me," he said, "You do."

"Do you know what he's going to tell me?"

"Yup."

"Then why can't you just tell me yourself?"

But my mom came in and I really had to get off the phone then.

FEBRUARY 3, 1998

My second period today was History. I was paired with Nathan. We were doing our work, but there was something… nervous and awkward about it. I noticed, for the millionth time, that Nathan has a very touchable face and very soft skin. His hair

1. I guess he and Lisa were still together, after that intense slow dance back in November.

2. I had forgotten that Matt could be nice sometimes. He was just an eleven-year-old boy, after all, not some kind of arch-villain. I wonder what he would have included in *his* diary, if he kept one.

is perfect and just the right shade of blond and his eyes… they're so big and the strangest shade of gold, and when I look into them, I just feel so guilty, I guess, compared to the innocence of his eyes.

But the thing about Nathan is that he knows, like, everything. He's kind of wise, I guess, in that he can tell I like him. He's not the biggest flirt, like Zach, but today his eyes seemed to say, "Come on, Emily, we both know we like each other. This is ridiculous—can't we just admit it?" It felt like a challenge and I looked away.

It's so weird. Nathan and I have this relationship between our minds; we've never actually said anything about it, but we both know it's there.[1]

Today after school, Zach called. He asked me what bra size I was and I said 34C, even though I'm just a 32B.[2] "Well," he said, "As long as your boobs aren't pointy. I hate pointy boobs."

What does that even mean? Of course they're not pointy.[3]

I wanted to change the subject, so I told him about my theory that you can't really trust anyone but yourself; everyone could just be lying to you, and you'd never know. He didn't seem to really get the concept: "But I can always trust Matt."

Then we talked about his being unpredictable. He said, "Name one time I've done something unpredictable." I couldn't, really—his dumping me became predictable after a while.

I didn't know what to say so I sighed and said, "I don't understand you, Zach."

"You understand me better than anyone else does." That really touched me.

1. A relationship between our *minds*. Really?! That's some deep, telepathic shit.

2. At our school, knowing a girl's bra size was a kind of social currency. Once a boy found it out (or made it up), it was a precious tidbit of gossip for him to lord over his less informed friends. So it's possible I lied in order to maintain a bit of secrecy, but I think it's more likely that I was trying to impress him so he would like me. Whether or not I wanted to admit it, I knew that Zach was mostly interested in me because of my developed body, so I wanted to play that up.

3. I'm still not sure what Zach meant by "pointy" boobs, but my guess is that he had seen some porn where the woman's nipples pointed slightly upward. It seems to me that most men would find that breast shape desirable, but as an eleven-year-old boy, Zach probably didn't know what to make of breasts at all, regardless of their often subtle variations.

Going back to the same person over and over again: is it love, or idiocy? I have to figure it out.[1]

FEBRUARY 6, 1998

This afternoon, I begged my mom to let me go to the dance, but she said no. I'm grounded, as usual. I had to babysit anyway, for the kids down the street.

Steph called me from the dance before the kids were asleep and said that she, Zach, and some other people were going to leave the dance and come to the house where I was babysitting. But that plan made me nervous because these kids I was babysitting aren't dumb. I said I had to go. But not long after the kids were in bed, Steph called back.

She said, "Zach likes you again."

My stomach did a flip. I said, "I don't want to talk to him—it will be too awkward!" But she put him on the phone anyway. I chatted about nothing, trying to keep the subject off of us going out again, but alas! It didn't work.[2]

He interrupted me to say, "So will you?"

"Will I what?"

"Go out with me, Stupid."

I groaned. "Zach, I like you and everything, but you keep doing this…"

"So we'll keep it a secret!"

"What?!"

"From my seventh-grade friends. So they won't convince me to dump you."[3]

Then Steph got back on the phone and said, "So you're going out again?"

"Yeah, I guess."

She went on, "Well, the dance sucks. There are

1. Well, it's not love. I do think I do think it was astute of me to recognize that his dumping me over and over again actually made him predictable.

2. Now, what kind of child says, "Alas!"? We must have been on a Shakespeare unit in Language Arts class or something.

3. If a guy suggests keeping a relationship a secret—at *any* age—it is a huge red flag.

too many dorky fifth-graders here and they haven't even played any slow songs. I haven't danced at all; we're just hanging around in the hall."[1]

FEBRUARY 9, 1998

Today, my first block was Drama. Zach and I ended up sitting next to each other. He was telling me how he and Matt had gone to the mall on Saturday and seen all the crackheads and men dressed as women and cool stuff like that.[2]

Once, a while ago, another one of the times we were going out, Zach asked me over the phone, "So, what do you think we're gonna do after high school?"

I said, "Do you think we'll still be going out then?"

He answered, "Why wouldn't we be?" and the conversation had ended there.

I hope he asks me that again, because this time I'll have an answer all planned out: "Well, first we'll go to college and we'll have to go to the same one, and then we'll get married and go to Europe on our honeymoon, unless you want to go somewhere else, like Disney World or something, but I think Europe would be very romantic, and then we'll move to San Diego and have three kids named Julie May, Angela Katherine, and Christina Sophia if they're girls; and if they're boys, then we'll name them Zach, Jr., but of course he'll have to go by his middle name so we can tell you apart, Ryan, with no middle name because no middle name really sounds good with Ryan, and Kyle Steven, Steven being spelled with a v."

1. "Just hanging around" describes what we were doing about 90% of the time. Our overwhelming, oppressive boredom likely led to a lot of our social conflicts, in hindsight.

2. I'm pretty sure this mall was an invention of Zach and Matt's imaginations. There was pretty much only one mall within driving distance of our town, and you were more likely to encounter a thirty-something mom in yoga pants shopping for her kids' soccer cleats there than crackheads or cross-dressers.

The Posters I Have —

Hanson Posters: ~~84~~ 85

Other Posters: 17[1]

FEBRUARY 11, 1998

In Science class today, I stared at the chalkboard without blinking until my eyes started to water. Then I raised my hand and asked to go to the nurse. I told Ms. Benson I had a stomachache and she was all concerned.

I was feeling pretty proud of myself for pulling that off, and I felt even better when I saw that Matt was also at the nurse. He was scooting around the room on a stool with wheels, eating saltine crackers.

The nurse let me stay until lunch, which was a half hour away. I went to lunch and then went back to the nurse, and this time Jenna and Lisa came, too. Jenna was trying to make herself throw up and Lisa was laughing.[2] Then Jenna and I pretended to be asleep on the cots so we wouldn't have to go back to class. We didn't leave for another hour and ten minutes. By that time, the school day was almost over.

Aaron came in at one point, took his own temperature, found it to be normal, and left. I was like, okay.[3]

Zach took the bus somewhere after school and he wouldn't tell me where. Matt said he was going to get braces put on. Oh, no!

2. I remember being fascinated by the idea of bulimia, but in this case, it's more likely that Jenna was trying to convince the nurse she was actually ill.

3. I hope that school nurse has since found a new profession, because it doesn't sound like she had things under control at *all*.

FEBRUARY 18, 1998

I was talking to Jenna on the phone today and she said that she thought everyone is born with a soul mate. Someone you were meant to be with.

She said, "My soul mate is probably in South Africa running around with nothing on but a leather thong. But you're so lucky! You and Zach are definitely soul mates. You are so perfect for each other!"[1]

I think we are soul mates, too. I can't think of anyone I'd be happier with.

FEBRUARY 23, 1998

Zach got braces but he doesn't look that bad. I can hardly even notice them. He's getting them off in October.

I saw Zach in the seventh-grade hall, talking with Amanda Collins at her locker. I was furious, but I quickly walked by without saying a word. I didn't confront him or anything, but in Drama class, he explained.[2]

He sat down next to me and asked, "Did you hear the rumors?"

I said, "No." Even though I had. There were about a zillion different rumors going around, all based on one thing: I had given Zach a blow job. I didn't want him to start talking about it, so I just said I didn't know what he was talking about.

He was like, "I think Matt started it. Ask Matt." Matt has a tendency to start rumors.

In the hall after school, I leaned over the railing near Zach's locker and shouted down to Matt, who was on the stairs: "Matt! Fuckhead! Hey, Matt!"[3]

He looked up and I said, "Why did you start those rumors?"

He said, "I didn't. Ryan did."

I was like, new mission. I hurried down the hall to Ryan's locker and said accusingly, "Who the hell do you think you are?"[4]

1. What a bizarre synthesis of sentimentality and racism, Jenna!

2. *Drama* class. How fitting.

3. Now *there's* a surefire way to get someone's attention.

4. Again, going with a strong opener.

He said, "What?"

I said, "Why did you start those rumors?"

He smiled. "I don't know what you're talking about."

I don't really give a fuck about the rumors. I actually think it's kind of cool. Zach pretends to care, but I think he really thinks it's cool, too. Everyone already thinks we had sex.

When I walked down the eighth-grade hall a few days ago, one of the eighth-grade boys yelled to his friends as I walked by, "Hey, there's the girl that Zach fucked!" And eighth-grade boys refer to me as "Zach's little girlfriend."[1]

Once, Zach was talking to me out near the busses, and one of the eighth-graders came over to us. He gave me the once over, nodded approvingly, and said to Zach, "So this is your girlfriend?"

Zach said, "Um… yeah." I felt so special.[2] Zach thinks that guy is gay. Whatever.

Jenna has a big crush on Aaron. I think I'm going to ask him out for her the next time I see him.[3]

FEBRUARY 24, 1998

Today Zach was flirting with me so bad! It was so cute. But in Gym, he didn't really talk to me at all, except to inform me, "Matt did it, he said so." I wasn't really that surprised that Matt had started the rumors. They don't really bother me.

But they certainly bother Zach. He called me today to tell me: "I don't know what to do."

"About what?"

"Everything."

I was like, "Oh…kay."[4]

He continued, "Amanda is so pissed off."

1. At this point, I really seemed to thrive on this rumor. It brought me to the attention of the older boys, and at least for now, I was enjoying it.

2. Apparently, it didn't take much.

3. Without her permission, of course. That's what friends are for!

4. Oh…kay.

"Why does she care?!"

"I don't know."

"Because she likes you, that's why."

He said, "She's always making fun of you."

"Why? I don't even know her!"

He said, "You have to confront her."

"What good will that do? None."

"Well, if you don't… you know. I'm just gonna have to listen to her. I can only take like, a week more of her bashing you." So if I don't confront Amanda, he's going to dump me. I hate it when he does this!!!

I said, "The only reason she bashes me is because she likes you!"

He said, "Okay. There are two possibilities why she hates you. One, she's a bitch. Or two, your theory… that… she likes me."

I said, "Yeah, either way, I'm right."

He sighed, "You know the last two times?" I wasn't sure what he was talking about. "Oh, my god, I can't believe you could forget, Emily. The last two times… I dumped you."

"Oh, yeah. The last two out of five times."[1] That comment was a little too sarcastic and he called me a bitch.[2] I didn't defend myself. I never do.

Then he said, "Well, those times were because of her." Right then, I wanted to pound in Amanda Collins's head. I always want to, but this time the temptation was stronger. Zach and I are soul mates, and Amanda is ruining everything.

I think I will confront her, only nicely.[3] If she likes me, even though I could NEVER like her, then maybe Zach won't dump me. I love him so much! Why does Amanda have to get in the way of everything?[4]

1. Snap!

2. The way I described this points to just how careful I felt I had to be around Zach. If I said something that was "a little too sarcastic," I risked falling out of his good graces.

3. Right. Kill 'em with kindness.

4. I have to say, I was really relishing the drama of this whole love triangle.

Zach still loves me though, I can tell. Even if he does dump me, we're still meant to be together. Seriously.[1]

FEBRUARY 26, 1998

Zach, Lisa, Matt, and I were all planning to go over Matt's house after school. It turned out Lisa couldn't come, so I went alone with them. It was scary walking into his house. I was like, inside Matt's house! With him and Zach!

I had promised Jenna that I would call her as soon as I got there, but Matt was on the Internet.[2] And they didn't want me to call her, anyway. Zach had his arms around my waist and was standing behind me. Matt told us to go down to the basement, and he came, too.

I sat down on the couch, and Zach sat next to me. He leaned over, so he was on top of me, and facing me, and he slid his hands under my back.

Matt said, "Wait—her legs." My legs were still hanging over the side of the couch. My body was kind of twisted. Zach got up, picked up my feet, put them up on the couch, and then lay back down on top of me.[3]

I put my hands on the back of his neck, and he nuzzled his face into the side of my neck. But we didn't kiss for a long while, because of me and my stupid excuses. I was really scared and nervous, and I kept making dumb excuses like, "But my breath smells like whiskey!" Because we had done a few shots earlier.[4]

But finally, we kissed. It was different than the other ones. It was better physically, but emotionally there was... nothing.[5] It ended, and I noticed that

1. Seriously? Because it seems like what I called "love" was actually emotional abuse. This type of manipulation plays out all too often in adult relationships, as well. The truth is, people in love don't constantly threaten to end a relationship if arbitrary terms aren't met.

2. Oh, the inconveniences of dial-up Internet connections!

3. The level of passivity on my part is disturbing, especially since Matt was apparently giving Zach instructions on how to move my body around like I was a puppet.

4. ... But only a few, because we were *eleven years old*. I don't think I had tried alcohol before that day, but I imagine I had sipped the whiskey to try to look cool in front of the boys. I don't remember where the alcohol came from, but I assume we had stolen it from Matt's mom's liquor cabinet. Most of our parents had stocked liquor cabinets from which we felt comfortable pilfering small amounts of alcohol whenever we needed to prove how mature we thought we were.

5. Not a good sign.

Matt was sitting on a really high stool, with his feet on the top rung, eating a bag of pretzels and watching us intently.[1]

Zach said, "Wanna go to second?" I nodded. So he started to stick his fingers up my shirt, but I freaked out and told him I had to call Jenna. He sighed and said, "No... come on." But I grabbed his arm, just above his wrist, and tried to push it away from my shirt. But he tried to get his hand up my shirt, and he was stronger. Finally, I gave in, but I still had my bra on, so he couldn't feel anything, anyway.

I sat up, took off my bra, and dropped it on the floor. Zach picked it up and tossed it across the room, where Matt picked it up and started playing with it and trying it on.

Zach slid his hand up the side of my shirt, but my elbow was in the way. I hesitantly wrapped my arms around his back, and he slid his hand the rest of the way up my shirt. "You have to kiss me while you're doing it," I told him, so he did. He slid his other hand up, too, while we were kissing.

Matt said he was bored and went back upstairs.

Zach grabbed my wrists and lifted my arms above my head. Then he grabbed the bottom of my shirt and started to lift it up. He was on his knees, straddling my hips. When my shirt was above my boobs he bent over and licked them. But not short, little licks, just one long, continuous sweep of his tongue across my chest.[2]

He started to put his hand down my pants and looked up at me. "Can I?"

I said, "I don't know..." I stopped playing with

1. At eleven years old, he was apparently experimenting with voyeurism.

2. This is *not* a move I would recommend, for the record.

his hair and pulled my shirt back down.

He said, "Why not? Come on." I told him I wasn't sure I trusted him enough, and he promised me he wouldn't dump me. During this chat, it became perfectly clear to me that he was drunk. Those few shots we had had earlier in Matt's dining room had really done a lot for him.

But he was on top of me and I didn't want to disappoint him. So I didn't say anything when he started to unzip my fly, and then he put his hand down my underwear. It didn't really hurt, but I just felt so slutty. Finally, I told him to stop touching me and he looked annoyed and ran upstairs.[1]

When I went back upstairs, Matt met me at the basement door and led me to the kitchen. We went out onto the deck, where Zach and Matt's brother were smoking. Matt's brother is in the ninth grade and goes to a private school. He is a known drug dealer, although he doesn't look like it.[2] Jenna thinks he is hot, and I guess he kind of is. He doesn't look at all like Matt. He put a new cigarette in his mouth and lit it, then asked me if I wanted it. He handed it to me when I nodded, and I took it from him. I made the fact that I was inhaling deeply very obvious, so they wouldn't think I was a loser.[3]

Then I had to call my mother to come get me, but we told Zach to leave first, so my mom wouldn't know he was there. But I still got grounded until the end of the school year for lying about where I was, and my mom doesn't even know what Zach did. Imagine how long I'd be grounded for if she did!

1. When I first started reading through these entries, I got to this point and had to stop. I put the diary down and didn't pick it up again until months later, when I decided to start The Un-Slut Project. That's because in the years that had passed since 1997, I had subconsciously accepted the version of events that Zach and Matt spread around school, which involved my supposed seduction of Zach. Even though I hadn't thought much about this interaction since about the time I moved out of my parents' home, I had still maintained the general belief that I had been the aggressor that afternoon. When I got to this entry, suddenly I realized that my memories and, as a result, my ongoing sense of who I was had been tainted by the rumors that followed this event. My consent hadn't been enthusiastic, and I certainly hadn't acted as the sexually knowledgeable seductress of Zach and Matt's rumors.

2. I'm not sure what I thought a "known drug dealer" should look like, or if there was any truth to Matt's older brother's reputation. At any rate, he was supposed to be babysitting us and making sure we didn't get into trouble. So… *that* didn't work out as planned.

3. The only other time I had smoked a cigarette was with Steph in the woods behind her parents' house; she had shown me how to tuck my lips under slightly when I put it in my mouth and how to inhale without coughing too much.

FEBRUARY 27, 1998

Today, Aaron called me! I told him he should go out with Jenna. She really likes him. He said he doesn't know what she looks like and to point her out to him on Monday.

We called Zach on three-way, and the first thing he said to Aaron was, "Go out with Jenna." Aaron said he didn't know.

Then we talked about all the rumors about what happened at Matt's house, and Aaron said he had heard that Zach "ate me out." I wasn't sure what that meant, but I said it wasn't true, just to be on the safe side.

I really like Aaron. When anyone else hugs me, it's like they like me, you know? But when Aaron hugs me, it's like, oh, that's just Aaron.[1]

MARCH 2, 1998

Today was an awful day. At lunch, Steph had detention or something, so I sat with Jenna, Lisa, and Michelle. Lisa told me that Emma, Catherine, and Hailey think I am a slut, and that they told her that if she doesn't stop hanging around with me, they are not going to be her friends. Luckily, Lisa stayed sitting with us, because she is just so cool.[2]

Right now, I really regret going to third base with Zach. I didn't know what I was doing.

I know Zach doesn't love me, because my sister's friend has a locker right next to Amanda Collins's locker, and she said Zach and all the seventh-grade girls were hanging around there making fun of me.

I almost cried when I heard that. We are not soul mates. How could I ever think that? It has taken me

1. Turns out, there was something to this: Aaron has grown into a wonderful, successful gay man. Come to think of it, that might explain his indifference to dating Jenna, despite the mounting peer pressure.

2. *Is* she? Because she felt compelled to deliver that nasty message from my other "friends."

too long to realize that I don't love him. I can't dump him now, because then people would think I am even more of a slut than they already do. How could one mistake cause my life to crumble like this?[1]

MARCH 7, 1998

My life is completely falling apart. Steph decided she doesn't like me anymore, and neither does Zach. But he can't dump me, because he promised he wouldn't. Jenna and Aaron are my only friends. Aaron has decided he is going to dump Jenna, so Jenna and I will just have to be miserable together.[2]

Jenna is really good friends with Zach, so we called him on three-way, only I was on mute so he didn't know I was listening. She asked him if he still liked me and he said, "No! She's a fag!"[3]

Then Aaron called him on three-way but with me on mute and said, "Oh, come on. You know you still like her." And Zach said hesitantly, "Yeah… I know. But she has no friends."

Aaron said, "It's only because of what she did with you."[4]

Two weeks ago I had the best life! I had everything I wanted and more than I could have ever imagined getting. I guess I was living in this world where everything was perfect, inside this little bubble. All of a sudden, one event caused that bubble to pop, and everything inside spilled out, making a huge mess.[5] I stared in the mirror tonight, watching myself cry hysterically.[6] I've never been in this situation before, where I have no friends.

And Steph… of all people. How could she betray me like that? She said, "It's because you like Jenna

1. Spoiler alert: it's about to get worse.

2. I guess Aaron and Jenna had started dating.

3. For my group of friends, "fag" was just about the worst thing you could call someone. I vaguely understood that it was a derogatory term for a gay person, but my classmates and I used it as a catchall term for things that were terrible and had nothing to do with sexual orientation.

4. Touché, Aaron.

5. As you can see, by age eleven I felt I had mastered the use of metaphor.

6. I definitely don't recommend doing this—it's self-indulgent and guaranteed to extend the duration of your wallowing session.

more than you like me." I told her that wasn't true, but she doesn't believe me. Can't she see I need her? We were best friends. What happened?[1]

I must deserve this. I must have done something so wrong—well, I've done lots of things wrong. So I guess I do deserve this, and God is just paying me back.[2]

Last night, I felt as if I were living in a dream—a nightmare, I guess. I was seriously considering just killing myself, but then I was like, "Come on, Emily, stop being such a retard. Stop trying to make your life into some dramatic soap opera." So I didn't kill myself.[3] But everything is going so wrong!

MARCH 10, 1998

So Zach hates me. Just great. I'm starting to hate him, too, mostly because he is so confusing. We're still going out, technically, I guess.

In Gym, Maggie ran up to me and said, "You're still going out with Zach, you know. He still likes you."

I sighed. "Tell him… that I said he can eat shit." She was like, "Cool!" and she told him.

After lunch, Matt came up to me, being nice, and said, "Zach is going to dump you."[4] I mean, it was nice of him to tell me, so I can dump Zach first.

Zach walked by looking at me, and I glared at him.

Matt said loudly, "Zach has this philosophy in life: hump 'em and dump 'em!"

I held up my hand, as if I was going to smack Zach, but he said, "If you hit me, I'll get Amanda Collins to kick your ass." So I put down my hand and walked away.

1. I wonder what Steph's diary would have looked like. What would she have included? Which interactions would she have picked apart and analyzed, if any? How would she have experienced the sequence of events that led to what I interpreted as her betrayal of me? I doubt she kept a diary though–Steph was always embarrassed of her handwriting and spelling. But I, ever self-centered, was just annoyed that she never wanted to exchange notes between classes.

2. My assumption that I must have deserved this is almost universal among targets of "slut" shaming. I was internalizing what others were telling me, even using my understanding of God to justify it.

3. This tactic of talking to myself reasonably still works sometimes when I'm feeling overwhelmed. But it won't always work for everyone. Especially when it comes to considering suicide, it's crucial to be able to depend on someone else for support, rather than taking it upon yourself. Luckily, there are now suicide hotlines especially for youth. I've included some of them in the Resources section of this book.

4. Maybe it was the "eat shit" thing, or maybe it was that he was always looking for an excuse.

Aaron hates Jenna now, and he has a crush on Lisa.

Zach and I have this hate thing going on, like trying to make the other person jealous and stuff. For instance, Zach saw me watching him from Jenna's locker, so he started flirting with Amanda Collins!

In study hall, Zach came in to do some homework or something, and he sat behind me. I got up and walked over to where Nathan and Tyler were sitting and asked Tyler to borrow his homework so I could copy it. He gave it to me, and I saw Zach glaring at me as I walked back to my desk.

Two seconds later, a wadded-up piece of paper whizzed by my head. I turned around and whispered, "You immature bastard!"

He hissed back, "You're an immature bitch!"

I whispered back, "I'm doing what I'm supposed to be doing in study hall! You're flicking fucking spitballs at my head!"

"Oh yeah, doing what you're supposed to be doing—copying from Tyler!"[1]

Even though I pretend to hate him, I have this place in my heart that's empty now that the stupid asshole is gone. I miss him.

MARCH 12, 1998

Today in Gym, Zach was sitting next to Maggie on the bleachers and I was sitting on the other side of her. Maggie was making a paper fortune-teller.[2] Zach and I started talking, and it started off as us throwing insults at each other but soon we got to something meaningful.

Zach said, "You're such a bitch!"[3]

1. Well, points to Zach for throwing spitballs in the name of academic integrity.

2. Next to compatibility tests, paper fortune-tellers were the best way to pass the time during and after school. First, you folded a square sheet of paper into what looked like an origami flower with spaces to insert your forefingers and thumbs. Then you wrote creative "fortunes" under the flaps and put numbers and colors on the outside. Finally, you accosted someone and demanded that they "Pick a number!" then "Pick a color!" moving your fingers and thumbs back and forth until you landed on their "fortune," which, you were sorry to have to inform them, was simply that "the person you have a crush on will fart next to you and it will be really loud and stinky."

3. Like I said… something meaningful.

I said, "You act as if I did something wrong to you!"

He said, "You did! You act all PMS y toward me, telling me to fuck off."

I screamed, "Well, you used me!"

"No, I didn't!"

"Then why did you all of a sudden hate me after we went to third base?"

Matt walked by and snickered, "Hump 'em and dump 'em, right, Zach?"[1]

Zach looked at me pleadingly and said, "I never said that." I glared at him. He said, "Fine, you don't believe me?"

I could tell he was getting mad, so I said softly, "No, I believe you."

He smiled. "Good."[2]

After school, he called me. He informed me that we were still going out: "I never officially dumped you."

I sighed, "Well, when you called me a whore you pretty much dumped me, and if you didn't, then I'd only be in my right mind to dump you."

He said, "Fine, then dump me."

"No…"

"Why not?"

"I don't know how to dump someone."

"Just say, 'I don't want to go out with you anymore.'"

"But I can't…"

"Okay." He gave up.

Then I confessed to him that I am bulimic, even though I am not, and so he decided to try to make himself throw up. I don't know if he succeeded. So we're on good terms now.[3]

1. Again, Matt with the perfect comedic timing.

2. I'd like to point out that this entire exchange took place *over* Maggie, who was just trying to make a fortune-teller.

3. I'm not sure what part of this last bit is the strangest: that I lied about being bulimic, that it could possibly be unclear whether the person on the other end of the phone had thrown up or not, or that this bizarre exchange somehow signified to me that we were "on good terms now."

MARCH 14, 1998

Today my life got worse! I was on the phone on three-way with Aaron and Jenna, talking about Zach. Jenna said, "Um, Emily... I think there's something I should tell you."

I said, "Is it about Zach? Is it that he doesn't like me anymore?"

"Well, not really."

"Is it that he likes Amanda Collins?"

She hesitated. "No... he doesn't like Amanda Collins."

"Then what is it?"

"I don't think I should tell you... you'd be really sad."

I sighed. "I'm already sad anyway, so just tell me."

She said, "Okay. Zach and Steph are going out."

I didn't feel the pain of it right away. I was just shocked.

Jenna told me, "Steph called me last night and said she and Zach were a couple. I thought she might be lying, so I called Zach to make sure. He said he kind of liked her and might ask her out."[1]

And that's when it hit me. Actually, it probably didn't. It probably won't hit me until I see them kiss or something. But I guess it was then that I realized that I no longer had Zach, and that Steph was a big bitch.

I said, "I'm going to cry."

Aaron said gently, "It's okay, go right ahead and cry." He is so great. He told me he would set me up with his cute cousin who is in eighth grade and goes to Catholic school. But who cares.

I remember how Steph was there, being hap-

1. Already "a couple," or "kind of liked her and might ask her out..." It's semantics, really.

py for me, when Zach and I first kissed. At least I know that Aaron is always there for me. Jenna too, maybe.

I just really can't believe that Steph and Zach… oh, gosh. I thought I loved him! How stupid was I? Pretty stupid.

I've been betrayed by the one person I thought I loved the most. But I'm not really angry, I'm just sad. Extremely sad, and feeling betrayed. I feel like killing myself, really. That would teach those two a lesson! But they probably wouldn't even care.[1]

MARCH 15, 1998

Today I spent lying in bed, feeling sorry for myself. I imagined slitting my wrist and leaving a suicide note: "Steph and Zach, I hope you're happy." But then I decided against it, because I would never be able to purposefully slice my skin. It would hurt too much.

So I went down to the cold basement without a blanket, hoping that I would freeze to death. But there would be no scars so everyone would think it was an accident. And I didn't want them to think it was an accident. I wanted them to know that I had killed myself because of Steph and Zach.

I went upstairs and lay down on my parents' bed, contemplating another way to kill myself.[2]

But then I saw a picture on my mom's dresser of my grandma and grandpa, looking happy and in love. I thought about how my grandma had died after living such a long, full, happy, successful life, and how if I killed myself now, I would be ending my life when it was still incomplete. So I picked up the

1. The limits of my perspective are most clear in the way I wrote about suicide. This wasn't just empty rambling: I really spent a lot of time coming up with ways to kill myself that wouldn't hurt very much and that I believed I could actually go through with. But even in instances where I was considering suicide because of the attention people might pay to me, or because I wanted to get revenge, it was no less serious. If I had gone through with it, I would still be dead. So many different factors go into a child's decision to end her own life, but one common thread is that, as children, we lack the understanding that life can get better. We've never survived emotional devastation before, so it's impossible to fathom how we *can* survive. That's why we need to rely on adults who have that perspective and lived experience to help us overcome it.

2. I didn't write about it, but I remember my mom coming in at a few different points and trying to comfort me. I wish I hadn't been so convinced that she would never understand.

phone and called Jenna.

"Now your bangs are curled, your lashes twirled, and still the world is cruel. Wipe off that angel face and go back to high school." —some guy from Grease[1]

MARCH 18, 1998

Some people are saying that Zach is going out with Steph just to make me jealous, but some people are saying that he really likes her. He goes out of his way to bug me.

Lisa and Catherine told me that all of them don't really like Jenna, and I don't know whether or not to tell her. I don't think I will. But it is so annoying when she stops walking down the hall with me to walk with them, and I know they don't want her to. Oh, well.[2]

I wish I could go back in time three weeks, to February 25th, the day before I went to third base with Zach. I wouldn't go over Matt's house and my life would stay perfect.[3]

Jenna is sleeping over Steph's house tomorrow night, and they are meeting Zach out somewhere. The thought of it makes me sick.

Tomorrow, I'm planning on telling Zach I'm sorry for whatever the hell it was that I did wrong, and I'm going to confront Steph. I'm going to say, "Why are you being like this? You know me too well, you know how much you're killing me… can you just stop it?" I'm going to see if that works.[4]

Matt called today. He said Aaron told him that he doesn't like me. But he was being really nice, too. He listened to me whine about Zach. Matt said,

1. I can only speculate about the mental leap I made to the lyrics of "Beauty School Dropout" from *Grease*: Was it the part about the world being "cruel" that resonated with me? Or did I just relate to every character with awesomely curled bangs? My parents didn't allow me to watch any movies rated PG-13 (not until I was thirteen, anyway), but somehow *Grease* had slipped through the cracks. We owned a VHS copy of it and my sister and I had memorized all the songs including, interestingly, Rizzo's ode to surviving "slut" shaming, "There Are Worse Things I Could Do."

2. I have a feeling the amount of bullying you encounter directly correlates with the amount of *halls* in your life.

3. I remember having this thought often over the next couple of years; I pinpointed the turning point in my life as that one afternoon at Matt's house.

4. Spoiler alert: it doesn't work.

"You know you still like him!"

I said, "No, I don't."

"Yes, you do."

I sighed, "Okay, I do."

He laughed, "You're stupid."[1] Matt told me he doesn't even like Zach. I'm kind of hoping all Zach's friends will ditch him and that he'll come crawling back.

Today in Gym class, Zach sat behind me on the bleachers with some of his friends.[2] I was sitting with Maggie. I didn't even know he was there until Maggie said, "Emily, look behind you!" I glanced behind me, saw Zach, and quickly turned back around.

Zach said, "Maggie, why do you always have to say stupid things like that?"

Some boys were like, "Um… Emily? Would you go out with… Zach wants to know… Zach has something to ask you." I looked at Zach. He looked away.

Finally one of them said, "Zach wants to know if you'd go out with… Scott." I glared at Zach, and he smiled. I turned back around, put on my sneakers, and left without saying anything.[3]

I heard someone say, "If you want to hook back up with her…"

And then someone else said, "Yeah, he wants her back." I pretended I hadn't heard.

But now that I know that he's meeting Steph somewhere tomorrow night… I'm so depressed. Zach thinks I'm going out with Aaron's cousin who is in the eighth grade and goes to Catholic school.

Matt called again, at 9 p.m. tonight. His brother was talking in the background, sounding drunk. I said, "Um… isn't it a little late?"

1. Like I said, he was being really nice.

2. Wasn't there any *activity* involved in gym class? It seems like we were always just sitting on the bleachers. I remember never wanting to participate in gym class because there was no time to take a shower afterward, and I was afraid of being gross and sweaty for the rest of the school day. An easy way to get out of class was to "forget" my sneakers (you can't play dodgeball in flip-flops!), and I pulled that trick almost every day. I think the gym teacher used to send us to sit on the bleachers as a punishment for misbehaving, too, which would explain Zach's presence.

3. Poor Scott. He was always on the periphery of the "popular" group of kids, but for some reason, no one ever seemed to take him seriously.

He said, "Is it a little late?"

"Yeah, it's 9 p.m." I sounded really annoyed on purpose.

He said, "Okay, never mind," and hung up.[1]

MARCH 22, 1998

Bad news. Bad, bad news. Jenna called and told me that she had just been at the pizza place, and Steph and Zach were there. The three of them went up to the train tracks, and Steph and Zach were making out.

I feel like I've been ripped in half and gutted and then had my guts stuffed down my throat.[2] Zach and Steph went alone to the pizza place and happened to meet Jenna there, and then… they were making out. How could she? How could he?

I feel so dead. Out of all my peers that I have ever loved, I've never loved anyone as much as I loved those two. And then they betrayed me… together. I can just picture them kissing, grabbing onto each other, so in love. Like Zach and I used to be. Only now it's Zach and Steph. And neither of them cares about me anymore. They don't even feel guilty.[3]

> You kiss a girl, you don't care who,
> As long as she's in love with you.
> Let's see how many you can do
> Without them knowing you're untrue.
> You get somewhere and then you're done.
> You use them and you think it's fun.
> You swear your love for every one.
> They fall for you, and then you run.

1. A drunk dial at age eleven! Matt started early. As I explained, his father had been killed a couple of years before, but I'm not sure where his mother was. Chances are, she was working more than one job to support her four kids and putting misplaced trust in Matt's older brother to look out for his younger siblings. Of course, it's also possible that neither Matt nor his older brother was drunk during this phone call, and I was just speculating based on what I assumed to be true about them.

2. Well. That was graphic.

3. And now, here it comes… *the poetry.*

MARCH 24, 1998

Steph dumped Zach yesterday. It doesn't really affect me much. Well, okay, yes it does.[1] But Steph hates me still, and Jenna is a poser to be like Steph.

I told everyone that I am going out with a boy named Mike from a different town, to prove that I am over Zach.[2] Zach was making fun of "Mike" in Library Skills class today.[3] This is how it happened:

I was sitting across the room from Zach. Michelle and Maggie were sitting near Zach, and they wanted to sit near me so they came over. I said to Maggie, "Let's all go back to your table."

She said, "Why?"

I said, "Because… then we will be far away from Ms. Albertson and we can goof off." Of course, it was really so I could be near Zach, but nobody needed to know that.

We were going to make the boys who were already sitting at Zach's table leave. I said, "Up, up! Go sit over there."

Zach thought I was talking to him and he said, "No! No! We were here first! I don't need to take that crap!"[4]

Finally, he said, "Well. You can sit here, but we're not moving."

I said, "Fine." And we sat there.

Zach leaned over and said in a low, sarcastic voice, "Mike."

I looked up. "What's wrong with Mike?"[5]

Zach said, "He's a fat shit."

"No, he's not. Besides, I'm not even going out with him."[6] I sighed. Then I made a puzzled face

1. Yeah, let's be honest here.

2. Wait, what happened to "Adam" from "camp"?

3. A decade after I took Library Skills, virtually all the material I'd learned had become completely obsolete. How much time was wasted memorizing the Dewey Decimal system and navigating card catalogs?

4. I have to side with Zach on this one. Where did I get off being so bossy?

5. Other than that, you know, he doesn't exist?

6. And also, he doesn't exist.

and stared at him: "Why do you even care?"

He made a mean face. "Why would I care?"

I shrugged and played innocent. "I don't know. Why do you?"

He looked at me in this way that I hate. He looked really angry and pissed off. But I like it more when he is mean to me than when he just ignores me, or when he snaps, "Shut up, Emily! I wasn't talking to you."

And I hate it when I open my mouth to say something to him and he moves away purposefully. It is much better when he's like, "Your dad is gay!"[1] Because, I mean, at least I'm getting some attention. At least he took the time to notice me and say something to me.[2]

MARCH 28, 1998

Today I went to the mall with Michelle. I bought jean shorts, a see-through candle with chunks of colored wax floating inside, funky sunglasses, and Michelle bought matching frog key chains and gave one to me.

Also we went into a photo booth and took pictures of ourselves with a frame around them that says, "BEST FRIENDS," and got the pictures made into stickers. So I guess Michelle is my best friend now.[3]

Jenna hasn't been calling me all that much. I guess she's really confused right now. She wants to be friends with Steph's group, but she wants to be friends with Erin's group, too.

Actually, she's kind of using Erin's group as a last resort. She knows now that Steph's group doesn't

1. As I said before, we thought "gay" was about the worst insult you could call someone.

2. As a girl, I was often accused of "just wanting attention," as if this were the worst possible motivation for doing or saying something. But why *shouldn't* girls—or anyone—want attention? We all deserve attention. I'd go so far as to say we all need it. But so often girls' feelings and actions are dismissed because we're expected to be humble and quiet, not cause trouble, and not draw attention to ourselves.

3. *That* was easy!

like her, but it's still hard for her to let go. Just like it was for me. I can empathize with Jenna.

In church today, I saw Aaron with his cousin who goes to Catholic school.[1] He is drop-dead gorgeous. I was staring at him all through the service, even though I knew I should be paying attention. I don't think he noticed.[2]

MARCH 29, 1998

Today it was like, 90 degrees out! Alicia called me and I went rollerblading with her. She is a seventh-grader who lives in my neighborhood and doesn't really care what's going on in the sixth grade.

Andrew rode by on his bike, and we ended up walking around the neighborhood with him for FOUR HOURS! He is so hot. At one point, my sister and some other boys who live nearby came out and started walking around with us, too.[3]

They are not cute or popular, and I am not attracted to them in any way, shape, or form, but they are boys, so I felt cool walking around with them. Andrew let me ride his bike and so I felt even cooler.

We walked by Steph's house and I felt confident so I yelled, "Steph! Come out and play!"

Her sister, who is sixteen, came to the window and said, "Is that you, Emily?"

I said, "Yeah."

She said, "Is there something you want to say?"

I said, "I just wanted to see if Steph wanted to come out."

She said, "Well, why don't you come to the door and say it?"[4]

I said, "No, we were just walking by."[5]

1. There were three Catholic churches in my town. My family didn't really belong to any one in particular; where we attended Mass each week depended on what time we woke up and finished eating breakfast. My older sister stopped going to church around this time and eventually refused to be confirmed into the Catholic faith. I had started to question the dogma, too, but almost all the boys I had a crush on also had parents who dragged them to Mass, so I saw that hour each Sunday as an opportunity to watch them surreptitiously from as close a pew as possible.

2. And neither did God, probably.

3. If four hours seems like an absurdly long time to be walking around the neighborhood, that's because it *is*.

4. I never spent much time with Steph's older sister, but I always thought she was really pretty and *really* cool in a scary kind of way. Like my family, Steph's family had recently moved to our town from a less-snobby Boston suburb but unlike me and my siblings, Steph and her sister never got in the habit of pronouncing their r's. To my ears, those missing r's made everything sound slightly tougher and even menacing.

5. Maybe we'll stop by again in four hours.

I told Jenna about it over the phone, and she laughed. Then she said she had to go. A little while later, she called back and said, "I was talking to Lisa, and she said that Steph told her that you guys went to Steph's house and were throwing rocks at it and pounding on the windows and calling her a slut."

Why would Steph lie about that? Oh, I know why. To ruin my life and build her own popularity. Maggie said that Steph is trying to get Amanda Collins to beat me up. I think I could hold my own in a fight against her, but the thing is, everyone would be rooting for her.

MARCH 30, 1998

Today before Homeroom, I was at my locker getting my books. The hall was almost empty. All of a sudden, I heard Steph's voice say, "Emily." I stood up and turned around, so I was facing her.

She had a smart look on her face and her hands on her hips. She said, "I heard you were at my house yesterday." I just looked at her. I didn't know what to say. Suddenly, her face turned angry and she pushed me into the lockers, hard. She said, "Don't mess with me!"

I just stood there, stunned, unable to really think about what had just happened. By the time I realized I should probably push her back, she was already down the hall.[1]

I ate lunch alone in Ms. Walsh's room. I felt sick. I so badly want to move to another town, another state, another *country*.

On March 24th, there was a shooting in Arkansas. Two boys pulled the fire alarm in their school, and

1. It was probably a good thing I didn't have a chance to push her back. Not that I would have, anyway—I never initiated fights, and the few times I found myself engaged in one, my mind kind of shut off in fear until the violence passed.

when all the kids were outside, they shot and killed four girls and a teacher. One of them was eleven and one of them was thirteen, and the thirteen-year-old had just been dumped by his girlfriend. He had tried to kill her, too, and right now she is in the hospital.

In Drama class today, we were supposed to write letters to the ex-girlfriend, whose name is Candace, telling her that we hoped she got better and stuff like that. Zach sat at the table next to mine and leaned over to read my letter. He said, "She'll be reading your letter and she'll be thinking, 'Wow! What a bitch!'"[1]

I am trying to be nice to everyone, but no one is nice back. It just makes them hate me more. I don't know how to act so that they'll like me. I want everyone to like me, but everyone likes different types of people, and how can I be all those types at once?[2]

APRIL 2, 1998

There is a dance tomorrow night, and I think it is going to suck. People are saying that Steph is going to beat me up. I just want to be like, fine, you hate me, who cares. But she has to drag it all out and she wants to fight me.

Today after school, I went over Alicia's house. When I was walking home later, I saw Andrew and Chris Walker riding toward me on their bikes. I tried to move to the other side of the street, but they kept swerving so they were right in front of me. Finally, they braked.

Andrew said, "Emily, I need to talk to you… over here." I went up to him and he said softly, "Will you hook up with Chris?"

1. Somehow, I think Candace Porter had more important things to worry about in the days following the Jonesboro massacre. The event shocked the country and rattled my classmates and me since the shooters, Mitchell Johnson and Andrew Golden, were sixth-graders just like us. They had pulled the fire alarm at school and opened fire when the students and teachers filed outside, killing four female students and one teacher. This was a time when school shootings were still rare, so I don't think there was any protocol for how our teachers should go about addressing it with us. As far as I can remember, aside from these letters we wrote in Drama class, we weren't really given any tools to cope with the news.

2. I know a lot of adults who still struggle with this conundrum. Myself included, sometimes, to be honest.

I said, "No, of course not!" And I walked away. Chris is Alicia's ex-boyfriend and I think they still kind of like each other.[1]

APRIL 17, 1998

Today, my last class was Gym. The guidance counselor was there, Mr. Shaw. Maggie and I were hanging out and talking instead of playing the game, and Mr. Shaw said, "So you guys aren't really participating that much in the game, are you?"

When Mr. Shaw was out of hearing range, Zach mumbled, "That's because the game sucks, because Emily's playing and Emily sucks."[2]

I turned around to face him and said, "Shut up, Stupid!" And I pushed him away from me.

He yelled, "That fucking hurt! You ho! Now I'll just get all the people who are going to beat you up already to beat you up even harder!"

In the locker room, Emma told me that he had asked her to beat me up, but that she wasn't going to.[3]

Why should I care, or want to live?
There's nothing more for me to give.
I'm only bringing others pain
And to myself I do the same.
There's no excuse or reason why
I should not end it all, and die.
Something sharp. A little slit.
And that would be the end of it.
The blood is trickling, pouring through
And all my troubles leave me, too.
Form a pool upon the floor,
Not inside me anymore.

1. The whole riding-a-bike-toward-you-and-braking-at-the-last-minute thing is quite terrifying to me. Why do people use it as a flirting mechanism? It's just threatening.

2. This is representative of my interactions with Mr. Shaw. I'd sit sullenly and stare at the ground when he tried to engage me in conversation, and as soon as he was out of earshot the bullying would start up again. He seems to have been trying to help, but I never felt comfortable confiding in him.

3. Gee, thanks, *Emma*.

And then I see my mother's face,
The tears that seem so out of place.
Why does she look so awfully sad?
What have I done that is so bad?
The blood is mixing with the tears,
Revealing all my deepest fears.
And with the setting of the sun,
I think, too late: what have I done?

MAY 1, 1998

Okay, I really don't understand Zach. Today, in Music class, we had a substitute who didn't care what the hell we did. Zach and I got into a huge fight about whose CD we were going to listen to. It was actually kind of fun—we made eye contact the whole time—but I don't think he noticed.

At the end of class, he had drawn this perverse picture of George Jetson masturbating that he and all the boys were looking at. I said, "Can I see?" He looked up to see if the sub was looking, and then handed it to me, quickly and secretly. I didn't think he would let me see it![1]

Right now, the entire eighth grade is on a class trip to New York City. The only kids who aren't allowed to go are the ones who have been suspended. There is one group of boys who have been suspended like, twenty times each, so they didn't go on the trip and they were in school today.[2]

Today in the hall, right after school ended, I stopped at Melanie's locker because I saw that Michelle was there, and I said "hi" to Scott, too, who started blushing so bad. I was standing with my back to the hall, facing toward the lockers.

1. If you want to know if someone likes you, first ask yourself: has he ever let me look at the drawing of George Jetson masturbating he made during music class?

2. Twenty times each was almost certainly an exaggeration, but that group of boys was always getting in trouble with the administration. One of them was always sitting outside the principal's office, waiting to be punished for smoking in the bathroom, yelling in a teacher's face, or, one time, throwing a trash bin through a window.

All of a sudden, I felt someone pinch my butt! I turned around and saw that group of eighth-grade boys walking by, and Chris Walker was looking back at me, smiling. I just looked after them and didn't say anything.[1]

MAY 6, 1998

Oh oh oh! Guess what! I am going out with Nathan! Yesterday, some of his friends told me that he liked me. I honestly thought they were lying. After everything that's happened, how could any boy ever like me again, let alone the most adorable boy in the sixth grade?[2]

At lunch, Jenna and Erin ran over to Nathan's table to make sure he really liked me. When they ran back, Jenna told me, "He said, 'I really like her. Why won't she believe me?'" So I told all his friends to tell him that yes, I would go out with him.

Today, I wasn't sure if we were actually going out, so I asked his really good friend, Daniel, who said, "Yes!" Then Nathan came down the stairs and I ran away. The weird thing is, I haven't said a word to him since we started going out.[3]

Yesterday, Melanie came over. We went bike riding to the library, and Andrew and Chris Walker were there. So Melanie and I got back on our bikes and rode away. We noticed that Andrew and Chris were following us at a safe distance.

Chris called out, "Emily!" Melanie and I rode a little faster. But soon Andrew and Chris were right next to us. Chris said, "Emily, why are you mad at me?"

I said, "I'm not mad at you."

1. One of the most upsetting consequences of being the school "slut" is that people think they have a right to your body. Once you have that label, it's assumed you've given up the right to decide who gets to touch you and when. This instance was notable because the boy who pinched my butt was one of the dangerous older boys, but this kind of thing happened almost every day; it was so commonplace that I didn't find it necessary to record every instance in my diary.

2. This rhetorical question demonstrates the damage that had been done to my self-esteem. Because of my reputation, I couldn't see a future where anyone would want to be associated with me romantically *ever* again. Pretty dismal.

3. Well yeah, because I ran away from him.

He said, "But... you're being rude. I thought I was your friend."

I laughed. "How am I being rude?"

Chris said, "You could be a little more friendly, Emily."

Andrew said, "All we're asking for is a helping HAND."

Chris said, "Those nice, pretty hands... just like you did for Zach."

I said, "I did not give Zach a hand job." Finally, they left us alone and we rode home.[1]

MAY 22, 1998

Today, Jenna and I went to the movies and met Nathan and Daniel there. Daniel sat down, then Nathan, then me, then Jenna. The movie was Godzilla, so there were lots of scary parts—Jenna and I would grab onto each other's hands and huddle together, even though I really wanted to grab onto Nathan.

My elbow was on the armrest between us, and every once in a while he would put his elbow on it, too, so it would touch mine. Movies are good for dates, because you don't have to think of anything to talk about.[2]

After the movie, Nathan and Daniel went into the bathroom. My dad came to pick up me and Jenna while they were in there, so we left. As we were walking out, I saw Nathan and Daniel, standing in the lobby watching us leave. I waved, but felt bad for not properly saying goodbye. Maybe he would have kissed me! That was my first real date, and my parents didn't know about it.[3]

1. This interaction strikes me as deeply creepy, especially since the boys behaving in such a threatening way were only thirteen or fourteen years old themselves. It's another example of how, once I was labeled a "slut," I was seen as no longer having the right to decide which people I wanted to interact with sexually. Boys assumed I was fair game.

2. Still true.

3. And now for some self-indulgent, dark poetry that doesn't even *rhyme*.

Love wraps itself around your heart.

It holds on tight and won't let go.

It floats in your mind like a cumulus[1] cloud,

Blocking out the logic

That you didn't want to believe, anyway.

Love lifts you up: you ride the wind.

Your insides melt away like snow.

It swims through your veins,

Touching every corner of your body and soul.

And then when it can't get any better,

When you feel like you're sitting on top of
 the world,

Love pushes you off the highest cliff

And laughs as you shatter on the jagged
 rocks below.

It betrays you,

Leaves you, wounded, to die

Or try to recover on your own.

But before it leaves,

It takes a chunk of your heart

Leaving a space that will remain empty

Forever.

1. In case people are wondering how I knew how to spell cumulus at this point, the answer is: I didn't. It was originally misspelled as "cumulous"–but we've corrected it here.

JUNE 4, 1998

Nathan wasn't in school today. Yesterday, I walked home from school with Scott. We stopped at his house and jumped on his trampoline, and then I walked home.[2]

Today in school, Matt said in front of his friends, "Have fun at Scott's house, Emily?" I just shrugged. He said, "Scott told us you made out with him."

I was like, "WHAT?!" Matt started to laugh. I ran up to Scott and asked him about it, but he de-

2. Trampolines were/are *so* much fun.

nied ever saying anything.

Today after school, Nathan called. He said, "What did you do with Scott?"

I said, "Oh, my gosh, I didn't do anything with Scott. You don't think I did, do you?"

"No! No. I mean, really. Scott?!"[1]

We talked about Zach and Matt in negative ways for a while. Nathan thinks exactly the same way I do. It's really cool. After about fifteen minutes, he said he had to go. "Should I call you back?" He asked.

I said, "Um... yeah, okay."

But then my sister got on the phone and stayed on all night, so even if he did call, he wouldn't be able to get through.[2] I think I really love Nathan. He would never hurt me like Zach did.

JUNE 8, 1998

Today is a Monday. Nothing really special happened today, but on Friday, we went on a field trip to the art museum. Nathan wasn't in my group, but Scott was, and he kept asking me, "How far would you go with Nathan?"

I was just like, "Um... I don't know."

After school, Nathan called. He said, "Hey, want to do something today?"

I said, "Sure, like what?"

He said, "We could go to the club."[3] I didn't really feel like going to the club, so I told him that. He said, "Want to go bowling?"

I knew he was joking. "Bowling?"

"Yeah."

"Seriously?!"

"Yeah."[4]

1. Poor Scott.

2. I guess we didn't yet have call waiting on our home phone line—either that, or I didn't trust my sister to interrupt her own conversation to take another call. My sister is two years older than I am and although we're close friends now, in middle school we didn't much care what happened to each other. She was aware of my reputation and from time to time advised me to steer clear of certain people, but overall she didn't have patience for the details of my life, because she was busy navigating her own social sphere. The only times we got along were when we were both grounded and had nothing to do but cut up old magazines to make collages together.

3. By "the club," we did not mean what one gets "up in" when one wants to do shots, dance, and behave in ways that inspire rap songs. We were talking about a much less glamorous recreation club our parents belonged to, where we'd often spend the day swimming in the lake, going on interminable nature walks, or taking boating lessons.

4. So... not joking.

"Well, let me ask." My mom said it was okay, so about ten minutes later, Nathan and his mom arrived to pick me up. His mom drove us to the bowling alley and we got out.

I felt really stupid wearing those dorky bowling shoes they make you wear, but hey, he was wearing them, too. A little while into the first string, Nathan asked me, "How come you never talk to me in school?" I just got up and took my turn. When I came back to sit down again, he said, "Do you like me?"[1]

I laughed, "Yes!"

During the second string, Nathan asked, "What was Scott asking you at the museum?"

"Not anything, really."

"Oh. Because I think he might have been asking me the same thing." I shrugged. We walked to McDonald's, which is across the street from the bowling alley. While we were walking, he asked me, "Come on. What was Scott asking you at the museum?"

I decided he already knew, so why not just say it? "He was asking me how far I would go with you."

"What did you say?"

"I said, 'Shut up, you're getting annoying.' And he was."

He said, "Oh, well..." He took a deep breath. "What would you say if I asked you?"

"I'd probably say, 'I don't know.'"[2]

"Would you go to first base?"[3]

"Yeah, but..."

"But what?"

"Well, ever since what happened with Zach, I

1. I'm impressed that Nathan had the guts to be so frank with me, especially since I was apparently running in the other direction whenever I saw him coming at school.

2. That sounds about right.

3. For us, first base meant French-kissing.

haven't really been able to trust that many people. I mean, I'm afraid that you could be using me, too."

"I'm not using you." We reached McDonald's and got to a small, two-person booth. He said, "Sit down."

"I need to go get some food."

"Just sit down for a minute." I sat down. "Emily, I'm not using you. Why do you think that?"

"I don't think you're using me. Just… if I went to first base with you and everyone found out, they would think I'm a slut even more than they already do."

"No one needs to know."

"I'd have to tell Jenna and then she'll tell everyone."

"Why do you think you'd have to tell Jenna?"[1]

"Well, she's my best friend. I tell her everything. Do boys do that? Do you tell Daniel everything?"

"Um… let's go get some food." So we did. When we got back to the table, I started eating a French fry. He said, "I don't understand you, Emily."

I said, "Oh, that's funny. I always thought I was pretty easy to understand."[2]

"You act like it in school, but… I don't know." We talked about all other important things: kissing, what second base even means, best friends, shallowness, how different people act in school, houses, money, people we like, people we don't like, parents, sisters and brothers, everything.

He is so good to talk to, and we never ran out of things to say. He is really a nice person—really deep and understanding. I love him. Really, I do. He understands me well. He's the type of person I want to end up with.

1. That's a valid question.

2. That wasn't true at all. In fact, I often purposefully went out of my way to be misleading. Most of the time, I had no idea what was motivating my behavior other than a vague desire to seem mysterious.

JUNE 12, 1998

Nathan is going to an all-boys Catholic school next year. He told me that he is scared I'll break up with him when he starts going there, because I'll never see him and I'll start liking other boys whom I do see a lot. I told him not to worry. We can keep in touch—it's called a phone. Plus, there are dances almost every Friday at his new school, and I can go to those with him. I love him so much—I don't know what I'll do without him next year.

He wants to kiss me, though—French-kiss me. Everyone's telling me that, and I don't know what to say. I like the kind of relationship we have now: honest, but kind of shy and unsure.

Nathan called today and Daniel was at his house, so I talked to Daniel for a while. He kept telling me how Nathan's not as sweet and innocent as I think he is.

I said, "But I always thought of him as such a cute, little… a little boy!"

Daniel said, "Nathan says if you ever say that again, he's going to come over there and beat you up."

I heard Nathan yell in the background, "And then I'd do her dead body!"[1]

I knew they were just kidding, because they were laughing, but I was shocked that Nathan would say something like that. And he keeps asking me why I won't go to first base with him.

So I'm getting really worried that he only wants me because of my body, which doesn't really look like most twelve-year-olds' bodies. Normally, I would be flattered.[2] But after what happened with Zach, I'd almost rather have no boobs, so if a boy liked me, I'd

1. I'm shocked now that such violent ideas were absorbed and uttered by this otherwise kind little boy. He most likely saw necrophilia referenced in a movie and decided to threaten me with it as a way to show off, somehow. But I don't want to make excuses for him—this kind of threat is definitely a red flag in any relationship.

2. Flattered that it didn't matter to him, sexually, whether my body was alive or dead?

know it wasn't just because of that.[1]

But I don't know. I certainly want to trust Nathan. He called again tonight and said, "Remember how you said you'd go to first base with me?"

"Yeah."

"Well, can I see you on Sunday?"

"I guess so. Call me on Sunday." Then my mom told me to get off the phone. It's so strange, but I'm kind of dreading Sunday. I'm trying to think up excuses why I won't be able to kiss him. I always thought, since the first day of fifth grade, that there was nothing I'd rather do than French-kiss Nathan. But now, even after everything I've done with Zach, I can't bring myself to do it.

With Zach, it wasn't kissing Zach that I liked—it was kissing. But when I kiss Nathan, I want it to be kissing Nathan that I like. I know I really do like him, but I don't know if he likes me. I think he's probably never kissed anyone before, so he's just curious about what it's like.

1. Key word: I'd *almost* rather have no boobs. I take that back, by the way. Within a few years, I would come to love my boobs.

SUMMER BEFORE SEVENTH GRADE

JUNE 25, 1998

Now that school is out, I'm going to this camp all day until 3 p.m.[1] Then as soon as I get home, I call Nathan. Today, he and Daniel came over. We hung out all afternoon and had a lot of fun—I realized that I really love him.

Then Alicia called and asked if we wanted to go for a walk. We did, and the whole walk Alicia was flirting her butt off with Nathan. Then when we got back to my house, we went into the family room and Alicia was still flirting with Nathan. And the bad thing is, he was flirting back! She looked really pretty today, and she was sitting back with her legs out in front of her, batting her stupid eyelashes, and I wanted to rip her head off.[2]

I confronted him about it when she went upstairs, and he said, "No! What are you talking about?" And then he started making fun of her. But… I don't know. I can tell this isn't going to work.[3]

JUNE 29, 1998

I don't know what's wrong. I don't know what's happened with Nathan. I haven't seen him for two days, and normally that wouldn't be too bad, but I can sense that something is very, very wrong. Otherwise I wouldn't miss him so much.

Oh, Nathan. If you're listening, if you can read my mind, then please know that I love you and that I would do anything for you and that I want to be with you forever.[4]

1. It was a musical theater camp, and it was glorious. No one at camp went to my school, so no one knew me as anything other than a really enthusiastic singer (and mediocre dancer).

2. Ripping her head off *sounds* like a good idea, but it might have been an overreaction.

3. From "I realized that I really love him" to "I can tell this isn't going to work" in one diary entry?

4. "Sorry, it's just me here."
   –Diary

JULY 3, 1998

Two days ago, I was talking on the phone with Nathan, and he asked me to call him back at 6 p.m. But I didn't because, well, it sounds kind of silly, but I didn't want to look desperate. So he called me at 6:24 p.m. and said, "I don't think you care about me."

I said, "Of course I care about you!"

And he said, "You never call my house."

"Sure, I do." Then we started talking about something else.

After a while, he said, "Can you call me back at 9:30?" At least it sounded like he said 9:30. But he called back at 9:26 and said, "You really don't care."

I said, "Yes, I do! It's not even 9:30 yet!"

He said, "I said 9:00."

"No, you didn't."

"Yes, I did. I said 9:00."[1]

I said, "Nathan, do you think I don't like you?"

"Kinda. I always tell you how much I like you, and you never tell me how much you like me."

I said, "Oh, Nathan, but I do!" He still didn't seem convinced. He really thinks I don't like him.[2] We got off the phone, but I called him back about fifteen minutes later, to prove to him that I do like him.

Daniel wanted to talk to me and he asked, "Emily, do you like it up the pooper?" Meaning, I guess, do I like anal sex? I just laughed. Daniel said to Nathan, "She said she does!"

Nathan said in the background, "Well, I can adjust."[3]

I said, "Tell Nathan to stop making fun of me."

I heard Nathan say in the background, "I'm not making fun of her."

1. Nathan was about ten years ahead of the game when it came to setting up manipulative traps.

2. Or he just really liked drama.

3. It seems significant that as I started sensing my relationship with Nathan was becoming more unstable, it also was getting more sexually aggressive. He went from politely asking whether I liked him at the bowling alley to suggesting we have anal sex pretty quickly.

I said, "Daniel, ask Nathan why he's always so mean to me!" Daniel did.

Nathan said, "I'm not. I love her."

Daniel said, "Nathan says he loves you." I knew because I had heard him. He is so incredibly sweet.

JULY 13, 1998

Today is Monday. I got back from a family trip on Friday and I called Nathan first thing. His mother said that she was on the other line and that he would call me back. Well, it's Monday afternoon and he still hasn't called me back. Maybe I should just call him. I'm really worried.

LATER ON JULY 13, 1998

Okay, I called Nathan. But his mother answered and said he was at the club with Daniel, but that she would leave him a note telling him to call me. And he did call me. We talked on the phone for about a half hour, and then he said he was going to go outside and burn ants with Daniel, but that he would call me back in about fifteen minutes.[1] He did call me back! We talked for about another fifteen minutes.

He said, "You know what sucks?"

I said, "What?"

He said, "That I can't go anywhere with you."

"Why not?"

"Because people give me shit about what you did with Zach."

I said, "I know. They should really get over it."[2] He agreed. Then he said he had to go but that he'd call me back. Well, guess what. That was at about

1. Is that all the time it takes to burn ants?

2. He managed to remind me of my abysmal social standing while simultaneously suggesting that he cared more about what others thought of me than he did about my feelings. The worst part is, I agreed with him.

5 p.m., and now it's 9:22 and he still hasn't called back. I really don't know what's up with him. I love him so much—I'm not going to give him up that easily.

JULY 26, 1998

Shauna's party was a major disappointment.[1] Nathan was going on vacation with his family, so he couldn't go. Daniel was there and he was being super funny as usual. He stole my sandal and hid it in the mailbox.[2] Louis was there, too. He is so annoying usually, but he was actually being okay this time. He's really funny and weird, but he's not cute at all.

Another boy named Mark was there, and I've wanted to get to know him ever since last summer when Melanie said he was super hot. Well, he's not super hot but he is semi-good-looking. He's really nice, too. I don't think I'd ever said a word to him other than at this party.

Shauna brought out her stuffed dog for some reason and said, "See this dog? This is my lesbian lover." I took it from her and started hugging it and stuff.

Then Mark said, "I don't think that dog is a lesbian." I said, "Why not?"[3]

He said, "Because I did her last night!" And he grabbed it and started running down the street with it.

I chased him and was like, "No! It's Shauna's lesbian dog!" And it was a joke we had between us.[4]

If I ever break up with Nathan, I think I'll want to go out with Mark. But I mean, it's not like I'm going to break up with Nathan anytime soon. Daniel says that Nathan thinks I still like Zach. Of course,

1. To be fair, all parties are major disappointments when you're hoping for something out of a teen movie and instead you find yourself sitting around eating Cheetos, hoping someone will suggest playing Spin the Bottle.

2. Like I said, super funny.

3. Because it is a stuffed dog?

4. Hilarious.

that's ridiculous. Well, maybe I do still like him a little. But Nathan is a much better person than Zach is.

It's been exactly five months today since I've kissed anyone. Maybe the next time I see Nathan, I'll kiss him. Or at least ask him if he wants to.

My sister French-kissed someone for the first time about two days ago, at the movies. She said it was awful. Her boyfriend is the one who kissed her. She said he had gross breath and he kept opening and closing his mouth on her tongue, and she was waiting for it to be over.[1]

1. Yup, that sounds pretty awful.

AUGUST 4, 1998.

I've been at overnight camp with Alicia and I forgot to bring my diary with me. Now that I'm home, Jenna has called. She went to sloppy second base with Erin's big brother, and she is very excited about that. She wouldn't listen to anything I said about camp. It's hard to readjust to her shallowness.

I don't know what to do. And I don't know what to do about it. And I don't know how to do it. I talked to Nathan two nights ago when I got home, and he said he'd call the next morning but he didn't. And he didn't call the rest of the day, and he didn't call today, either.

Something has got to be up, but I don't know what to do about it. I wish my life was like it was at camp, where everyone liked me and respected me and nobody hated me or sneered at me. I was popular at camp.[2] And I used to be popular at home, too. I know how it feels to be popular. But I'm not popular anymore and everyone just thinks I'm a slut and I hate it.

2. Camp felt like an escape from my reputation at home. It was a protestant Christian camp with a casual, kind atmosphere, and I enjoyed what felt to me like a more inviting alternative to the Catholicism my parents practiced.

AUGUST 13, 1998

Today, around 7 p.m., Alicia and I decided to go for a walk. A car full of boys drove by. It was Andrew, Chris Walker, and some of their older friends. They pulled into the driveway of one of their houses, right next to where we were standing.

They walked with us down to the pond, and they had beers, so I had a few sips. It tasted okay. Chris started trying to grab my boobs, and he wasn't drunk, he is just always like that.[1] They weren't flirting with Alicia as much, and I was kind of glad.

Then one of them was like, "Want to go swimming?"

And we were like, "At this nasty pond?"

And he said, "No, at my house." So we all walked to Andrew's house, and he has an aboveground pool, so we sat in the chairs around the pool.

They said, "Emily, strip down and jump in!" I said no, so Andrew grabbed my arm and started to drag me toward the pool. Then Chris joined in. I finally managed to pull away and ended up falling in the dirt.

I really didn't want them to take off my sneakers, because I wasn't wearing socks and my feet would have smelled awful.[2]

Alicia and I decided we wanted to leave. So Chris and Andrew said they'd walk us home. The whole way, Chris was wrapping his arm around me and grabbing at my boob. I stood still and told him to stop it, without sounding too mean, and he reached out and stuck his hand up my shirt. I don't know how to feel. I technically went to second base with Chris, even though I told him not to.[3]

1. If he had been drunk, it wouldn't have been an excuse for this behavior.

2. I distinctly remember the terror of this moment. Although in hindsight, I should have been afraid for my safety, at the time I was mostly just afraid that they would discover how bad my feet smelled.

3. There is such an important distinction to be made between what Chris did to me and what would actually constitute cheating on someone. He touched me without my consent. The fact that I blamed myself for this interaction is really telling, as is my reluctance to sound "too mean" in insisting that he stop touching me. I believed what other people were constantly telling me: that I was a slut.

It would hurt too much. So
down to the cold cellar wi
nket, in hopes that I wou
e to death, but there woul
rs, and everyone would th
s accident. ~~⬤~~ And I did
te think it was an accid
d them to <u>know</u> that I h
f because of ~~⬤~~ and
nt upstairs and lied down e
s bed, contemplating anothe
nit suicide. But then I sa
e of my Nonna and Nanno,
and in love. I thought a
nna had died after living
ll, happy, successful life, a
illed myself now, I would
while it was still incompl

SEVENTH GRADE

OCTOBER 25, 1998[1]

Things have changed a lot since I last wrote! Nathan and I broke up because he found out what I did with Chris Walker. I felt really awful—really awful—about that for a while, especially because I don't even like Chris, even as a friend.

At the dance two days ago, I spent a lot of time hanging out with Tyler, who is obviously cool and who I think likes me. I don't think I like him as a boyfriend.

Zach and Matt are in my History and Math classes. Matt makes fun of me most of the time, but at least he's noticing me. It's much worse when he just completely ignores me. That means he really hates me.[2]

Zach is going out with Kaylee and that doesn't bother me that much, and so he and I are semi-friends again. Not like we call each other or anything, but we talk in class and we were hanging out together at the dance a lot.

Steph and Jenna are like, glued together, but actually, that doesn't really bother me that much, either.[3]

NOVEMBER 1, 1998

Last night was Halloween. I went out with Stacy, Melanie, Gina, and Michelle. We were armed with shaving cream and eggs. We ran into Daniel, Nathan, Tyler, Louis, Jacob, and a few more of their friends. Nathan hates me now because of what I did with Chris Walker while I was still going out with him, so he started attacking me with shaving cream and stink bombs.

1. I can't say for sure why I didn't write at all for the next couple of months. It might have been that I wasn't sure how to process what happened that evening in August, or how to make sense of Nathan's decision to break up with me because of it.

2. This strikes me as a particularly pathetic outlook.

3. It probably should have bothered *them* though, since being glued together sounds uncomfortable and inconvenient. But seriously, I'm sure this did bother me. Steph and Jenna had been my best friends, and now they had both turned against me.

I guess it was kind of funny.[1] He is still as hot as ever, but he doesn't go to our school anymore. I was completely covered in shaving cream and I was freezing cold.

We walked around the neighborhood where Stacy lives, and I had major bonding time with Jacob, who is really popular. He said, "I was over Tyler's house and we were looking for you. Why didn't you come outside?" The truth is, I had seen them walking around, and Alicia and I had purposefully gone out looking for them. Isn't it ironic that in such a tiny neighborhood, we did not find each other?[2]

Jacob said, "You are covered in shaving cream!"

I said, "I know, it's freezing cold. But I'm hot anyway, right?"

And he grinned. "Yeah, but not as hot as you usually are." He said it in a joking way, but it was still flattering.

Melanie was covered in shaving cream, too. I was standing with her, and Tyler said to her, "You look ugly with shaving cream all over you."

She said, "Hey, don't call us ugly!"

He said, "I didn't. I called *you* ugly. Emily is hot." I laughed. I know I shouldn't have. I should have stood up for her.[3]

NOVEMBER 3, 1998

I miss Nathan. He is too smart and complicated for me, but I still miss him.[4] I realized that on Halloween.[5]

I decided I am starting to really like Jacob. He always knows the right thing to say, and he comes off as calm, cool, and collected but not as snobby.

1. No, it wasn't. But pretending to find it funny was probably preferable to confronting my real feelings about having my ex-boyfriend throw stink bombs at me as retaliation for an incident that we both misunderstood.

2. "Isn't it ironic..." had become one of my favorite ways to start rhetorical questions since Alanis Morissette's "Ironic" was released in 1995.

3. Ugh. I was a terrible friend.

4. Being "complicated" was about the highest compliment I could give at the time. Forget being friendly or handsome—nothing made a guy more interesting and deserving of my attention than being frustratingly opaque.

5. Because nothing makes a girl want you back like attacking her with shaving cream and stink bombs.

And he's funny. And he doesn't seem to judge me because of the reputation I have for being a slut, and he does not try to grab my boobs or anything.[1] But he is so laid-back that he can sometimes seem cold, like Nathan.

Most boys are easy to manipulate with a coy smile or a witty comment, but Nathan is different. He doesn't seem to like it when I flirt with him.[2]

Possible boyfriends:

1. Tyler
2. Nathan
3. Louis
4. Jacob

Melanie is my really good friend, but she's always so negative. I am always having fun, but she's obviously not, and then I feel bad and can't have fun anymore. It seems like our whole friendship is me telling her my guy problems and her helping me fix them. So I can see why she's so depressed all the time. I think I really want her to have guys like her. I know I really want her to have fun and be happy.[3]

NOVEMBER 22, 1998

Alicia told me she doesn't like me because I follow her around. I don't know what she means by that.

Yesterday, I was on the phone with Stacy. Louis, Tyler, and Daniel were on three-way.[4] Daniel and Louis were like, "Will you go out with Tyler?" They asked about a million times and I just laughed.

I told them, "I'm going to go over Stacy's house and you guys should come over, too." So I went over

1. Cool but not snobby? Check. Funny? Check. Doesn't try to grab my boobs or anything? Check. If I didn't remember Jacob as a particularly sweet kid, I'd say this was a pretty low bar to clear.

2. I wonder what I was even trying to "manipulate" boys into doing, anyway. Pay attention to me?

3. Melanie is still my really good friend, and I can report that she is happy. In middle school, I recognized that she was much more in touch with reality than I was, but I mostly saw her as existing to support my emotional needs. Our friendship was one-sided and probably not that fun for her. She's still wonderfully snarky and wise. I visit her, her husband, their beautiful baby boy, and their silly puppy whenever I can, and it's always wonderful to hear about her full life.

4. Our three-way phone conversations were precursors to Google hangouts or whatever people are using these days to have remote group chats. They could even turn into four- or five-way conversations if we had friends over and they picked up the phone in another room of the house. In most cases, there was some romantic tension between two of the participants and the other people were just there for a buffer, because having a group on the line didn't feel as formal or intimidating as a one-on-one phone call.

her house but I could only stay for an hour because I had to go to church at 4 p.m. Stacy has her own problems. James is mad at her for some reason, and she is like, in love with James so she is all upset about that. And there's this other guy who likes her and he is her semi-friend, but she doesn't want to go out with him, so she vents on me about that, too. I don't mind—I think she's funny. I tried to help her though. I talked to James and put in a good word about her. But you know, I have my own things to worry about.[1]

Anyway, Tyler, Louis, and Daniel came over to Stacy's house, but as soon as I answered the door, my mom came to get me. So that was retarded.[2]

Ugh, but my main problem right now is that Alicia hates me. She wants to become tight with Steph and Amanda Collins, and to do that, she needs to cut all ties with me. So that sucks.[3]

DECEMBER 1, 1998

Stacy is having a party on the 5th. It is probably going to be good—not great, though. That is because all the boys going think I am a slut. It will be in her basement, and there is a closet with the mattress from an old futon in it. All the boys are going to want to get me in there, and normally I love the attention, but it is getting out of hand lately.

Today, at lunch, Louis asked me to give every boy at his table a blow job. What nobody understands is that I am a really big flirt, but deep down I am a really big prude. I am extremely terrified of being alone in a closet with Tyler. I enjoy the thought of making out with him, but it makes me so nervous!

1. Sheesh.

2. No! I hate that I used the word *retarded* like this. As a special-needs teacher, my mother prohibited us from calling each other "retarded" or even "stupid" at home, but I suspect that just made the word even more enticing and fun for me to use in private. Saying it aloud also provided me the opportunity to demonstrate how far I had come in pronouncing my *r*'s, which was one of the ways I had changed the way I spoke in order to fit in at my new school. There was a socioeconomic chasm between "retarded" and "wicked retahded," and it was vast.

3. That *does* suck. Alicia had been my best friend for the whole summer.

I don't know.

Oh, and Stacy is going out with James now. I'm happy for her! Now she doesn't have to be depressed because she thinks no one likes her.

Yesterday everyone found out that Jenna gave an eighth-grader a hand job. He's been her boyfriend for about a month, and she is totally in love with him, so I don't consider it slutty at all, but half of her friends do consider it slutty, so they've ditched her.[1]

I called her today and we had a conversation for the first time in over a month. I really love Jenna. She is really confused right now, and I can totally understand that. Right now, I am making it my job to be there for her to vent on. I needed her after my friends ditched me, and she was there, so now when she needs me, I will be there for her.

But she is still best friends with Steph, and that's okay, because it proves to me that no matter what Steph says, Jenna still likes me. So she is my real friend, and I am not going to lose her.[2]

DECEMBER 7, 1998

Stacy had her party and it was pretty fun! We played Spin the Bottle and I didn't get to French-kiss anyone, but I regular kissed almost every person there.[3]

Stacy spun the bottle and it landed on Mark, who is Shauna's boyfriend now. But it was the third time she had gotten him and so they had to French! Then James landed on Gina three times and they had to French.

James was so pissed off that Stacy had kissed Mark![4] And Shauna was pissed that Mark kissed Stacy, too, but she is only thinking about dump-

1. Even if this bit of news ended up being true, it's off-putting that I blindly accepted it as such, given my own experience with sexual bullying. My reaction to Jenna's predicament reveals a bit about how I defined "slutty" at the time; having been in a relationship for a month and being "totally in love" with the person apparently meant Jenna didn't fall into that category.

2. Odd that I didn't consider the possibility that Jenna not speaking to me for a month might have had something to do with Steph's opinion of me. I think it just goes to show how desperately I wanted to believe that I could trust her. Jenna and I—and every girl in our class, for that matter—needed to believe we had people we could trust because at any point, a rumor could convince all our "friends" to abandon us. That constant state of paranoia had to have contributed to our emotional volatility.

3. How funny that I used "regular kiss" as a verb! I wonder at what age you stop distinguishing between a French kiss and a "regular" kiss.

4. Even though he had just kissed Gina. Sounds fair.

ing him. I hope they don't break up. Anyway, the party was fun for me, too, because I played Twister with Jacob![1]

After school today, Stacy and I went over Gina's house. Stacy was crying because James dumped her. She was unreasonably sad.[2] She was curled up in a ball on Gina's couch, crying her eyes out, and I was trying to comfort her. I called James from Gina's house and he said he absolutely would not go out with Stacy again. I don't really care all that much.

I decided I really love James. Not as a boyfriend, of course, but he is such a sweetheart! I told him how nervous I had been about going to the party. I said, "I think I'm just, like… bewildered by everything." I thought that sounded so corny!

But he said, "Yeah, like everything's happening too fast." And I couldn't believe it, because that is just what I feel like. James really listens to me.[3]

At the party, Scott called me a slut and that bothered me. I sat on the couch and sulked, and nobody noticed and that made me sulk even more. But then James came over and put his arm around me and told me that I could vent on him, so I did and I felt much better. I told him that I'm going to stop acting so outgoing so boys will not call me a slut.

He thought that over for a minute and then said, "Emily?"

I said, "What."

He said, "Remember in fifth grade, how I used to tease you about your boobs being so big?"

I said, "Not really," even though I did remember. Back then, I was too stupid to appreciate my boobs.[4]

He said, "Well, I'm really, really sorry."[5]

1. Twister: facilitator of acrobatic flirtation since 1966. Early Twister detractors apparently accused Milton Bradley of selling "sex in a box." Perhaps there was some truth in that.

2. I wasn't necessarily the best judge of what was reasonable though.

3. Not to detract from the power of listening—and James really was a good listener—but it really is a low bar to set for friendship. James is another example of someone whom I desperately wanted to be able to trust, just for the sake of trusting someone.

4. My reference to "back then" implies that I felt a lot of distance from my fifth-grade self. In seventh grade, I apparently identified Boob Appreciation as a marker of maturity. The truth is, my outlook on breasts had changed along with everyone else's as more of us went through puberty and started thinking about sex. In fifth grade, my breasts had attracted awkward wonder from my new classmates because hardly anyone else had developed them. By seventh grade, they still attracted a lot of attention, but it was more intentional and sexually charged. I was starting to recognize my body as a source of power, even if that power was still tinged with embarrassment.

5. This marks the first time a boy had apologized for sexually bullying me. It meant a lot to hear James not only acknowledge that he was aware of how his behavior had affected me, but say he was sorry.

DECEMBER 19, 1998

Yesterday after school, I went over Stacy's house. We were on AIM (AOL Instant Messenger), chatting with James about how much I like Jacob. He said I should tell Jacob that I like him, and that in fact he would call Jacob for me right then. After a few minutes he said that he'd called Jacob but Jacob wouldn't believe him, so Jacob was coming online and I should talk to him. So we started a conversation with Jacob, about Stacy and how much she loves James.

Then, randomly, Jacob said, "Emily, you still owe me a kiss from Stacy's party." I don't think I wrote about this, but at Stacy's party when we were playing Spin the Bottle, I landed on Jacob. We were just about to kiss, but then Stacy's dad came in so we forgot about it. I was really disappointed, but I pretended not to care.[1]

I was so excited that Jacob remembered! So we're kind of half going out. There are some girls who are going to rip my face off when they find out.[2]

There was a dance that night and I went with Stacy. Jacob couldn't go because he had basketball practice. But it was fun anyway! I slow danced with Mark and Louis, and I was being friends with Zach. He was pretending to have Tourette's syndrome so he was running around, screaming out swears randomly and having muscle spasms. We were cracking up.[3]

DECEMBER 21, 1998

Oh, God. Everything is changing so quickly. It feels like a whirlwind! Shauna and Mark went to third base over the weekend, and everyone is making a big deal out of that.[4]

1. Stacy's dad would often drop in at inconvenient times, and now I suspect he was purposefully sabotaging our sexual exploits but making sure it seemed random in order to avoid humiliating Stacy. A lot of our parents struggled with the balance between maintaining order in their homes and allowing their kids to participate in the social scene. Stacy's dad managed to pull it off better than others, but Stacy was still kind of a mess.

2. Ow!

3. Was there any group of people Zach *didn't* find hilarious to mock? I remember Tourette's syndrome as being a favorite source of cruel humor, since we misunderstood it as an excuse to "scream out swears" at each other.

4. There's no way to know if this rumor was based in truth, but that didn't matter to me.

I don't know what's going on with Jacob. Today, I went online at Stacy's house, and we were talking to James again. He had Jacob on the phone again. He asked Jacob if he liked me, and Jacob said, "I did, and I kinda do."

I said, "Well, ask him if he is going to ask me out."

James said, "He says he will, when the time is right."[1] I don't know what that is supposed to mean.

I don't know about anything anymore. Time is flying by so fast and it is taking with it millions of events that I don't understand. My friends are growing, and I'm growing, slowly but surely, and I know it sounds corny, but I feel lost and bewildered by it all.[2] Some people depend on me to be down-to-earth and something solid to hold onto.[3] But I don't feel like that at all.

I don't know what is going on! Seventh grade is flying by so fast! It seems like from this time last year on, my life has been in fast forward. I desperately want it to slow down, so I can have a chance to sort out my feelings about everything.

Here's a song lyric I like: "How am I supposed to live without you, when all that I've been living for is gone?" —Michael Bolton

DECEMBER 23, 1998

Things are really weird between me and Jacob. I've never really talked to him about what's going on between us, but I've talked to about fifty other people about it.

I'm becoming closer with Emma again. Ever since last year, she's been like, my worst enemy aside

1. Jacob just loved to speak in riddles. Of course, it wasn't even an option for me to ask him out.

2. With this reflective outburst, I was performing the role of the angst-filled teenager I aspired to be. It's absurd that I would have felt "lost and bewildered," since I literally *could not have had* more opportunities for guidance from the adults in my life. In addition to my parents, I went to a school with four full-time guidance counselors, for Pete's sake. But for some reason, their attempts to engage me in conversation went ignored.

3. And I have some bad news for those people.

from Steph. I was okay with that until I started my whole Be Nice No Matter What thing. She'd say something mean and I'd smile genuinely and say, "I don't feel that way about you." At first, she'd give me a weird look, but after a while she just stopped being mean. And now we sit next to each other in chorus, so we sometimes joke with each other.[1]

Also, Hannah is being awfully nice to me. But her sister is a bitch and I'm suspecting it might run in the family. Hannah is really pretty and popular, and she's going out with Matt now, so it's good to be friends with her. She is always telling me nice things Jacob says about me.

Zach is being nice, too. I've been successful in almost entirely erasing any romantic feelings toward him, and now I'm beginning to realize how cool he is. It is fun to get to know someone you already know. Maybe Emma has been putting in a good word for me. But maybe not, because if he were to diss me, she would not stand up for me against him.

Matt has power over everyone—it is so annoying! Jacob might not go out with me because he thinks Matt might disapprove. Come on. And that's how it is with everything! I am trying to work my niceness on Matt, and maybe it's lowering his hate level of me a little bit.

DECEMBER 30, 1998

It is Christmas vacation so I am not seeing anyone at school, but my dad got AOL for a month! So I am always online chatting with Stacy, James, and Jacob. It is so much fun.[2]

1. I don't remember ever feeling particularly close to Emma in the first place. Most of our interactions seem to have involved her telling me whom to date or whom I better not even think about dating. But at the time, it was important for me to feel like she at least didn't *hate* me. And for the record, I still pull out the Be Nice No Matter What strategy in certain situations. I can't say that I stand by it in every case though, especially when there's a severe power imbalance.

2. Christmas vacation was a welcome break from the maintenance of so many complicated peer relationships and part maddening containment. I enjoyed playing Parcheesi with my family, going "coasting" at the golf course ("coasting" was what my mom called sledding without a proper sled), and curling up with the latest *Fear Street* book. But at the same time, I felt a creeping panic that everyone was hanging out without me and that when school started up again, my tenuous friendships would have disappeared.

But I was chatting with Stacy last night and I got a new chat. It was from the screen name DieEmilyLindin and it said, "Hi Emily." I just stared at it and didn't respond. Then I closed the chat box and went to get some cheese in the kitchen.[1]

When I came back to the computer, the chat box was back and this time it said, "Why haven't you killed yourself yet, you stupid slut?" I know it sounds stupid, but I felt like the chat box could see me through the computer screen.[2]

I asked Stacy if she knew who had made that screen name, DieEmilyLindin. She said it was Steph and that Steph had also made a webpage called Die Emily Lindin, and that it had been there for six months, but Stacy had just found out about it from Emma. I didn't try to go to the webpage. I felt kind of sick, like I could throw up, and I just signed off AOL.

Stacy is in one of her ultra-depressed states, and James and Jacob aren't helping. They are always like, "Why don't you ditch Stacy?" And I know I would never do that! She's worried, though. But I know how it feels and I am NOT EVER going to ditch her! I am a stronger person than that.[3]

James and I have become super close. I trust him. He is probably the first boy I have really liked without having a crush on him.[4] And it's great. Right now, I think he and Stacy are my closest friends, and it's weird because they HATE each other.

1. Cheese makes everything better.

2. "Cyberbullying" wasn't even a term yet, but this interaction was a precursor to what happens so often today. Until that message from DieEmilyLindin, home had been a safe place where I could, for the most part, escape the sexual bullying. I didn't have a cell phone (no one my age did in the late '90s), so once I made it through my front door, I had been protected from the way people thought of me and interacted with me at school. The Internet was about to change all that, but I didn't know it at the time. All I knew was that somehow, someone who wanted me to die had accosted me in my own home and that I could really go for some cheese.

3. "Ditching" someone as a friend was what you did when the damage they were doing to your social status outweighed your kind feelings toward them. It often entailed telling them off publicly, but it could also mean purposefully fading out of their life by not inviting them to things and not sitting with them at lunch. Practically speaking, we treated "ditching" friends almost exactly the same as breaking up with a boyfriend or girlfriend—except getting ditched was worse, because it often happened en masse.

4. At my school, genuine friendship between a boy and a girl was rare. So having that kind of relationship with James, especially given my reputation, was worth commenting upon.

JANUARY 6, 1999

Daniel is being horribly mean all of a sudden. He keeps calling me a ho and a whore and a slut.[1] I am trying not to care because I've kind of always thought he is weird. James is still nice, at least. So is Louis, most of the time.

I'm still tight with Stacy, Gina, and kind of Shauna. We don't buy lunch ever but we sit together and have fun. I sit with Michelle at lunch, too, but only out of tradition.[2] We are not tight. Scott is going out with Gina now, and so he and I are friends now, too.

Catherine and Hailey were online today, and they IM-ed me and were being nice! They invited me into a chat room twice, but I was already in one with James. I don't have anything against them except that they are friends with Steph. And her screen name is DieEmilyLindin. Every time she comes online, I sign off.[3]

JANUARY 8, 1999

Rules to Live By:[4]

- Be nice or at least nonchalant to everyone.
- Let people vent on you.
- Never make fun of losers.
- Sing really loud in church.[5]
- Never wear white tights.[6]
- Flirt with hot guys.
- Never wear push-up bras, because people who notice if you do are perverts.
- Sing in the shower.
- Be really happy if a guy brings you flowers for no apparent reason other than that he

1. I'm not sure what was going on with Daniel, but it's possible his friendship with Nathan was behind this shift in behavior.

2. You know what else is a lunchtime tradition? Eating food. But that's not a tradition I felt inclined to uphold, apparently.

3. It seems like there should have been a way to block her, but either AOL hadn't developed that tool yet or I just hadn't figured out how to use it.

4. This list was likely inspired by Baz Luhrmann's 1998 hit "Everybody's Free (to Wear Sunscreen)," with which I was obsessed for a long time. The song is just a spoken-word version of a 1997 essay by Mary Schmich over a remixed version of Rozalla's "Everybody's Free (to Feel Good)," which Luhrmann had featured in his 1997 interpretation of *Romeo + Juliet*. I'm not sure if it was my vague association of that music with the film's star, the beautiful Leonardo DiCaprio, or my desire to be the type of person who could understand and bestow general wisdom that spurred my obsession with "Everybody's Free (to Wear Sunscreen)," but I remember writing out all the lyrics and pondering them, line by line.

5. I'd always loved the sound of my own singing voice, and church gave me an excuse to belt loudly in public under the guise of praising God.

6. I still maintain that white tights are supremely unflattering on almost everyone.

is madly in love with you.[1]

- Make sure your deodorant works.[2]

- Lies almost always snowball against you.

- Never convince yourself of anything stupid.

- Colorful socks are good.

- Never wear underwear that gives you wedgies if you are going to dance.

- Never wear underwear that gives you wedgies anyway.

- Don't trust guys who are full of themselves.

- Keep a diary and read it when you get old.[3]

- Save notes people write to you.

- Take a lot of photos of your friends.

- Make a bulletin board.

- Going out with someone is confusing.

- Never name your son a cross-gender name like Nancy.

- Make sure you don't smell bad.[4]

- Don't talk about yourself too much.

JANUARY 10, 1999

I just lay on my bed and listened to the "You and Me Song" five times straight. That was my and Zach's song. I am so stupid! I'M IN LOVE WITH HIM GODDAMMIT! WHY THE FUCK DO I LOVE ZACH?!!

I'm not supposed to love him. He is HORRIBLE to me. But I'm in LOVE with him! I have realized that I will always love him! There is absolutely nothing I can do about it, either.

The "You and Me Song" was playing on Jenna's CD player when Zach and I kissed for the first time on Halloween. It's been almost a year since we went

1. I don't think this had ever happened to me, but I'd clearly read enough romance novels and seen enough romantic comedies to know that it was something that *happened*, in theory.

2. A few weeks before I made this list, my mom had bought me "natural" deodorant for some reason. It made me smell like patchouli for a couple of hours before fading away entirely, so I spent the rest of the day panicking about the rank stench I was certain my body was emitting. Finally, I went to the girls' room and dabbed my armpits with wet, soapy paper towels. That only made matters worse, because my wet armpits stained my shirt in the same way sweat would have, and now my body odor was mixed with the aseptic scent of the liquid soap from the girls' room. To this day, I harbor suspicion of "natural" deodorant.

3. Check!

4. See above, "Make sure your deodorant works."

to third base and my life changed forever. It doesn't seem like that long at all.

JANUARY 20, 1999

James and Gina are going out! Gina used to be going out with Scott, but he dumped her. I asked him why, and he said, "Because I like you." I guess I knew deep down that he wasn't joking, but I just laughed like I thought he was.[1]

Later, he came up to my locker and plain out said, "Will you go out with me?" I smiled hugely like it was a joke and it was funny, and I walked away. I shouldn't have done that because it just led him to believe that I didn't understand.

Today at lunch, he randomly asked me again. I pulled the same smile routine as before. Then after school today, Louis called me and said, "Would you ever go out with Scott?" I told him I'd have to make sure it was okay with Gina, stalling. He called back about an hour later and told me he'd checked with Gina and she thought it was okay, so would I go out with Scott?!

I'm not sure what drove me to say it, but I painfully murmured, "Yes…"

And he said, "Great! I'll call Scott and tell him that you two are going out!" I hung up without saying goodbye, completely disgusted with myself. It wasn't fair to Scott!

I called Stacy and she put Gina on three-way. I explained to them what had happened, and they expressed their sympathy for me, but told me there was really nothing they could do.[2]

So I called James. He said he'd call Scott and

1. Props to Scott for having the courage to come right out and say it, but shame on me for not reacting honestly and kindly. To be fair, the whole laughing-and-pretending-that-never-happened act does work *sometimes*.

2. I'm sure Gina really enjoyed hearing about all this, seeing as Scott had just dumped her to ask me out.

dump him in a nice way for me, and not to worry. He called back a minute later and said, "Okay, I did it, but he really likes you, Emily. He is pretty sad." I knew he would be sad. I should not have said yes. I also know that Scott has liked me for two years.[1]

A little later tonight, James called me again. He said, "Gina is mad at you because she says you treat her like crap."[2] The thing about James is that he always seems to be on your side. He's so good to talk to because he knows exactly how I feel and exactly what to say. I don't think I treat Gina like crap, I mean, I don't mean to. I'll have to try to be a lot nicer to her from now on![3]

Also, Jacob didn't spike his hair today.[4] It's the first time he's worn it regular in like, a year. Everyone made a big deal out of it, but it wasn't that big of a deal. He still looked hot. But I'm not going to like him so much because I really don't think he likes me. I hate liking someone who doesn't like me back.[5]

FEBRUARY 6, 1999

Today is a Saturday. Last night, there was a dance! People asked Jacob to dance with me, and he said definitely, for the last dance. That was about an hour away. But during that hour, he got in a Sprite fight with Louis, so they had to spend the rest of the dance cleaning it up.[6]

But I was having fun anyway! On a slow song, some boy was like, "Emily, you have to dance with Tyler!"

And I was like, "Um…" and then we were thrown together. But I realized that I didn't mind being that

1. I had been wrangled into this situation, but there were a few obvious points when I could have brought it to a halt. I'm ashamed that I managed to bail myself out of it in the least confrontational way possible, without taking responsibility for hurting Scott's feelings—or Gina's feelings, for that matter.

2. Well, duh.

3. It seems impossible that I could have missed how inadvertently cruel I had been to Gina that day. Perhaps because I didn't care about Scott romantically, it was hard for me to wrap my head around how someone else could.

4. Jacob and most other boys in my class used gel to spike the front of their hair so that it stood one to two inches out from their forehead. Sometimes they bleached just the ends of the spiked part. It's a look I can only hope stays firmly in 1999, where it belongs.

5. Maybe Scott would have some advice about how to handle that.

6. Sprite fights always ruin *everything*!

close to Tyler. And we couldn't have been much closer! When he breathed, I could feel his stomach go in and out, because my stomach was pressed up against his.[1] And my right ear kept touching his. Dancing with him is okay, because he is the same height as me.

When the slow song was over, I danced with Stacy and Gina for a little bit. Then another slow song came on, and for a moment I was standing around looking like a retard,[2] but then I looked up and saw Tyler coming across the gym. I started talking to Gina, trying my best to look pretty. Tyler came right up to me and said, "Emily."

I turned toward him and smiled. "Oh, hi, Tyler."

"Do you want to dance?"

"Sure," I said, as I wrapped my arms around his neck. Again, I could feel him breathing. Whenever he adjusted his hands around my waist, I got the shivers. I so wanted to turn my head and kiss him, but I just couldn't! I was afraid I'd miss his mouth and lick his nose or something.

When that song was coming to an end, I was dreading having to let him go. But luckily, "From This Moment On" by Shania Twain came on, and we didn't even have to start to pull apart. I am not in love with Tyler, as I was with Zach and Nathan, but I like him a lot, and so why not go out with him?

Except there is the Jacob factor. The last song was a fast one, which was pretty gay, but I guess Jacob had finished cleaning up the Sprite, because I saw him talking to James.[3] James started to come toward me but Jacob blocked his way. James easily picked Jacob up and out of the way.[4] I figured James

1. At least his stomach wasn't twitching like last time.

2. Seriously, Emily? That word again? Ugh.

3. It makes me cringe to imagine the effect this casual, derogatory use of "gay" must have had on my classmates who *were* gay. They grew up surrounded by all of us using "gay" interchangeably with "stupid," "ugly," "annoying," and any other negative thing we wanted it to mean. We were so cruel in our carelessness when it came to language.

4. Jacob was pretty small for his age.

would probably find something embarrassing to say in front of Jacob, so I frantically said something that had nothing to do with me. "Why are you so mean to Gina?" I asked.

He said, "I'm not." And he isn't, either. So I felt like a pretty big loser, and I walked away.

After the dance, everyone was waiting outside for their parents to come get them. I was standing in a group with Stacy, Daniel, Louis, and Tyler. Daniel was talking about how he judges girls by how hot they are and how big their boobs are. I said, "Well, I judge boys by how long their schlong is."

Louis said, "How can you tell?"

I told him to hold up his hand, and I explained that from the tip of his middle finger to his wrist was how long his schlong was. He was fascinated by this.[1]

Tyler said, "Well, I judge girls by their personalities," which caused all three of them to burst out laughing.[2]

Then my dad pulled up, and Stacy and I got in the car because we were giving her a ride home. Stacy said, "Why did you walk away from James and Jacob?"

I said, "Because I was done talking to them."

She said, "Well, they were calling you back. They were probably going to ask you out for Jacob. They thought you were ignoring them so they walked away."

OH STUPID, STUPID ME!![3]

1. First of all, "schlong"?! Second, this little test is, unfortunately, not true at all. I'm not sure where it came from, but it seems like an example of "wisdom" passed down from someone's older sibling.

2. Either the idea of a girl having a "good personality" was already a punch line for us, or the boys' laughter was the result of nervousness. From the way I wrote about it, I believed the former to be true; at least, I was under the impression that my own personality was far less important than my looks.

3. My reaction to this little moment is an example of my tendency to attach way too much meaning to events in my life. Based only on Stacy's report that James and Jacob had been calling after me and her further speculation about their intentions, I became convinced that I had missed what might have been my only chance to start going out with Jacob. In reality, if they were calling after me at all, it was probably to ask me more about schlongs.

FEBRUARY 7, 1999

I just finished watching *The Basketball Diaries* starring Leonard DiCaprio. It's about this sixteen-year-old boy who lives in a bad section of New York, and he gets hooked on all sorts of drugs and gets kicked off the basketball team and sees his friend murder someone. And all the while, he keeps this diary filled with poetry and his thoughts on everything.

I almost wish I had a screwed-up life so I could be cool and record all of my thoughts.

I like being pretty, even though I know I shouldn't. I'm such an awful bitch. Faces mean nothing. But really, faces mean everything. Sometimes I think that beauty is mostly everything. It should not be, but it is.

There is nothing I love more than a demonstration of a cute boy's love for his mother. The relationship between boys and their mothers amazes me. I want to have a son someday and I will name him Carson, after Carson Daly from *TRL*.[1]

I will name my second son Scott. My daughters will be named Auralee, Vivia, and Evangela. Vivia will go by Vivi and Evangela will go by Angela or Eva or Eve or something.[2]

Love is nothing. Death is nothing! Nothing is anything but nobody cares. Why would they? They are nothing, too. Neither am I.[3]

FEBRUARY 13, 1999

Today is Saturday. Yesterday, Gina had a party! I thought it was going to suck because no boys were going. But after school, I went over Stacy's house. She has AOL, and we could go on as my screen

1. *TRL* (*Total Request Live*) was a countdown of the most requested music videos every afternoon. And yeah, I'm definitely not naming my son after Carson Daly.

2. I have always maintained an ever-changing list of my favorite names for potential babies. I still have one, and zero of these names have stuck around.

3. At twelve years old, I was quite the nihilist.

name. Nobody was on and we were about to get off, but then Jacob came on. He sent me an instant message as soon as he came on! He was with James and Louis and he said they were going. So obviously, Stacy and I started primping for it!

When we got to the party, it was all girls, most of whom we're not even friends with, except for Gina and Michelle. I'm starting to think Michelle is extremely annoying. There were only three boys there: James, Louis, and JACOB!!! And they all arrived together.

Nobody really did anything—we all just kind of stood around and talked.[1] After it got dark, we all went outside on the deck. There was a table in the middle of the deck, and a couple of candles were on it. Jacob had a lighter on him for some reason and he took it out to light the candles.[2]

I said, "Can I try?"

And he said, "Sure," and handed it to Michelle, who handed it to me. I couldn't get it to work, though, and he said, "Here, let me do it," and put out his hand. When I was handing it to him, our fingers touched, and everyone noticed.

Michelle, who also likes Jacob, said, "Emily, everyone knows the only reason you came to this party is to make out with Jacob." That statement caught me off guard, but only for a second.

Everyone was startled and Jacob said, "Michelle…"

She said, "Well, it's true!" I just turned and went inside. Stupid Michelle![3]

Anyway, Gina was in the living room sulking, because she and James used to be best friends and then they went out and broke up, and now

1. That's all we ever really did at any party, unless someone had the guts to suggest playing Spin the Bottle. Sometimes we turned on music and tried to convince each other to dance, but parties were mostly a chance to gossip about each other, plot about who should date whom, and start passive-aggressive fights.

2. Ahem… Jacob always had a lighter because he was rumored to be a bit of a pothead. Like Matt, Jacob had access to pot through his older brother, who was in high school and supposedly carried a beeper. I didn't know much about Jacob's older brother except that he appeared truly not to care one bit about anything. That made him *really cool.*

3. Seriously Michelle, WTF.

he hates her. I went into the kitchen where he was, and talked to him about it. A few other people, including Jacob, were standing around the kitchen, too.

James said, "Emily, come here." He put his hands up like he was going to tell me a secret, and I leaned toward him. He whispered to me, "You know what, Emily? I'll make a deal with you. I'll ask Gina to dance if you ask Jacob to dance."

I said, "No."[1]

He said, "Fine." Then I went into the dining room for a second.

I came back into the kitchen and started talking to James and Jacob. The conversation kind of drifted to Gina, and then Michelle flounced in. "Emily!" she yelled in a super annoying voice, hands on hips, "Stop talking about Gina!" I was taken aback, considering I wasn't even saying anything mean. I guess Michelle was just trying to show off for Jacob, but it backfired.

He looked at her in disgust and said, "God, Michelle, chill." I love how he stands up for me.[2]

Anyway, I went back into the dining room, where the boom box was, and danced with my girlfriends for a while. The party was almost over. James and Jacob came into the dining room just as someone put on "All My Life" by K-Ci & JoJo.[3]

James went up to Gina and said, "Come on, Gina, let's dance." She obediently put her arms around him. I knew what was coming!

I heard Jacob say, "Hey, Emily..." in a really cute way. "I guess we have to dance."

I looked at him and he had a super-hot half-

1. Why did I refuse? This seems like a great opportunity to put my plan to be extra nice to Gina into action while also getting to dance with Jacob.

2. Okay, now I feel a little bad for Michelle. She had a crush on Jacob, and being dismissed in this way by someone you have a crush on really hurts.

3. And you know what *that* means.

smile on his face. I said, "You made a deal, didn't you?" James had this huge grin, and Jacob nodded. I said, "I don't like to be part of deals, do you, Gina?" But she just stared moony-eyed at James. I sighed, smiled, and put my arms around Jacob, who wrapped his arms around my waist. His stomach doesn't do weird twitchy things, like Tyler's does.[1]

I had socks on, and he had on his sneakers, so he was almost as tall as me, not counting his one inch of spiked hair. As soon as we started dancing, he stepped on my toe. I said, "You just stepped on my toe!"

And he said, "Oh, sorry." After a few seconds, he stepped on my toe again. Before I could say anything, he whispered, "Is Gina pissed because you were talking about her?" His breath tickled my ear.

"No," I whispered back. I almost died of happiness, just holding him.

Then Stacy, who is a saint and I love her, took a PICTURE! She said, "Okay, we need a picture of this," and she picked up my disposable camera. Thank goodness I reminded her of the flash, or it wouldn't have come out![2]

AHHHH!!! I LOVE JACOB SO MUCH!!! HE IS SOOO PERFECT!!!

FEBRUARY 16, 1999

I just got off the phone with Melanie, and she told me something that really hit home. She said, "Emily, you set these way-high standards for people and expect them to be fulfilled. Jacob can't possibly meet your expectations of him, and one day you are going to be very disappointed when you realize he's not perfect."[3]

1. Well, that settles it, then.

2. None of us had digital cameras, let alone camera phones, so disposable cameras were our method of capturing memories. Each camera had enough film for twenty-seven pictures, and you had to turn a little dial after taking each one. The flash was a separate button you had to hold in until a light started blinking, and then you had one shot to get the picture you wanted. My mom used to drop my disposable cameras off to be developed at CVS or Costco, and I remember the feeling of anticipation when the photos were finally ready. I would grab the stuffed envelopes from my mom as soon as she walked in the door and run upstairs to my bedroom, where I would sit crosslegged on my bed with the door closed and ceremoniously flip each photo over, one at a time. Sometimes, weeks would have passed since I had taken them, so I wasn't always sure what to expect. The satisfaction of discovering a photo where a boy I liked looked particularly cute or where I looked particularly skinny was usually tempered by disappointment at having forgotten to turn on the flash for a good portion of the roll, and finding the last five or six photos to be completely black.

3. Melanie always gave sage advice for a twelve-year-old.

That is so right. I know Jacob, but I've never seen his bad side, so I have just assumed that he doesn't have one. But he must—everyone does. And one day when he does or says something un-perfect, I'm going to feel let down, and he won't know what he did wrong.

But I can't keep analyzing situations like this! Things keep happening and I spend so much time thinking about them that I miss out on feeling infatuated, which is, although fake, a great feeling.[1] That's how I felt the day after Gina's party. Just picturing Jacob's face made me curl up in a ball and squeal. It made me feel stupid, but it was still a great feeling.

Yesterday I went to the mall and bought the Britney Spears CD. There is this song on it called "Sometimes," and it so describes my relationship with Jacob! Well, okay, so it doesn't really describe our relationship, but it's still fun to sing along to.[2]

FEBRUARY 22, 1999

At school today, Mark had just gotten back from a vacation in Aruba. His little sister told Shauna that he had met a girl there. Shauna laughed, and she didn't believe it. But everyone was talking about it and the boys were giving him high fives. Well, after school I went online and Mark was on. He told me everything because I promised not to tell Shauna. But I didn't promise that I wouldn't tell anyone else.[3]

Apparently, the girl he met is fifteen and they went to sloppy second base, and now they're going out. So Mark has another girlfriend. I immediately

1. I disagree with this characterization of infatuation as "fake." Sometimes it's an important step toward love, and sometimes it's just a fun feeling to have. Just because it's not love doesn't make it "fake."

2. In my attempt to make all things meaningful at all times, I was compelled to force myself to relate to the timeless genius of Britney Spears: "Sometimes I run, / sometimes I hide, / sometimes I'm scared of you, / but all I really want is to hold you tight, / treat you right, / be with you day and night, / and baby, all I need is time."

3. How transparently sneaky of me! Maybe I was jumping at the chance to be on the outside of a piece of gossip, for once. Maybe it felt like a privilege to be the one going behind someone else's back, rather than fearing other people were going behind mine.

sent the whole conversation to Stacy and Gina, and Gina called Shauna. Shauna called me and told me that Mark had apologized, and asked if she should forgive him.

I stared at the phone.[1] "No!" I shouted. "Shauna, he cheated on you and he is going out with another girl! You can't trust him."

She seemed desperate. "Then what should I do?"

I said, "Tell him you can't trust him and break up with him. If he goes out with someone else immediately after, get over him. If he seems really depressed and begs forgiveness, then give him about two weeks to realize what he did wrong, and if he asks you out again after that, say yes."[2]

Shauna thought this was a good idea, but I doubt she'll have the guts to break up with him. She worships the ground he walks on. It's really pathetic. But I think I'm really jealous of their relationship.[3]

FEBRUARY 23, 1999

Today, Shauna said she was going to dump Mark at lunch. We were all excited and helped her plan how she was going to do it.[4] When lunchtime finally rolled around, all the people at Mark's table already knew, but they weren't saying anything. Boys can be such horrible friends to each other![5]

Anyway, I went over to the boys' table and talked to them and shared secret smiles with James, because we knew what was coming. Shauna, followed by our whole table and about three other tables, boys and girls, came over. She planted herself in front of Mark and said nervously, "Mark, you disrespected me, so…"

This wasn't going as planned at all. She was sup-

1. Which I could do, because it was a *Clueless* Hands-Free Phone. Even though the little earpiece made it technically hands-free, you were still tethered to the wall by the cord while you were talking on it. But that's not what made the phone cool, anyway. Sure, you could push a button and hear Cher's voice exclaim, "As if!" or "I'm outie!" But for my purposes, the phone's selling point was its voice changer. I could turn a little dial to the right and become a chipmunk, or turn it to the left and become what I thought was a pretty believable-sounding teenage boy. As you can imagine, the potential for prank calls was endless.

2. I just loved being in the position to give what I thought was pretty stellar advice. This was, no doubt, a variation of something I had read in a *Seventeen* column and had tweaked so that it made more sense to me.

3. …? What's there to be jealous of? Maybe just the fact that they were in a relationship, no matter how unstable and unhappy that relationship was.

4. The whole thing was collaborative, naturally.

5. Oh, the irony.

posed to stomp up to him with an attitude and bash him in front of everyone. Instead, she looked reluctant, completely reassuring him that he had all the power in their relationship. After about a thirty-second speech, she concluded, "And so I don't think we should go out… right now."

"Or ever!" I added, trying to save her pride. The crowd of people who were watching started cheering and laughing. Mark started laughing, too! He laughed so hard he nearly fell out of his chair.[1]

The crowd had departed, and now it was just me and the boys. I leaned across the table and said, "So, Mark, who are you going to go out with now?"

He shrugged. Then Scott said something really mean. He said, "Well, Emily, who do you have?"

Carefully controlling my features, I made a cute little puzzled face and walked away. I am so fake. Whenever I realize a boy is looking at me, I make my face into a prettier expression. Whenever I am around boys, I am constantly aware of my facial expression, my stance, my hands, my body language, everything. I like showing some cleavage sometimes, too.[2]

MARCH 3, 1999

Shauna and Stacy are in a fight for some reason or another—I think because they called each other bitches behind the other one's back, and then the other one found out. Today at recess, Shauna slapped Stacy. Everyone was really into it, especially the boys.[3] After school, they were supposed to have a real fight at Curb Café, but Shauna couldn't go. I decided to go with Stacy and Gina anyway.

1. I wonder if this was a nervous reaction because of the humiliating scene we had set up, or if Mark was so malicious that he would laugh in Shauna's face.

2. I remember this feeling of supreme self-consciousness at all times, but especially around boys. Much later, I would finally realize that everyone else is too busy worrying about themselves to notice the things we're most insecure about.

3. Despite the seemingly constant passive-aggressive fights among my classmates and me, physical altercations were a rare occurrence and thus reason for excitement. Sometimes they were outbursts of honest anger, other times they were grabs for the attention we all sought.

When we got there, James, Jacob, Scott, Mark, and Louis were there, too. They all hate Gina, so when they saw us, they went across the street to the playground. Then another group of girls, including Michelle, arrived and we weren't sitting with them because they are immature and annoying.[1]

Those girls got it into their stupid heads to follow the boys to the playground and spy on them. Stacy, Gina, and I were too cool for that, so we stayed and ate our French fries while Michelle's group ran across the street to no doubt make fools of themselves.[2]

When we were done eating we decided to walk to my house because it is closest, and Stacy had to call her mom and tell her. The closest pay phone was in the library lobby and the library is right next to the playground. We decided to keep it on the down low, go in, use the pay phone, and leave. If the boys thought we were there to find them, we could just explain that we were there to use the pay phone.[3]

As soon as we got to the library's front steps, Michelle ran up to us and giddily said, "The boys are playing football! Come watch!" I was really getting annoyed with her, but followed her to the side of the building where we could see the boys. But it wasn't like they didn't know we were there—Michelle's group would let out obnoxious, high-pitched screams whenever one of the boys did anything.[4]

I was embarrassed to be with them and I wanted to go home. But I stayed because all of a sudden, Jacob ran out from behind the bleachers IN HIS BOXERS!!! He was still wearing his baggy black

1. Quite unlike *my* friends and *me.*

2. I don't remember who exactly was in "Michelle's group," but by this time I had decided Michelle was annoying and it's likely I just lumped anyone she happened to be hanging out with that day into her "group," so I could more efficiently deride their collective behavior.

3. Now *there's* an excuse that doesn't make sense anymore.

4. Whether or not the boys intended it, their football game had become a kind of performance for us. It was a reversal of the gender roles I was used to, where I felt as if everything I did was scrutinized by ogling boys. Now we were the oglers.

T-shirt and backward baseball cap, and they kept playing football as if there was nothing weird.[1]

Then Stacy realized she still hadn't actually called her mom, so she, Gina, and I went back into the lobby. She was talking to her mother when all of a sudden, Louis slammed himself into the glass door of the library, holding it shut. Michelle was yelling behind him, "They're taking your back-packs!" Louis moved so we could get out, but by that time, Mark, James, and Scott were already back at the field holding our backpacks. Of course, we ran to catch up to them and reclaimed our backpacks.

I was like, "Screw this," and walked back across the parking lot, figuring Gina and Stacy would catch up.[2]

They did, and Stacy said, "The boys told us to stop following them and leave them alone!" I didn't know whom in particular she was referring to when she said "the boys," but I hoped it wasn't Jacob.

MARCH 4, 1999

Today Stacy and Gina came over again, and the phone rang. It was Louis. I said, "Why were you guys being mean yesterday?"

He said, "We just wanted to hang out with the guys, and then you girls followed us."

I said, "We did not follow you," and I explained to him how we ended up at the field. I said, "Are they like, mad at us?"

Louis said, "I don't think they like you guys." Louis has a habit of telling the truth, even if you don't want to hear it. I asked him about it and he said, "Well, I don't think they have a problem with

1. I have no explanation for Jacob's no-pants demonstration. My only guess is that he accidentally spilled something or peed on himself and ditching his pants was the simplest solution. I doubt it was for our benefit as audience members to their football game.

2. Rather than being like, "Screw this," I suspect I had actually been stricken with fear that Gina and Stacy would *not* decide to follow me, and that I would find myself stranded alone on the other side of the parking lot, pretending to be too cool for this nonsense.

you, just with Gina."

I said, "You're just saying that because I'm the one you're talking to."

He said, "No! I'm serious, they all like you. But I think Jacob likes you as just a friend." I almost cried when he said that. Louis always tells the truth.[1]

I said, "If I were talking to Jacob, would he be thinking, 'Go away'?"

Louis said, "No, he'd be thinking, 'Come sit on my lap and let me squeeze your—'" but I cut him off before he could finish. I don't want to believe Jacob is a pervert.[2]

As soon as I got off the phone with Louis, the phone rang again. This time, it was James. He was at Jacob's house. At first I was being very hostile toward him. He said, "This is James."

And I said, "I don't want to talk to you."

But he just said okay, and I thought he was going to hang up, so I said, "No, no, I'll talk to you."[3]

He said, "Do you want to talk to Jacob?"

I said, "No." Because I really didn't.[4]

He said loudly, "What? You don't?!"

And Jacob's voice in the background said, "What? She doesn't?!"

I asked James, "Do you guys hate us?"

He said, "No, we don't hate you."

I said, "Because I just got off the phone with Louis, and he told me some stuff."

"What? What did he tell you?"

"Nothing, just that the reason you like me and none of my friends is because of, um…"

Stacy said into the receiver, "Her boobs!"

James seemed shocked. He said, "What? No,

1. Of course, it's much more likely that Louis did *not* always tell the truth. Even if he was generally averse to lying, who's to say whether what he believed to be true was actually "the truth"? It was just easier for me to simplify his personality so that I could make decisions about how to react to him.

2. Since I apparently believed Louis to be a truth-telling oracle, I took his words at face value and thought they would reflect poorly on Jacob. But even if Jacob *did* want me to sit on his lap so he could squeeze my… whatever Louis would have said… would that really have made him a "pervert"? After all, to some degree, I *wanted* him to want that. The way I used "pervert" here to describe Jacob seems uncomfortably similar to the way others were using "slut" to describe me.

3. Way to call my bluff, James.

4. As Britney Spears put it so eloquently, "Sometimes I'm scared of you." I guess there were parts of that song I really could relate to, because I was definitely scared of Jacob… sometimes.

Jacob doesn't like you because of your boobs!"

"He doesn't like me? Because I have big boobs?"[1]

"No! No, wait! I meant, the reason he likes you is not only your boobs."[2] So maybe Louis was confused. Anyway, they had to go so James could call his mom, and later they called us back. So they really did want to talk to us.

Soon James went home and then we were just talking to Jacob. One time Stacy mentioned something about asking someone out for someone else. He said, "I hate it when people ask me out for someone else. It's annoying. If they really like me, why can't they just ask me out themselves?"[3]

Jacob just got AIM and his screen name is Bizkit plus some numbers because his and like, every other guy's favorite band is Limp Bizkit. He does not like to cook biscuits or anything like that![4]

MARCH 8, 1999

Okay, this might sound really bizarre, but this is a fantasy I have. I would have long, curly, blonde hair, and I would be wearing a flowing, pink skirt down to my ankles and I would be barefoot. Jacob would be in a white suit, and he wouldn't look hot, he would look beautiful. And we wouldn't want each other, we would love each other.

We would be standing on a rock ledge, behind a waterfall, and we would be dancing. His hair would be matted to his forehead because it would be wet. Music by Enya would be playing.[5] Oh, maybe I would be in a white dress. No, no! Then Jacob would be able to see through it and it would make him horny and that would just completely ruin my fan-

1. I used to do this a lot. I would feign misunderstanding for the sake of extending a conversation and, hopefully, gleaning more information from my source. It must have been exhausting for all involved.

2. In case you haven't picked up on this, we cared a *lot* about boobs. Our preoccupation not just with their size but with whether or not they were being squeezed—and by whom—bordered on obsession.

3. Hint, hint.

4. I, on the other hand, wasn't allowed to listen to Limp Bizkit, nor did I particularly want to. I was all about jumping up and down at school dances and shouting along with Fred Durst that I "did it all for the nookie," but that was the extent of my Limp Bizkit knowledge. While we're on the subject, what ever happened to Fred Durst?

5. Of *course* it would.

tasy. So it is light pink.

I like to have conversations with people online more than I like to talk on the phone. Because online if you write something embarrassing, you can just be like, "Oh, sorry, that was my brother" or something, and you can't do that on the phone. Plus, if I have a really good conversation online I can print it out. Then I can read it over and over again whenever I want to.[1]

I think that's why I like photographs so much, too. They are like, solid memories. Memories that you can touch. Some pictures make me smile just looking at them, or some trigger bad memories.[2] Like this picture I have of me and Zach from sixth grade. It makes me remember how Steph had one that she took of him and Hannah hugging, and then Steph and I went into the woods behind my house and burned it. It burned really cool, like the layer of shininess on top of it bubbled up and turned brown and then the whole thing caved in.

Also, some other stuff: goals are important to have, but I've also realized that if you set definite goals for yourself, you are unlikely to reach them. If you know you want something to happen but you're not sure what, something usually happens and you end up liking it. Oh, well, I'm setting goals for myself anyway.

Goals for the Rest of Seventh Grade—
Become better at:
1) manipulating boys[3]
2) dancing
3) being trustworthy
4) not talking about people[4]

1. The qualities of online interaction that I was picking up on have only gotten more significant. You don't have to take immediate responsibility for what you say, the way you would have to in person; some people behave online as if they'll *never* be held responsible for their words. There's also a very real permanence to online interactions, although printing out conversations seems absurd now, since their permanence isn't dependent on a hard copy.

2. I still really like to have hard copies of photographs. Even though it's technically safer to store them online, the memories captured in photos somehow feel more real to me if I can put them in a frame.

3. This isn't the first time I've written about my desire to be better at manipulating boys. For some reason, "manipulation" was attractive to me as a skill to be honed. It seems really creepy now, but I must have associated it with the all-encompassing quest for social power. The release of *Cruel Intentions* at right about this time in 1999 didn't help things; Sarah Michelle Gellar as the beautiful, seductive, terrifyingly *manipulative* Kathryn basically became my role model.

4. I'm glad I recognized talking about people as a problem I had to work on, but achieving this goal would prove to be a struggle. In order to be part of the hypercritical social environment I was so committed to, I had to engage in the constant gossip upon which it depended.

MARCH 9, 1999

I am thinking about my whole situation with Jacob. Lots of times, things have happened, or rather, haven't happened, and I've been really mad at myself later for not doing what so obviously was the right thing. And here I am, blowing another chance, and later I am going to be thinking, "Emily, you are so gay! It was so obvious he liked you, so you should have just ASKED HIM OUT!"[1] And I will be thinking this after he has given up on me and moved on—when it is too late.

I need to let him know I like him back, and I have been trying to do that through James. James is obviously telling Jacob everything I say, but I'm pretending like I don't know that. I am so sneaky!

Its 9:52 p.m. and I'm about to go to sleep, but I was thinking about some stuff. I wonder what happens to you when you die? I almost want to kill myself to find out, but I think I am too young. I am at the perfect age: twelve to fourteen. It's the age for Spin the Bottle, trying to be older, showing off, and being anything but myself. I feel awful for people who are not "popular" because they cannot enjoy it.[2]

I always think, "I wish I could go back in time to the first time I saw Zach," and then I expect something to happen so that when I open my eyes, I will be sitting on the bleachers in the high school gym during band practice, staring at a younger, immature, innocent, better Zach, and being a younger, happier, shallower self. Then I would never get involved with him, I would never go to third base with him, and everything would stay the same.[3]

1. Unfortunately, I am 99% sure I meant "gay" as a derogatory synonym for "stupid" here; I wasn't actually questioning my sexual orientation.

2. How do those people even get through the day? Seriously, though, this strikes me as an attempt to deny my own persistent unhappiness by projecting it onto vague, "unpopular" people who I imagined must have had it worse than I did.

3. I had this thought often enough that I can remember it clearly, many years later. I would actually close my eyes and recite, "I wish I could go back in time…" as if it were a magical incantation. I wasn't naïve enough to believe it would actually work, but it was impossible to resist at least *trying*.

I wish I could write music. But nothing ever comes to me. Sometimes I am like, inspired by a tune or lyrics or something, but then I always forget it before I can write it down.

MARCH 13, 1999

Yesterday after school, Gina and I went over to Stacy's house. We were planning on having a snowball fight with Daniel, Louis, and Mark. That didn't sound like that much fun, but whatever. We were online as my screen name and Steph was online as the screen name DieEmilyLindin. She invited me into a private chat room. I went in, but only for a second, because nothing happened.[1] Matt instant messaged me from his screen name: "Emily?" But I didn't answer him. I didn't want to deal with Matt.

Anyway, we went over to the schoolyard to have the snowball fight. While we were walking there, I felt like a really big loser because I know Louis doesn't really like me. I was afraid that when we got to the schoolyard, they wouldn't be there. But when we got close, we could see them, and they ran to meet us. My pants were soaked through, I had snow down my shirt, and my hair was a wet mess. We were playing "full body contact," meaning I got picked up and thrown in the snow about a million times and broke about a billion bones. It didn't really hurt though because there was about a foot of snow to cushion my fall. Daniel tackled me and as soon as I got to my feet, Louis knocked me back down, and all the while Mark was chucking hunks of snow at my face. Then Louis had to go home, so it kind of died down.[2]

1. I still remember the visceral apprehension I felt every time I saw that screen name. I was so afraid of what she would say to me online. Whatever she said or did to me in person, I at least had the knowledge that there would be some kind of consequence for her if I decided to tell an adult. Online, there was no way to hold her accountable.

2. Even though it sounds violent, this snowball fight was probably not cruel-natured. I think it gave the boys an excuse to be physical with me and perhaps to get out some sexual frustration. At any rate, it doesn't seem like I minded being knocked down and having snow chucked at my face as much as one would expect.

So Stacy and I started to build a snowman, and Daniel built a snow prostitute.[1] Our snowman turned out to just be a snow midget because it was taking too long. But Mark randomly decided to knock over Daniel's prostitute, so Daniel got mad and started chucking snow at our snow midget. He made a hole in the bottom of it and yelled, "Look, now your snow midget has a pussy!" And Mark ran over, dove onto the ground, and buried his face in the hole! That was so out of character of Mark.

Today, Daniel was acting a lot like Nathan. Every time he'd say or do something, I would imagine Nathan doing the same thing. It was weird and sad. I miss Nathan a lot. He hates me though, and it's not funny because he hates me with a passion. He's very into hating me and I don't like it at all. It's not my fault our relationship got boring. It's not my fault Chris Walker practically assaulted me.[2] So for shit's sake, Nathan, STOP BLAMING ME!

MARCH 22, 1999

Today is a Monday. On Saturday, Stacy, Melanie, and I went to the movies with Daniel, James, Louis, and Jacob.[3] Nothing really happened, except this:

Stacy was getting bored with the movie so she asked if anyone wanted to go to the snack bar with her. James said he would go and then we all started giving them money and telling them to buy us something while they were there. Anyway, about a half hour passed and they were still not back. Jacob turned to face me—he was sitting in front of me—and said, "Where the hell are Stacy and James?" I contemplated the possibilities.

1. I wonder how he indicated that it was a snow prostitute, specifically.

2. Atta girl!

3. I never really went to the movies for the purpose of watching a movie. It really didn't matter what movie was playing—I was much more concerned with who would be there and who would sit next to whom.

"Oh, my god," Daniel whispered, "I bet they're having sex!" We were getting really loud, so the other ten people in the theater were paying more attention to us than to the movie, which was *Carrie 2: The Rage*, and might be a pretty good movie if I ever get the chance to concentrate on watching it.[1]

So James and Stacy eventually came back and these two black men who were sitting behind us jumped up and started going, "Yeah, James! Way to go, man!" James, obviously, didn't have any idea what the hell they were talking about.[2]

After we explained it to him, he caught onto the joke and yelled, "Stacy! Was it good for you?"

Then a guy who worked there was like, "If you don't quiet down, I'm going to have to ask you to leave."[3]

I think there is this way that everything's perfect, just like it should be. You know, when you are completely satisfied with everything and you can just sigh and think, "Everything is exactly as it should be." I've only experienced that feeling once. It was over a year ago, but the feeling was so strong and distinct that even now, I can remember exactly how it felt. I was walking out of Ms. Covey's room and I turned and there was Zach, waiting for me at my locker. He was leaning up against it, hands clasped in front of him, head down, and he didn't see me. As I approached him he looked up slowly, and when he saw me, this huge smile came over his face. And it was a genuine smile, not a "Your tits look huge in that tank top smile" but a "You are the only person I want to be with ever" smile. I smiled back at him and he touched my arm, and I thought, "This is so right. Here is how everything should be." It was the

1. On second thought, nah.

2. I noted that the men were black because they were some of the only people of color I had ever interacted with. The movie theater was in the next town over, which was much more economically and racially diverse. My town was overwhelming white—there were a handful of families of Asian descent but only two black families. A couple of years later, I would develop tentative friendships with some of the black students who were bused to our suburban high school from Boston as part of the METCO (Metropolitan Council for Educational Opportunity) desegregation program. But in middle school, my world was almost entirely monochromatic.

3. Being reprimanded in this way was satisfying for me because it made me feel like I was part of a borderline delinquent group of friends. For someone who romanticized the idea of getting into trouble with authorities, being told to quiet down by the disgruntled teenager who worked at the movie theater was a triumph.

greatest feeling in the world, of complete and genuine satisfaction; my life was at its high point and it couldn't possibly be any better.[1]

The scary thing is, I think I missed my chance with Jacob. There's been all this for nothing—we'll never go out, and I'll be left feeling empty and disappointed. I really want Jacob, I just feel as if the excitement has passed and everyone's moving on—nobody cares anymore. They think we're pathetic for not going out already. Well, if I did miss my chance with Jacob, I am going to make it a point to be more bold and to never miss anyone again.[2]

MARCH 23, 1999

Today in the locker room before Gym, I was talking to Emma. She is my semi-friend again, I guess. She said, "I was talking to Jacob yesterday and he said he wasn't going to go out with anyone this year. I asked him, 'What about Emily?' and he said, 'Well, yeah, but the only reason I would go out with her would be to get some.'"[3]

I just about cried. The rest of Gym class was ruined and I had to face Jacob in Science! I decided not to say anything to him about it. I told James what Emma had said. He was a little bit pissed at me for stealing his seat, but he shook his head and said, "Emma is full of shit."[4]

That was reassuring until lunch, when Gina confirmed Emma's story to be true. "He said that," she told me, "But he said it in a joking way. He was only kidding."

Louis came over and asked me, "Do you still like Jacob?"

1. Thank goodness *that* didn't turn out to be true. It's remarkable how much the "high point" of my life depended on other people's approval of me. The only thing that had changed since the scene I described here was my classmates' general opinion of me—and, consequently, Zach's attraction to me—yet that was enough to make me yearn for a time of perceived perfection.

2. Strange how I determined whether or not I had "missed my chance" based on the interest of others, not that of Jacob himself. It would be such a waste of everyone's energy if we never ended up going out, after all—they would have been scheming to get us alone together at all those parties and dances for *nothing*. Tragic.

3. "Getting some," which referred vaguely to kissing and maybe even going to second or third base, was seemingly the number one priority for every boy in my class. Because it was dependent on a girl's cooperation, few boys ever actually "got any" in middle school—but that didn't mean they spent any less time plotting about it.

4. Emma really was full of shit. Everything she said to me seemed carefully crafted to hurt my feelings.

I said, "No. I hate him." He went back to his table, but I forgot to watch and see if he told Jacob.

At about 3:30, the phone rang. It was James, at Jacob's house. He's always the one who asks for me! Jacob must be chicken or something. Anyway, James asked, "Are you mad at Jacob? He wants to know. He's not on the phone or anything. In fact, he's in the bathroom taking a dump." I heard the muffled sounds of Jacob trying to take the phone away, and then James continued, laughing, "No, no, he's right here. But he wants to know if you're mad at him."

I said, "I don't know who to believe."

James said, "Emma is messed up. She asked Jacob to dance at the last dance but he said no, because he was getting up the balls to ask you to dance. So Emma said, 'You only want to dance with Emily because she's got big... titawkaninnies.'[1] And Jacob was like, 'No.' And he told her to shut up and walked away." Then James changed the subject and said, "Jacob says you owe him a kiss from Stacy's party." I couldn't believe he remembered that! That is SO CUTE. Of course I remember it, but guys aren't supposed to remember things like that! Oh wow, he is too perfect.

I was just listening to "Wear Sunscreen." I don't know the name of the guy who sings it, but he doesn't really sing, he just talks the whole time and says very deep and meaningful things.

My favorite line is: "Don't be reckless with other people's hearts. Don't put up with people who are reckless with yours."[2]

1. Did I spell that correctly?

2. I was referring to Baz Luhrmann's "Everybody's Free (to Wear Sunscreen)" again. I was trying to cultivate an appreciation for "deep and meaningful things," and that song presented them in bite-size pieces that I could try to apply to my own life.

MARCH 25, 1999

Today, Jacob brought into school all these "Romance Coupons." I don't know where he got them, but they were really funny![1] At lunch, James came over to our table and gave one to Gina. It said, "Gives Bearer Permission to Be Nervous." I don't get it, but oh, well. He gave one to Stacy that said something about NOT COMPLAINING.

Then he went back to his own table and yelled back to us, "Hey, Emily! I think Jacob has one for you!" Jacob was looking down at his lap.

I said, "No, they're all mean. I don't want one."

But James said, "No, they're not all mean." Then he ran over and handed me one. It said:

"Allows Bearer Naked Cuddling (Maintaining the Boundaries We Set!)."[2]

Then after school, Jenna called! That is so weird because I haven't talked on the phone with her for the longest time. She said, "It is pathetic how you and Jacob are not going out yet. Can I call him and ask him out for you?"

I was like, "Okay." But she called back and said he wasn't home.

Jenna and Hannah have started hating Steph, and they think I do, too, so that's why they're being particularly nice to me. But I never really hated Steph. Right when I got off the phone with Jenna, Steph sent me an instant message. This is how it went:

DieEmilyLindin: hi[3]

Me: hi

DieEmilyLindin: I feel really bad talking to you when this is my screen name.[4]

1. These painfully corny coupons can be found in any novelty shop around Valentine's Day as a last-minute gift idea for uninspired spouses.

2. I appreciate how this coupon enforces consensual naked cuddling, maintaining set boundaries.

3. No matter what Steph actually typed, the very use of the screen name DieEmilyLindin was threatening. This kind of casual malevolence is prevalent in online bullying today and it's all the more hurtful for implying that the bully is too cool to really *care* that much about their target. I felt embarrassed that Steph's screen name upset me, as if I were overreacting. She was able to hurt me while giving the impression that she was rolling her eyes and shrugging about the whole thing, which only made me feel more ridiculous.

4. But alas, everyone knows it's impossible to make a new screen name that doesn't call for someone's death.

Me: that's ok

DieEmilyLindin: I don't want you to die.

Me: ok

DieEmilyLindin: I don't want to be friends, but can we not like, be enemies?

Me: ok

So we are not enemies anymore. But you know what? My plan to be nice to everyone is not really working. I find myself being mean to people without even realizing it. Stacy and Gina are mean to people who used to be their friends, and those people think it's my fault. But I couldn't care less who else Stacy and Gina are friends with. I am friends with other people, too, but not people I'd feel comfortable sitting with at lunch. Except for Melanie, who is my best friend.[1] If my group ditched me, I would have nobody to fall back on. I have to start building stronger friendships with everyone.

MARCH 27, 1999

In English class, we were supposed to go through these poem books and pick out deep poems that meant something to us. That was a pretty challenging task, considering the poem books we had were all children's poems. I managed to find a reasonable one, about a girl named Samantha who gets eaten by a panther.[2]

I purposefully gave myself laryngitis by screaming a lot into a pillow and clearing my throat in this way that like, ruptures your vocal cords. I like how my voice sounds now: all squeaky and sexy.[3]

I have been thinking about life. I am young right

1. There was always something special about my relationship with Melanie, and it was heightened by our shared love of descriptive writing. I recently visited her at her home outside Boston, and she pulled out boxes of saved notes she and I had exchanged throughout middle school. We read them aloud, laughing and sometimes tearing up. In addition to our awkward incorporation of hip language from magazines like *Seventeen* (boys we were "crushin' on" and situations we were "totally buggin' about"), they were marked by detailed, comprehensive descriptions of everyone sitting near us in class and what they seemed to be up to. We described each other, too, and there must have been something solidifying about putting our appreciation for our friendship into writing.

2. That does sound reasonable.

3. This day just keeps getting more and more reasonable. There might have been an element of stress relief behind all the pillow-screaming, but it's more likely I was just trying to make my voice sound like Britney Spears's.

now, but soon I will be like, fifty, looking at pictures of the younger me, feeling nostalgic. That means thinking about the past and missing it. I feel that way a lot now—just imagine how I will feel when I'm fifty!

Last night, I was in the mood for a good cry, so I took out my diary from December 1997 and started reading about Zach and all my old friends. I came to that letter he wrote me about how he is so sorry for breaking up with me, and could I ever forgive him? It is still folded in exactly the same way as it was when I got it. I opened it and read it and did not feel one twinge of pain. I did not, in any way, feel depressed to not be going out with Zach anymore. I can't yet go so far as to say that I laughed at myself for ever being so stupid as to like him, but I think I'll be able to do that soon.

MARCH 29, 1999

I HATE MY DAD SO MUCH! HE IS SUCH A FUCKHEAD! For some reason, he is against letting me go on AOL.[1] When I am over Stacy's house, we always go on AOL and I accidentally let it slip out in front of him, and we got in this HUGE FIGHT. He was like, "YOU CAN'T GO OVER TO STACY'S HOUSE ANYMORE BECAUSE I CAN'T TRUST YOU!"

And then I yelled, "DAD, GO TO HELL!" and I ran into my bedroom and locked the door.[2]

I also hate Ms. Metcalf. She doesn't understand that I am a strong person and that I should be allowed to express my opinions. Teachers should be encouraging me to find my good qualities—one of

1. Restricting my use of AOL was one way for my parents to feel in control of my behavior. They didn't know about the DieEmilyLindin screen name, but they were deeply suspicious of the online environment in general and probably felt that just shutting the whole thing down was the best way to keep me safe.

2. This would have been impossible, since my bedroom door didn't have a lock on it. More likely, I shoved my clothes hamper up against it as a barricade. It's not like my parents would have been trying to get into my room, anyway; they were probably relieved to have a break from my antics.

them is standing up for what I believe in—and then they should help me go with it. Ms. Metcalf suppresses my good qualities by making it obvious that I am not allowed to have an opinion. Instead, she laughs when Matt calls me a slut in class.[1] She always sends me to the office and lets Mr. Jones deal with me.[2] But I like Mr. Jones. He is nice. When we are alone, talking in his office, it almost seems like he understands how frustrated I am.

It is so hard for me to express what I'm thinking in words right now. I guess I just have these thoughts going through my head, but they are not thoughts, really, they are feelings. It is hard for me to put them into words that other people will understand.

APRIL 4, 1999

It is 10:37 at night. I was just getting ready for bed and I heard my parents talking in the kitchen. My dad just got back from my perfect cousins and aunt and uncle's house, and this is what he was telling my mom: "They said their kids *want* to go to Mass. When it was time to go, the kids dropped everything and ran to the car. Maybe Catholic school is necessary."[3]

My mom said, "Well, she goes to CCD..."[4]

"It's not making a difference!" my dad yelled. "Look what she wanted to leave the house wearing today![5] And do you know what she told me last night? She told me SHE DIDN'T BELIEVE IN JESUS!" My mom gasped.

FOR GOODNESS SAKE! My parents are considering Catholic school so I will realize how wrong I am to question the Catholic religion?! Forc-

1. Ms. Metcalf's behavior would be disturbing in any adult, let alone an educator. Along with most of my other teachers, she had a sense of my reputation. It wasn't her job to fix my social life, but she could have at least made an effort to maintain a safe classroom.

2. Mr. Jones was the soft-spoken, kindhearted vice principal of the middle school. He wasn't aware of the details of my social situation and as far as I know, he never reached out to my parents about it, but knowing that he was even willing to listen meant a lot to me.

3. Being sent to Catholic school was a quiet, constant threat hanging over my head. Besides stricter teachers and less room for intellectual curiosity, it would have meant wearing an ugly uniform, which I simply could not abide.

4. CCD, or "Confraternity of Christian Doctrine," is basically Catholic Sunday school, but it takes place during the week. I went every week until my confirmation ceremony sophomore year of high school.

5. When it came to style choices, it didn't take much to scandalize my parents. I'd probably attempted to leave the house in a tank top that revealed my bra strap if it accidentally shifted a tiny bit, or shorts that didn't come down as far as my fingertips when I held my arms at my sides.

ing Catholicism upon me is not going to make me believe in it! Honestly, sometimes my parents can be the biggest shitheads.

I believe that God is not a being, but a feeling. I think He is the idea of goodness—God is like, a metaphor.[1] I don't believe in Hell, either. If God created us as sinners, why would He punish us for just being what He made us? He wouldn't. I believe that God understands us, and that we are stupid and shallow and that in the end He forgives us, because even if we are too stupid to be sorry for our sins, He takes pity on us and lets us be in Heaven with Him.[2]

APRIL 7, 1999

Yesterday, Louis told me that Mark liked me. He said it seriously, but Louis is an extremely good liar and the type of person who would play a joke like that on me. So I didn't believe him and dismissed it as one of those stupid things Louis says.

But today, in Math, I was getting bored. My eyes were wandering around the room and they stopped on Mark's face. He was staring at me as if he were studying me. There was a mix of sadness and determination in his eyes, and it made me uncomfortable. I looked away.

Math was the last class of the day, and when I was at my locker, putting my things in my backpack, Gina ran over all excited. She pressed a note into my hand and said excitedly, "It's from Mark! He told me to give it to you! Can I read it?"[3]

"What?" I asked, not sure how I felt. I couldn't deny a little tingle of happiness that ran through me, but I was also frightened. Mark used to go out with

1. I was really into metaphors.

2. I had forgotten the extent to which I was already questioning Catholicism at this point in my life. My religious rebellion was inspired by my resentment at being told by adults that some questions just didn't have answers and that therefore I should stop asking. That never sat right with me. My parents, for the record, were deeply shaken by the 2002 scandal in the Boston Archdiocese—when Catholic priests were found guilty of sexually abusing minors—and now they no longer attend Mass or tithe. Also, three out of my four "perfect" cousins who went to Catholic school are now on nasty terms with their parents.

3. We were constantly passing notes back and forth in class, but letters were a weightier matter. They almost always contained a declaration either of romantic interest or of a breakup, and they were usually delivered by a third party who had promised *not* to read them under *any* circumstances.

Shauna, and he wanted her to give him a hand job but she said no. Then he grabbed her and tried to force her to do it. That is one of the reasons I was unsure of how I felt.[1] The other major reason I was unsure is because I am totally, completely, hopelessly in love with Jacob. But at this rate, we'll never go out![2] There is a dance this Friday, and if I am going out with Mark, I won't be able to dance with Jacob!

Stacy, Melanie, and Michelle had also gathered around me, waiting to hear what the note said. So I opened it and let them read it over my shoulder. It said:

Emily,

I really like you and I think you're hot. I know that what happened with Shauna was wrong, perhaps it was entirely my fault.[3] I know you probably don't like me at all, but I know what I did was wrong and I wouldn't let it ever happen again. I really like you, at least since December I've thought about asking you out, now I did, and if it's no, all right I'll deal with it. I really like you. I think you're really hot and nice. Please go out with me.

Mark

P.S. Write back if you want.

Everyone gasped and started saying things like, "Oh, he's so cute!" And he is cute. But as much as I want to say yes, I feel like I'm bound to Jacob. And today at lunch, Jenna told me she had written him a note about how he should ask me out, and he had written back saying, "I really like Emily, but I don't want to go out with anyone right now." So if he's not going to ask me out, why not go out with Mark?

1. That's a pretty huge reason. What Mark did to Shauna was not okay, but unfortunately it doesn't seem like any of us recognized that.

2. My drawn-out courtship with Jacob could have been dealt with in a simple, face-to-face conversation or even in an honest phone call. But I have a feeling we both enjoyed the struggle.

3. Yeah. It was.

But my mom said I should tell Mark that I like a bunch of different boys and I don't want to be tied down to just one of them.[1] That way I can dance with both Jacob and Mark at the dance, and if Jacob finally decides to ask me out, I will say yes, of course! And I can just tell Mark I changed my mind. But if Jacob keeps being retarded, I can just be like, "Mark, does your offer still stand?" and see what he says.

Gina's locker is two over from Mark's, and she talks to him all the time in Homeroom. She said he talks about me all the time and is in love with me. That makes me feel good, except I'm kind of worried—I'm always worried! Mark doesn't really know me as a person. From what Gina tells me, he seems to think I'm perfect. I know some other boys do, too, and I have myself to thank for that. Wearing short shorts and skintight shirts certainly doesn't help.[2] But I know that I am not perfect inside. I am afraid that Mark will get to know me and realize I'm not perfect, and be disappointed.[3]

MARCH 10, 1999

Today is Saturday. Last night, there was a dance. Everyone wanted to know if I was going to go out with Mark. Tyler and Daniel were like, "Will you go out with him?"

I said, "Let me dance with him first. I want to see if he makes me feel tingly." I meant tingly as in nervous because I liked him, like butterflies, but they took it a different way.[4]

"You mean horny?" Tyler laughed.

"No!" I said, but they ran off to tell Mark. A few

1. Way to go, Mom! It wasn't often that I confided in her about my relationship worries, so it's likely she had overheard a conversation with one of my friends and offered this advice unsolicited.

2. I should point out here that the way I dressed wasn't any different from the way most girls in my class dressed. Shorts that fit my hips and butt looked shorter on me because I was taller than most girls my age, and anything that wasn't designed to be baggy looked "skintight" on my body. With that said, it doesn't matter *how* I dressed. Mark and the other boys in my class were responsible for their own behavior toward me, regardless of the clothes I wore.

3. I think by "perfect," I might have meant "willing to be sexual." It's unclear. Although I was rather typically attractive, no one would have ever called me "perfect"-looking, least of all myself.

4. Yeah, "tingly" might not have been the best word choice, in hindsight.

minutes later, they came back.

Daniel asked, "What does Mark have to do to make you feel, er… tingly?" This sent them into another fit of giggles.

I sighed. "Tell him to just be himself." I danced with him, and I saw Jacob.

He and Matt were running around yelling out, "We're pimps! We're pimping!"[1] Matt lifted Jacob up like a baby and charged through a group of people. When the song was over, Mark went back to his group of friends.

Tyler and Daniel ran up to me. "Will you go out with him now?" While I was thinking about what to say, I noticed that Jacob was still with Matt, pretending to be pimps, whatever that means.[2]

I mumbled, "Okay."

"Really?!" They cried. "All right!" Like it was as much of a victory for them as it was for Mark.[3] They ran over to tell him. All my girl friends started congratulating me. I felt sick to my stomach. Mark came over and stood next to me.

Melanie whispered, "You look miserable."

I whispered back, "I am."

She said, "Well, at least pretend to look happy, for Mark's sake." We looked over at Mark, who was beaming from ear to ear. I plastered a smile on my face, pretending I was in a play and Mark was playing the part of my boyfriend. He reached over and took my hand. Our fingers intertwined, and his hand was sweaty. He took my other hand and began playing with my fingers. It was a romantic gesture— if I liked him, I would have been swooning.

His hands started to move my hands downward,

1. I doubt either of them had a clear idea of what a pimp actually is, but they knew "pimping" was a cool thing rappers wanted everyone to know they were doing.

2. What would pretending to be a pimp even *look* like?

3. Because dating is a team sport, obviously.

toward my waist. I got stiff, remembered his incident with Shauna, what happened with Zach, and also what happened with Chris Walker, all at the same time somehow. I was petrified. If he tried anything, I wouldn't be able to move.[1]

Luckily, Melanie turned to talk to me at that instant and Mark dropped my hands. Then another slow song came on. Mark wrapped his arms around me. We were really close. I looked to the side and his eyelashes fluttered against mine. I leaned my head against his and closed my eyes. It felt good to be holding someone this close, even if it wasn't Jacob. Mark turned his head to look at me. I was suddenly very aware that he was going to kiss me. I kept my head turned to the side and bit my lip. He took the hint and turned his head so that his face was pressed into my neck. I couldn't feel anything. Another slow song came on, annoyingly. Mark turned his face up, as if to kiss me, and I kept looking to the side. He kissed me on the cheek and waited for my reaction. I didn't do anything—I just kept staring off into space.

He kissed the corner of my mouth and I decided to just get it over with, so I turned my head so that his lips were pressed against mine and opened my mouth a little bit. Kissing Mark was nothing like kissing Zach. With Zach, we both opened our mouths and our tongues kind of met in the middle. Mark shoved his tongue into my mouth, surprising me so much that my eyes flew open. Everyone was watching us. I closed my eyes and tried to get into the kiss, but that was impossible. His mouth kept opening and closing and I couldn't move my mouth at all. Mark owned the kiss. I tried to end it, but wasn't able to until the song ended.[2]

1. I didn't have the emotional tools to come to terms with any of these things, so when they came up, my body reacted by becoming completely helpless. Mark's experience of this moment must have been the complete opposite of mine; he was getting to dance with the girl he had a crush on! He had no way of knowing what was going on inside my head.

2. What a nightmare.

Then I pulled away and ran to the bathroom. Gina was right behind me. I could feel tears start gathering in my eyes. Steph came into the small bathroom. She looked at me, smiled, and said, "What have you been doing?"

"What?" I didn't understand. She patted her own neck, applied some makeup, and left.[1] I looked in the mirror and nearly died. There were red marks all over my neck from where Mark had been sucking on it. Then I really started to cry, and I took out my makeup and did my best to cover the marks.[2] Stacy, Michelle, and Melanie arrived and crowded into the bathroom.

"Mark asked us where you went," Melanie said. "I told him you were in the girls' room. This is the one place he can't follow you." My friends are very understanding. They told me I should wait a while to break up with Mark.

"He really likes you," Gina reminded me. "Give him a chance."[3]

APRIL 12, 1999

Last night I talked on the phone with Jenna about what to do about the whole Mark situation. She had me convinced that breaking up with him would be for the best. After all, is it fair to be going out with Mark when I am also in love with Jacob?

But when I got to school today, Mark had the sweetness turned on full blast. He defended me when Hunter drew naked pictures of me. Stupid guys do that a lot and I've kind of gotten used to it, but it really pissed Mark off. He also waited for me after Math class so he could walk me to my locker. I

1. Phew. That could have been worse.

2. Hickeys were usually seen as badges of honor. Not only were they tangible evidence that you had hooked up with another person, they proved that the hookup had been heated and aggressive. But in this case, I felt branded by the hickey Mark had left on my neck, as if he had marked me as his own.

3. The strange power dynamic stands out to me here. I seemed to have social power over Mark, since he kept sending his friends to beg me to go out with him, but in our physical interaction I clearly felt powerless. He doesn't seem to have done anything blatantly wrong toward me, but for some reason I associated his attention with negative, threatening interactions I'd had before.

just couldn't bring myself to break up with him.

Melanie told me, "On the bus on the way home today, a bunch of retarded eighth-graders were like, 'Who thinks Emily Lindin is a slut?' And they all raised their hands. Mark turned around and said, 'Anyone who doesn't put their hand down right now is going to get a serious beating.' They all put their hands down." I sighed. She continued, "That was sweet of him, Emily. Do you remember when you were going out with Zach? Did he stand up for you when people dissed you? No. Yet you were madly in love with him. Mark is a good kid, and it is a shame. Otherwise you might be able to find a reason to dump him." She is so right.[1]

I wrote this poem that I guess is kind of like from Mark's perspective. It's like Mark writing a poem to me, I think. It makes me sad.

1. Melanie was always a wise source of advice. Also, I am nostalgic for the word "diss" ("dis"?) as an abbreviation for "disrespect."

I wrote you a poem, but it sounded like shit.
So you read it through once, then forgot about it.
I brought you some flowers and knocked on
    your door,
But you said, "Don't come back to my house
    anymore."
I gave you some chocolates for Valentine's Day,
"I'm allergic to chocolate," is all you could say.
My shoulder brushed yours; you recoiled at
    my touch.
Why do you hate me? I love you so much.

APRIL 16, 1999

This week, everyone has been ditching Jenna![2] All because of Steph. What a bitch. She asked Jenna,

2. The worst part about getting ditched was that it wasn't final—your friends would usually drift back slowly, only to ditch you again. This is what had happened to Jenna.

"How's life on welfare?" in front of everyone. Jenna and her mom just stopped living with her grandparents, and I guess they're on welfare. I hadn't known that.[1]

Today at lunch, I was walking by Zach's table and he called out, "Is that a tank top, Emily?" I was wearing a tank top but I had a zip-up sweatshirt over it. I became conscious of every muscle I moved, every face I made, and everything I said.

Hunter laughed and said, "Zach, are you looking at her boobs?"

Zach nodded and said, "Yeah, actually I am."

"Me, too," Matt piped in. Hunter nodded. They were all scrutinizing my chest, and I felt very self-conscious. I zipped up my sweatshirt and kept walking, back to my table.[2]

A few minutes later, Louis came running over from his table and said, "Mark wants to know if you're wearing a bra." I looked over at Mark, who was obviously oblivious. I just laughed. Of course I was wearing a bra.

Melanie called after school today. She had another story about what happened on her bus on the way home![3] She said, "Mark was sitting near to me, Stacy, and Gina, instead of with Louis or Tyler." Louis is on her bus, and Tyler must have been going over his house. "Louis was so mad that Mark wasn't sitting with them, so he stood up and yelled, 'Tyler had a wet dream about Emily Lindin last night! So did I! Oh, Mark, you're on the bus—oops!' Mark was about ready to kick the shit out of him." I think it's nice how Mark gets so angry and jealous when other people talk about me.[4]

1. Jenna's mother was significantly younger than most of our classmates' mothers. She had grown up in our town, accidentally gotten pregnant with Jenna at the end of high school, and raised Jenna with the help of her parents in the same big house she had grown up in. They eventually moved out of Jenna's grandparents' home, into a small condo in another town with a lower cost of living. Jenna could still attend school in our town though, using her grandparents' address. This situation is certainly not uncommon, but Jenna was unlucky enough to be the only one of our classmates going through it.

2. Their words weren't exactly threatening, but the fact that they felt so comfortable making me feel objectified like this is really disturbing. It seems motivated by a mixture of sexual curiosity and a callous desire to humiliate me.

3. I trusted all of Melanie's stories. Unlike me, she had no real motivation to exaggerate.

4. "Nice" is one way to describe his reactions… "Red flag" is another. In Melanie's account, Louis was using me as a tool to bother Mark, but in doing so in a public, sexual way, he was really reinforcing my reputation to everyone on the bus and humiliating me.

APRIL 17, 1999

Nothing matters, when you think about it.

In the long run, no one cares.

All your problems are irrelevant:

The whos, the whats, the wheres.

Doesn't matter where you spend your life,

Or what you say and do.

The only thing that counts is

If you're happy when you're through.

—Me

In Health class, we're learning about reproduction. It's weird to hear the boys say things like, "woman," "menstruation," and "breast," because we're not allowed to use slang terms.

My legs feel really smooth because I just shaved them.[1] I'm glad I'm a girl because I get to shave my legs, have big boobs, and complain about PMS.[2]

MAY 5, 1999

Today is Wednesday. After school, Melanie, Michelle, Erin, and I all went over Shauna's house. Jacob and Tyler were at Louis's house, and Louis lives right behind Shauna. When we got to Shauna's we started primping, because the guys said they were going to come over. Then we looked out Shauna's bedroom window and saw the guys were in her backyard, jumping on her trampoline. Erin got the brilliant idea to crawl out the window and onto the flat roof, and then jump down onto the trampoline from there.[3]

I was scared, but I did it, and it was so fun! Then we pushed the picnic table up next to the porch and

1. I had been shaving my legs since the fifth grade, when Steph had shown me how. I had begun feeling self-conscious about the dark hair that stood out starkly on my shins whenever I wore dresses, and when I mentioned it in passing to Steph, she suggested we shave my legs together. She had already started shaving hers, so I trusted that she knew what she was doing. My mother had noticed the next day, but hadn't really made a big deal about it; I guess she figured she had to choose her battles when it came to puberty-related decision-making in our household.

2. Er... "get to" shave my legs?! And what about not having PMS in the first place? That would be nice.

3. What could go wrong?

stacked chairs on top of it so we could easily climb up onto the roof and jump off, instead of having to run up to Shauna's room and climb out the window. Then the guys ran inside and grabbed cushions off the couch, and we had a pillow fight on the trampoline![1]

Eventually we got too tired to keep fighting, so we ended up sitting around in a circle on the trampoline. The guys were like, "Emily, you have to flash us!"

I said no, because of Mark, but Erin said, "I'll flash you!"

And they were like, "Okay." So she did.

Then they decided they still wanted me to flash them, and Louis said, "If you don't flash us, I'm going to tell Mark you gave us a strip show!" I said no again, but Louis went inside and yelled behind him, "I'm calling Mark right now to tell him about your strip show!" So I panicked and flashed them really quickly.[2]

Then my mom came to pick me up and I had to go home. When I got home, Melanie called and said, "Twenty minutes after you left, Louis dared Erin to kiss Jacob, and she did, and they made out for like, a minute!"

Okay, I like the relationship I have with Jacob—I feel pretty comfortable around him as a friend. But I can't deny the pang of jealousy I felt for a moment when Melanie told me about

Erin hooking up with him. I think maybe I still love him. I don't know. I just can't stand the idea of him loving someone other than me.

Anyway, Jenna and I have become really good friends again! We talk on the phone like, every day, and I feel like I can completely trust her again. I think she feels the same way about me.

1. Trampolines are basically death traps... but they are so *fun*.

2. Not only were they were willing to back me into a corner this way, I let them because I was sure Mark would believe them over me anyway. Actually, a lot of the flirtatious episodes in my life involved this kind of mild extortion. I was an easy target since my reputation as a "slut" meant I had limited credibility—I knew people would assume that I had willingly engaged, regardless of what had actually gone down.

MAY 14, 1999

Jenna is sleeping over and she's already fallen asleep.[1] There was a dance tonight, and it was so fun! Mark couldn't go but that was okay, because I wanted to flirt with other guys anyway. I wore a pink shirt that is skintight and comes down almost to my boobs.

I was talking to Tyler, and he said, "Will you dance with me on the next slow song?" I said yes, so when the next slow song came on we started dancing. I put my head against his shoulder and closed my eyes. It was so comfortable. Then the song ended and we parted, and I went over sit on the bleachers.

Zach came over and was being quite talkative. I realized that I'm starting to feel comfortable around him, for the first time ever. We started to talk about when we went to third base, and he said, "I'm so sorry for everything that happened after that. Really." He looked like he genuinely meant it, and so of course I believed him. He still has that hold on me. I decided I wanted to dance with him.[2]

But there was just fast song after fast song, no slow songs, so I kept talking to him and waiting. Zach decided to get up on Matt's shoulders, so they'd be really tall.[3] Then Zach looked at me and said, "No, Emily, you get on my shoulders!"

I was like, "I am too scared to get on anyone's shoulders!"

Then a slow song came on and Stacy pulled me aside and said, "Oh my god, I think Zach likes you again. You should dance with him!"

Then Zach was right there, and I covered my face and hid in Stacy's shoulder, so she whispered to him,

1. I didn't have that many one-on-one sleepovers. When they happened, it was usually out of convenience for the friend's parents, who might have been too tired or busy to come pick up their child and figured it was easier just to wait until the morning. Slumber parties with four or five girls were even rarer but much more fun and almost always involved making prank calls on my *Clueless* Hands-Free Phone.

2. Uh-oh.

3. Naturally.

"Will you dance with Emily?"

And I heard him say, "Yeah." Then I looked up and started shaking my head no.

Zach opened his arms and said, "Come on." So I wrapped my arms around his neck and leaned close against him. Matt was flicking Altoids at us.[1] Everyone who passed by raised their eyebrows and whispered something, sometimes something mean, but I felt like I belonged in Zach's arms. I felt like holding him was the way it should be.

1. Seriously, Matt? Well, Altoids are better than Airheads, I guess.

MAY 16, 1999

Last night was Saturday, and we had a surprise birthday party for Shauna at Stacy's house. It wasn't really a surprise because she helped plan it, but only Stacy and I knew that.[2] I had an outdoor disposable camera, so we went outside to use it before it got too dark.

2. Birthday parties were a way to establish who was inside your group of friends and who was, inevitably, outside. They were, like all parties, an excuse for us to socialize with limited adult supervision, but they had the added purpose of proving to everyone just how many people –and *which* people–thought you were important enough to celebrate.

All the girls were posed for a picture and James was ready to take it, but then Louis ran by and dumped a pail of water on us! We were soaked and extremely pissed off. We ran inside, grabbed two paper cups each, filled them to the brim at the kitchen sink, and ran outside to dump them on Louis.

Then Louis came up behind me and grabbed me around the waist. I screamed and kicked my legs in the air, but he lifted me off the ground and turned me toward Daniel, who had grabbed the hose. Daniel unmercifully sprayed the hose at my face, drenching both me and Louis. When Louis let me down, my T-shirt was sticking to my body and Daniel yelled out, "Everyone, you can see Emily's nipples! Look!" I ran inside before anyone could see and changed into some of Stacy's dry clothes.

When I got back downstairs, almost everyone was in Stacy's family room, watching *Fear*.[1] I sat down next to Stacy. Everyone was like, "Emily, go sit next to Mark," who was sitting in a loveseat across the room. But Mark got up, grabbed my hands, and led me back across the room to the loveseat, where he put his arm around my shoulders and sat very close to me.

Daniel sat in a chair right next to us and said, "You guys should make out."

I nodded but said, "Not right now. I have a cough drop in my mouth."

Daniel put out his hand and said, "I'll hold it while you two kiss."[2] But before I could give it to him, everyone decided they wanted to go outside.

There is a lake across the street from Stacy's house, and most of it is surrounded by trees, but there are three steps down to this little beach. We were walking across the street and Mark and I had our arms around each other. Daniel came up and put his arm around me from the other side and was like, "Let's have a threesome!"[3]

We were like, "Yeah!" so we went down to the beach together, and then Mark said, "All right, Daniel, get lost."

Daniel turned to me and asked, "Can I kiss you?" I shook my head.

Daniel made a pouty face and so I said, "On the cheek, you may." And he leaned over and touched his lips to my cheek.

Scott then randomly popped up and said, "I

1. Classic Marky Mark Wahlberg. One of my favorite lines to quote with my sister was: "It could've all been different, Mr. Walker. You should have let nature take its course, but in the end, it will anyway... *So let me in the fucking house!*" Our parents would inevitably scold us for using the *f-word*, and we would whine, "But it's what he says in the *moo-vie*. We're re-creating *art*."

2. Aw, thanks, Daniel! Always such a good helper.

3. He was really committed to working out a threesome somehow.

want to kiss Emily, too!" I rolled my eyes but let him kiss my cheek, which he did, but not as gently as Daniel had.

Then Mark was like, "All right, now get lost!" And they ran back up to the street to join the rest of the party. Mark and I started making out. We made out for about five minutes. Every once in a while, someone up on the street would say something funny and we would stop kissing to laugh, then start again. From what I could hear, it sounded like the people up on the street were playing Truth or Dare.

I pulled away from Mark and said, "I want to go play Truth or Dare. Will you come up with me?" He just looked at me for a minute, and then he put his hands on my lower back and pressed me right up against him. I wasn't really kissing him anymore, I was just smashed up against him and I couldn't breathe.[1] Finally, I said, "Hey! Stop!" and dragged him up to the street. By the time we got there, Truth or Dare was over and we all just sat around talking.

Mark wandered away with a few of the guys and Daniel said to me, "Eat some of my candy necklace so it looks like we're making out." I rolled my eyes, leaned over and bit off one of the pieces of candy, then had another because it was good. Daniel said, "Can I have a kiss?"

I sighed. "Again?! All right, turn your cheek." He did, and I leaned forward, but when my face was just about touching his, he turned back toward me so I would kiss his lips. I jerked back quickly and said, "Daniel! Don't do that!"

He smiled. "Okay, I'm sorry." And he turned his cheek again, and again I leaned forward to kiss it,

1. I didn't realize it at the time, but Mark's behavior was borderline violent when it came to kissing me. I never felt in control or enjoyed our intimate exchanges.

and again he turned his face at the last minute.[1] I pulled back without kissing him, just as Mark possessively wrapped his arm around my waist and glared at Daniel.

Daniel grinned. "Mark," he said, "I'm stealing your girlfriend."

Mark said, "Daniel, it was funny at first, but now it's just getting kind of creepy."[2]

MAY 19, 1999

Steph is the biggest bitch. What goes around comes around, and I think it's about to hit her full force. Steph and Erin are in a fight. This is why: Steph is going out with Matt now, and she saw Erin giving him a back rub. I guess that really pissed her off.

Today at the beginning of fifth period, Erin and I passed Steph in the hall. Erin wanted to make up, I guess, and she started to say, "Steph..." gently touching her forearm. Steph completely flipped out and screamed, "Don't you EVER fucking TOUCH me again, you STUPID SLUT!" Then she put her hand on Erin's throat, pushed her up against a locker, and tore out a chunk of hair from the side of her head. It all happened really quickly, and then Steph turned and left. She didn't make eye contact with me at all.[3]

I ran up to Erin, who was just standing there staring after Steph. I led her to the nurse's office, and she had her hand on the side of her head but didn't say anything the whole time. I'm not really good friends with Erin, so I didn't know what to say to her.

1. Fool me once, shame on you. Fool me twice... Actually, just stop trying to kiss me. Daniel was the only person in my group of friends who acted like this; he could get away with it because he generally played the role of the goofball, not to be taken too seriously.

2. Agreed.

3. Erin was targeted as a "slut" for giving her friend Matt a backrub without knowing that he was dating someone else. This incident demonstrates that really, "slut" shaming has nothing to do with the target and everything to do with the person doing the shaming. It scares me to think about what this must have been like for Erin. It also scares me to think about what might have been going on in Steph's life outside of school to elicit this type of anger.

Steph was suspended for the rest of the day, which doesn't seem like too horrible of a punishment.[1] But everyone really likes Erin. She has a brother in the eighth grade, and all his friends are saying they're going to kick Steph's ass.[2]

I know it sounds mean, but I hope everyone turns against her. And because she was so cruel to everyone else, she won't have anyone to fall back on. But she's still friends with Kaylee, Catherine, Emma, and all them, and Matt won't dump her because he is a good boyfriend.[3] I feel bad for her, but it was crazy how she attacked Erin like that.

MAY 25, 1999

Right now, I feel the same way about Zach as I did in sixth grade: hopelessly in love with him. There is just something about him—he has this certain effect on me. I guess I never stopped loving him for the past two years. For a while, I became infatuated with other people, but in the back of my mind I've always hoped we'd end up together.[4]

Today, Zach, Matt, and Hunter had to miss school to go to court because Matt threw a rock at some lady's windshield.[5] So Zach wasn't in Math class with me, and we had a test.

After school, I had play practice, and the play is in about a week, and I have all my lines memorized, and I guess it is going to be good. But anyways. I got home from play practice, and the phone rang.

I answered it, and a familiar voice asked, "What is the math homework?"[6] I knew the voice, but I decided to pretend like I couldn't quite put my fin-

1. There could have been more to this punishment, depending on how Erin's parents reacted. If I were them, I would have considered getting Steph expelled or perhaps enrolling Erin in a school with a zero-tolerance approach to bullying.

2. Having an older brother who would threaten to beat up anyone who bullied her probably helped Erin in the short term, but it only perpetuated the cycle of bullying.

3. Really? *Matt* is a good boyfriend? I might have seen him this way because he was, if nothing else, fiercely loyal. In the world of my seventh-grade class, where social structures were always shifting, loyalty was valued highly.

4. Well, getting back together in middle school doesn't *quite* mean ending up together, but...

5. Throwing rocks at someone's windshield is not just destruction of property—it could end up killing someone. The way I just casually mentioned this is a bit off-putting, but it reflects how this kind of behavior was expected from those boys. They were testing the limits of the damage they could do without facing any real consequences.

6. Ah, the old what's-the-homework tactic! It's tried and true.

ger on who it belonged to. I politely asked who it was, and the answer was, "Zach," in a tone that said I should have known that, and also surprise and disappointment that I hadn't.

"Oh, hi," I said pleasantly. "It's page 219, all questions."

"Thanks," he said.

I said, "Okay?" as if to say goodbye, but he said, "Yup. So, how was the test?" We got into a conversation about that, and he told me about court. We had been talking for about fifteen minutes when the conversation landed on me and Mark.

I told him, "My relationship with Mark is awesome because it's like, I don't really like him, and I don't think he's that obsessed with me, so all we do is make out. And that's the most fun part of going out with someone, anyway, and this way if we break up, it won't be too painful. Besides, it's not like we're going to get married or anything."

Zach said, "Well, you could."

"Get married? To Mark?!"

"No, not necessarily to Mark. Just, if you were going out with someone in middle school that you really liked, and you stayed going out with them, then you could get married right after graduation."

I thought about that for a moment and then said, "Well, so you'd probably lose your virginity to them, right?"

"Yeah, probably."

"Well, then you'd get married, and that means you'd have sex with only one person in your whole life."[1]

1. I'm glad that this concept sounded like BS to me, even as a twelve-year-old. Sexual compatibility is such an important part of most marriages that leaving it up to chance seems like an irresponsible and ill-fated decision.

Zach answered, "Well, you might have periods where you're broken up with them."

"But what if you never got back together?" It was at this point that I realized we were talking about ourselves. I think Zach did, too.

He was silent for a moment, and then he said, "You would always end up getting back together. You'd be like, soul mates."[1] I considered what he had said. I still can't decide what to think about him. We talked for about an hour, and then I had to go out to eat with my family.

As soon as I got home, the phone rang, and it was Scott. I guess he and Zach are sometimes friends.

The first thing Scott said to me was, "Do you really like Mark?" With the question just thrown upon me like that, unsure of the circumstances, I didn't know what to say.

I decided to tell the truth. "He's okay. I don't really like him, though."

I could hear Scott's smile in his voice as he said, "Oh. 'Cause I know someone who likes you."

"Who?"

"Zach."

"Oh, jeez." I was not disappointed, by any means. I told that to Scott. I don't know what to do. Zach and I are soul mates, but I don't want to hurt Mark.

MAY 26, 1999

Today, I knew I was going to have to break up with Mark. I'm sorry, I know I'm pathetic, but I love Zach too much to go out with anyone else.[2] I didn't know how to dump Mark—I really didn't want to hurt him. But everyone knew that Zach and I liked

1. I don't remember when I stopped believing in the concept of a "soul mate," but whenever it was, it wasn't soon enough. Once you decide someone is your soul mate, you're basically taking the idea of ever ending the relationship off the table, even if it's obviously the right thing to do.

2. Maybe I imagined my diary could forgive me for being pathetic, or maybe I was just apologizing to myself. Sometimes I wrote in this voice, addressing my diary as if it were an intimate friend. It makes sense, considering how few intimate friends I actually had.

each other again, even Mark.

Right before lunch, Daniel came up to me and said, "I have to tell you something that you probably won't care about. Well, Mark doesn't want to go out with you anymore." I smiled, because really, this was good news. I wouldn't be hurting him by breaking up with him, because he had broken up with me. Of course, it was because he knew I was going to dump him so he wanted to dump me first. But whatever.

I went to lunch, and Scott came up to me and said, "Mark just called you a slut and a whore."[1] That offended me, but not too much, because Mark was actually helping me out. He was turning around the situation by being mean to me. But I know it was because he was hurt.

Everyone was bombarding me with the question, "Are you going to go back out with Zach?" I just shrugged, not sure what to say. I knew I wanted to go out with him, but I am so paranoid—deep down inside, I was terrified that this was a joke he was playing on me.[2] I was talking to Scott and I let it slip that I was going to say yes to Zach.

He ran off to tell him and a few minutes later came back and said, "Okay, so you're going out with Zach." I smiled and nodded, feeling a satisfied sense of déjà vu. Had this not happened five times before?[3]

But anyway, in Math, Zach was like, "Are we going out?" and I nodded, and he was like, "Okay, then."

But I was feeling really guilty about hurting Mark, so I decided to write him a note saying I was sorry. As I was writing it, I began to cry, thinking about how much Mark must be hurting. Zach leaned over

1. Not just a slut, and not just a whore. A slut *and* a whore. I had become used to these insults; they no longer hurt in a surprising, stinging way, but instead just piled on, contributing to an enduring state of low self-esteem. But it must have been a bit of a relief in this situation for me, since it meant I didn't have to see myself as the only one doing the hurting in this breakup.

2. This fear that people were secretly making fun of me, even when they were expressing romantic interest or acting nice, was constant and pressing. Because that fear had been realized before, it was almost impossible to shake.

3. It's not déjà vu when it actually *has* happened before.

as if to comfort me, but then stopped. He just looked at me, not knowing what to say. I almost laughed. We'd been apart so long that he'd forgotten how to deal with me. I just smiled at him through my tears. I gave the note to Melanie, because she is on Mark's bus, and she could give it to him.[1]

She called me after school and told me, "I gave it to him. He read it and said, 'That dumb slut.' Then he crumpled it up in a ball." Hmm. I am not going to try to analyze Mark's behavior—I don't know him well enough.[2]

MAY 28, 1999

Next year, Zach is going to an all-boys Catholic school. I said I would miss him, and he said, "Well, you'll get to go to two sets of dances—yours and mine. Plus, you'll get to sound cool when you tell people you have a boyfriend who goes to Catholic school."[3] That means he's planning on us going out for a long time! Yay! I'm so glad we're back together. We are definitely soul mates.

MAY 30, 1999

Today, I got this e-mail from Nathan:

Hey Emily!!!!!!

It's Nathan, remember me, the only guy that went out with you for a reason other than your tits! OH YEAH... I remember now!!

I hear that you are even more of a slut than you used to be. You're going out with Zach again, huh? Oh yeah, that's a bright move Emily!! You're practically asking him to finger you (or further) then dump you. Then you'll put on the "I've

1. I believe the idea of writing Mark an apology note began with sympathy, but it was also a kind of performance for the sake of our classmates, so they wouldn't judge me too harshly for breaking up with him.

2. What's there to analyze here? I'm not surprised he took it so hard. "Slut" was an easy insult for Mark to call me; he was echoing what he had heard all our peers saying about me.

3. I guess that was all it took to sound cool.

been hurt" act so everybody will be sympathetic toward your dumbass decisions.

Going out with Zach again was just about the STUPIDEST thing you could ever do. I seriously thought that you were smarter than that, that's the only reason I ever went out with you... but now I know that you aren't.

—Nathan

P.S. You can e-mail me back if you want to bitch about how it wasn't your fault that this all happened.

P.P.S. Daniel told me all this, and he agrees with me.[1]

I asked Melanie what she thought about the e-mail and she said Nathan was a dumbass. My sister said that he is probably just jealous.[2] I was talking to James on the phone today, and I told him about it.

He laughed and said, "What a loser. He's obviously jealous because he wants to be going out with you." I'd like to think Nathan is jealous. But the thing is, Nathan is really wise. It's like he knows and understands everything about me—he is the only guy I cannot manipulate easily. It's like he can see right through me, to my insecurities. It makes me feel so stupid that he hates me.[3]

JUNE 4, 1999

I haven't kissed Zach yet since we've been going back out, and I want to kiss him on the field trip on Thursday. We're going on this field trip as a class, and the trip itself shouldn't be that fun, but the bus ride there and back—three hours each way—should be lots of fun. Zach is on my bus! And we stay with our bus groups the whole day! I really can't wait.

But there is something that makes me upset.

1. The act of printing out this e-mail and pasting it into my diary seems a little self-punishing on my part. Some of what Nathan had written definitely reflected my own view of myself.

2. I rarely confided in my older sister, but when I did, she usually gave me sound advice. We still didn't care too much about each other's life, but we were becoming closer.

3. This e-mail was pretty mean, but Nathan did have a point. This was as close as anyone I cared about ever came to shaking me by the shoulders and telling me to get a grip. With that said, it was about time for me to get over my perception of him as an abundant fount of wisdom. He was clearly trying to hurt me.

I wrote on my Trapper Keeper "Zach + Emily 4 ever."[1] In Social Studies, right before class began, when not everyone was there yet, I was talking to Hunter. Hunter and I aren't really friends, but he is very good friends with Zach and is popular. He was standing by my desk and he saw what I had written on my Trapper Keeper.

He smiled, picked up a pen, and wrote beneath it, "Or until Zach gets some." I asked him if that was the only reason Zach was going out with me. He shrugged and said, "I dunno."

"Well," I said, "I just won't give him any! And if he doesn't like it, he can dump me." Maybe Hunter told him that. I'm pissed that now my Trapper Keeper says, "Zach + Emily 4 ever—or until Zach gets some."

Tonight, I was over Stacy's house, and we called James's house. James was there with Jacob and Daniel. Stacy was on the phone with them and she was overly flirting. Then she said, "She's sitting right next to me. Why? Oh, okay." She handed me the phone.

I took it and said, "Hello?"

"Hi," Daniel said. "Do you know you have a perfect body?"

I said, "Thank you for pointing that out to me."

He said, "So. How does it feel to have such big boobs?"

"Daniel..."

"Can I touch them?"

"No."

He sounded worried. "Don't tell Zach I asked that, okay?"

"I won't."

Then he said, "Emily?"

"Yes, Daniel?"

"May I put my tongue on your stomach?" That seemed like a weird thing to ask.[1]

"What? Why would you want to do that?"

"I don't know. But may I?"[2]

"No." How bizarre.

I am getting the bad feeling that I am just a phase. I was on the phone with Zach and he was like, "All the guys want you so bad." I noted that he used the word "want." I also remembered how some eighth-grade girls had sudden popularity with guys and then, not too long after, an even more sudden popularity crash.[3]

JUNE 17, 1999

I haven't written in so long! The bus ride to the field trip was awesome—Zach and I made out! He is still a great kisser. Someone took a picture of it.[4] School ends on the 23rd. Zach is leaving to go to Virginia to visit his cousins the next day! He is not coming back until July 2nd, and then on July 3rd he is going away to camp. Next year, he is going to Catholic school. I am going to miss him so much!

But I am not worried about us breaking up.[5] We are so in love! Yesterday on the phone, we were discussing what we are going to name our children. I told him I like the name Carson and he said okay, but Carson's middle name has to be Michael (that's Zach's middle name).[6] Then he came up with the name Angela Mia, because it means "My Angel" in Italian.[7]

1. At least he asked politely?

2. Daniel's attempt at suggesting a sexual interaction is telling of just how limited our understanding was. Somewhere—a music video, a book cover, a snippet of a TV show—he had likely seen a man putting his tongue on a woman's stomach in a sexual context and felt compelled to at least try to replicate it.

3. For girls, popularity among boys was a tricky, even impossible balance: perceived sexual availability could make a girl suddenly popular, but once that perception became a reality, the boys' attitude toward her would change. It wouldn't be that they necessarily lost interest, but rather that their interest became tainted by disdain.

4. Luckily, this was before smartphones, so the picture was taken with my disposable camera and it ended up safely pasted in my own diary.

5. The drama surrounding my romantic relationships was what mattered to me. Breakups brought sadness, of course, but more importantly they brought an opportunity for attention and visibility among my classmates.

6. Really? *Still* with the Carson Daly thing?

7. Neither of us spoke Italian.

Another person I've had bonding time with recently is Tyler. I think if Zach and I ever break up, I will go out with Tyler.[1] Tyler and I both have AOL Instant Messenger, and we told each other our passwords. Mine is "emily"[2] and his is "bonerface." I didn't ask why that is his password.[3] So we can go online as each other whenever we feel like it. That might come in handy if I ever want to find out what a guy thinks about me. I can pretend to be Tyler and ask the guy whether he likes "Emily."

1. But what about Carson? And little Angela Mia?

2. Password strength = unbelievably weak.

3. I didn't have to ask.

...le to pop, and everything inside s...
making a huge mess.

I stared in the mirror tonight...
...hing myself cry hysterically. I'...
...r been in this situation befor...
...e I have no friends. And ▓▓▓...
...ll people. How could she betray...
...that? She said, "It's because y...
▓▓▓▓▓▓ more than you lik...
...old her it wasn't true, but she...
...n't believe me. Can't she see...
...her? We were best friends. W...
...ened? I must deserve this. I...
...e done something so wrong - we...
...lots of things wrong. So I g...
...eserve this, and God is just pa...
...back.

...ast night I felt as if I was living...
...n - a nightmare, rather. I was se...
...idering suicide, but then I wa...
...Come on ▓▓▓▓, stop being such a...

SUMMER BEFORE EIGHTH GRADE

JUNE 25, 1999

Tonight, Lisa threw a going away party for Hannah, because she's moving to another town. This is a group of people that I don't hang around with too much anymore. I mean, they are cool and everything and we sometimes talk in the halls, but I usually wouldn't be invited to one of their parties anymore.

It was in Lisa's backyard and kind of in her basement, too. Erin and I were making up "porno dances" by ourselves in the basement to "Crazy" by Britney Spears. We were being really immature, but it was fun. We had this move we called "Hump Me" and we leaned over, putting one hand on the ground and the other on our butt, and then bounced up and down and backward. It was ridiculous. We also had this move we called "Cleavage," and it is when we wrap our arms around ourselves, pressing our boobs together, and say "Cleavage" in a sexy voice.[1]

Jenna was furious because her eighth-grade boyfriend showed up with his best friend, and they were both completely trashed. They just wandered down to the basement and passed out on the couch. I think she had every reason to be mad at him.[2]

I was sitting in a lawn chair next to Tyler, and some of the girls started saying I was being slutty because I am going out with Zach. But Zach is visiting his cousins for the summer! I am not going to sit in a corner and sulk because he is not there.

Emma pulled me aside, looking very serious. She said, "Emily, I was talking to Zach on the last day of school. He said he was going to miss you very much over the summer. I asked, 'You like her a lot, don't you?' and he said, 'I would take a bullet for her.'"[3] At

1. Coming up with creative names for dance moves was not one of our strengths.

2. In all likelihood, that was the first time he and his friend had ever tried alcohol. But I assumed this was regular behavior for them, since they were cool, dangerous eighth-graders.

3. Well *that* seems a bit extreme, Zach. But of course, it's possible Emma was making this whole conversation up.

this point, Emma looked at me very seriously and said, "I just thought you might want to think about that. Zach is willing to die for you, and here you are, flirting with every guy here." I didn't really listen to her.

Toward the end of the party, people started getting sad, because they realized that Hannah was really moving far away. Everyone started to cry—all the girls and Scott, anyway.[1] I wasn't really crying at all because, like I said, I'm not that great friends with Hannah anymore.

When he had to go home, Jacob hugged me last. He pulled away and looked at me and said, "All right, call me or something... I mean before school starts..." I nodded. He's going out with Kaylee, so I didn't want to really talk to him anymore and get called a slut again. He shook his head, "No, I mean, not just as a friend..."

His voice sounded really weird, so I asked, "Are you drunk?"[2]

He shook his head, no, and continued, "Well, cause like, Kaylee and I... I don't know... she's being a retard... I don't know... I'll see ya." Then he turned and walked into the front yard.

Erin came up beside me and whispered, "Did he just ask you out?"

I answered honestly, "I don't know. It sounded like it, didn't it?" She nodded and looked excited. I was very confused.

When I got home, the first thing I did was go upstairs and wash off my leg where Louis had thrown cake at me. As I was going downstairs, the phone rang. I answered it and it was Tyler, with Jacob on three-way. Jacob said, "Emily... I really need some

1. Poor Scott.

2. Nobody at that party (besides Jenna's boyfriend and his passed-out friend) would have been drunk. We didn't usually have access to alcohol, and even if we had, I'm sure most of us would have felt uncomfortable actually drinking around each other. Rather, by asking Jacob whether he was drunk, I was demonstrating that I knew about that kind of thing and that I wasn't fazed by the idea.

help on the situation with Kaylee." He explained that he was trying to hug her tonight and she pulled away and wouldn't let him get close to her. "I don't know what to do," he said. "I think I want to be single again. I just don't know how to deal with her."

I didn't know what to say. If I gave him good advice, then their relationship would be good again, and I know it sounds horrible, but I'm not sure I want that. I kind of like Jacob in the back of my mind, still. It flattered me that he thought of me to call for advice.

He made up a hypothetical scenario: "Okay, so what if we were going out. And I went to kiss you— would you be a loser like Kaylee was, or would you kiss me back?"[1]

"I would kiss you," I answered truthfully. I think Jacob wants to dump Kaylee and go out with me. I never really stopped liking him after that whole relationship we had going that wasn't really a relationship at all, but you know what I mean, when we liked each other. He is just so perfect. And I know that Zach and I are soul mates and that we have already planned our wedding and what we are going to name our kids, but... I really, really hate to admit this, but... I don't know. I don't think I like him that much anymore.

Jacob is so perfect, and I mean, if Zach and I were really soul mates, I wouldn't be attracted to anyone else, would I?[2] I mean, I like how things are right now with my guy friends: I like them as a little more than a friend, and they like me as a little more than a friend. That way, we flirt a lot, but there are no relationship crises or anything retarded like that. I

1. Wow, that sounds so *hypothetical*. No wonder I had been so attracted to Jacob for so long, what with our shared commitment to setting up elaborate, playacting scenarios.

2. Another reason the concept of having a soul mate is ridiculous. My outlook was naïve, but the romantic novels I read inspired and constantly reinforced it.

really don't know where to go from here. I like Zach a lot. I know how upset I would be if he hooked up with someone else over the summer, and judging from what Emma said about how he would die for me, I'm guessing he feels the same way.

But I have this problem: I really like guys who seem out of my reach—like way too popular or something. But once they come within my reach and start liking me back, like Zach has again, I lose interest in them because they seem boring. That has kind of happened with Zach.[1]

JUNE 30, 1999

Today at 9:30, Jacob and Tyler called using Jacob's three-way. We talked until 11:15—that is an hour and forty-five minutes! Tyler is funny, but I think he is very insecure with himself. He always makes jokes when I ask him serious questions that he'd rather avoid. Jacob, however, is very deep. He is the type of person I can discuss anything with, but also joke with. Tonight we were discussing lots of things, including the saying "What goes around comes around," each of us explaining why it was or wasn't always true. We also talked about bisexuality, and how Erin is a slut, and talking about people behind their backs. We didn't do that, we just talked about why other people do it.[2]

We also talked about how if you go out with someone you're friends with, when you break up, you'll hate each other. But that only happens in certain cases, and I think Jacob understands that. He is the coolest person in the world. He is easygoing and never makes you feel awkward. He also agrees with

1. Unfortunately, the same thing would continue to happen for the next decade or so. It's resulted in a lot of off-and-on relationships with rather aloof men. In the case of Zach, I was probably more concerned that a stable relationship resulted in lost opportunities for drama.

2. Except for the whole "Erin is a slut" part. I wish I had been self-aware enough to recognize that I was judging her by the same criteria that I suffered under myself.

me on most things.

Oh yeah, I got a letter from Zach today. I miss him, but I'm kind of mad at him. That is because I was on the phone with him the night before he left, and he said this to me: "You know, the day after I come home, I am going to camp. There will be all boys there. I'll give you my camp address, so you can write to me."

"Okay," I said.

He said, "Also, send me pictures."

"Okay."

"But you'll have to use a Polaroid camera—you don't want your parents seeing them when they get developed."

"Zach!" I said, "I am NOT sending you naked pictures of myself!" I was appalled that he thought I would even consider doing that![1]

"But Emily! It is an all-boys camp, and I will miss you so much."[2]

"Oh, I get it," I said. "All you will miss is my body." I was so mad I could hardly speak. The letter I got from him today did not apologize for his rude behavior. He wrote it when he was on the plane, which was six days ago, and I just got it today. I think I am very angry with Zach. But maybe I am just trying to find a reason not to like him anymore. I would probably forgive him a lot more quickly if Jacob weren't in the picture.

JULY 2, 1999

I got another letter from Zach today. I got two yesterday and one the day before, so that's four letters total. I don't know how I feel about him. I think

1. Thank goodness this was before the time of smartphones. Taking a naked picture, getting it developed, and sending it in the mail to someone seems a lot more drastic than quickly snapping a picture and pressing "send." Nowadays, Zach's request for nude pictures would be commonplace, and I doubt I would have the same reaction.

2. I wonder how many times that line has worked.

I love him but I don't know. He is not perfect, like Jacob, but he is mine. He may be horny, but I won't be able to stay mad at him for long. His letters imply that he cares about me very much. I do care about him, too. In fact, I desperately want him to be here with me. He is coming home late tonight. I called at 10 a.m., and his mom said he wouldn't be home until very late, and that he is leaving very early tomorrow morning to go to camp, but that she would tell him I called. I ache for him right now, literally. I want him so bad it is making me sick. I don't really want to make out with him or anything, I just want him to hold me and not to let go, ever. I feel so safe in his arms. I know that is ridiculously corny, but it's true!

But then there's Tyler. Here is an e-mail he wrote me yesterday:

> hey emily its been one whole day since i saw u and im already missing u so i just e-mailed u to say i love u also i want u to let me squeeze ur boobs over the summer so this will hopefully persuade u ok so write back or call me or sumpin i luv u

And today he wrote me this one:

> hey emily
>
> if u called me between 3-7 i was at jacob's house
>
> i really wanna do sumthing with u seriously
>
> and i'll be really disappointed if u write back saying "tyler you can't squeeze my boobs." i will probably start crying so i advise you not to say it
>
> write back soon
>
> did u dump zach yet?????
>
> im missing you![1]

1. Now *there's* a tactic I haven't encountered in many, many years: "Let me squeeze your boobs or I will cry." Manipulation comes in many forms, I guess.

JULY 16, 1999

Today after camp, Stacy and Melanie came over. I had gotten a letter from Zach, which I read half-heartedly and then tossed in the box where I save all the letters I receive.[1] We walked to Dunkin' Donuts to get fruit Coolattas and on the way back, we passed by Jacob's house.[2] He and Tyler were outside on their bikes. We stopped to talk and they came with us back to my house. We hung around in my driveway for about a half hour. Stacy told me she had been talking to James, and he had told her that Scott likes me. I definitely don't like Scott as a boyfriend.

Anyway, Melanie's dad came to pick her up and then Stacy, Tyler, Jacob, and I went downstairs to my basement, which is full of interesting things to do. It has a huge chest full of dress-up clothes, a piano, tiny bicycles, weird board games, a Nordic-Track, and lots of other random things.[3] We weren't really having deep discussions or anything, we were just fooling around. We went upstairs and made a video, lasting about two minutes, mostly consisting of Tyler trying to get the rest of us to look at the camera. The guys didn't leave until 9 p.m.![4]

I decided to definitely break up with Zach. There is no question about it. The next time he calls I have to do it. And I have to do it myself, not get someone else to do it for me, and I have to do it nicely, so he won't end up hating me and telling everyone I'm a slut again.[5] I'm not going to go out with anyone else now, not until high school.[6]

1. Ouch.

2. I loved fruit Coolattas. If it had been up to me, I would have been drinking them constantly. They're just blended ice and some kind of fruit flavoring, and to my seventh-grade self, there was nothing more refreshing.

3. At the time, my family's basement was unfinished and my parents used it for storage. It had a cement floor and pink insulation padding the walls, and the only people who ever went down there were my sister and me when we wanted privacy from our parents.

4. This was *really* late for friends to be over at my house. I guess since it was summer and it stayed light out later, my mom and dad just lost track of time.

5. It had to be carefully planned and executed, like defusing a bomb.

6. This declaration that I was deciding not to go out with anyone else until high school points to the things that likely went on that afternoon in my parents' basement, but that I had carefully left out of my written account. My memories of those hours spent "fooling around" in coed groups are saturated with anxiety. The pressure to allow the boys to tease me, touch me, and otherwise remind me of my status as simply a "slut" was often reinforced by the girls in the group, even those I considered my best friends. I'm not sure why I didn't represent this more often or more clearly in my diary entries; perhaps I wanted to pretend things were different.

JULY 26, 1999

I haven't written for a while, but I broke up with Zach. He called as soon as he got home. I was set on doing it right then, but I just couldn't bring myself to do it. I knew I would never be able to do it myself, so I told him I had to go have dinner, even though I had already eaten, and I called Stacy. I literally begged her to call him and break up with him for me. She finally agreed, and called him with me on three-way, but he didn't know I was listening. He took it well, because I think someone had already warned him. He told Stacy that he was going to call me later.

I told my mom that if Zach called later, I wasn't home, and then I told her the whole story. She said, "How could you have such little respect for Zach's feelings?! When he calls back, you are talking to him and telling him yourself why you're breaking up with him."[1] So when he called, I did talk to him. We talked for about a half hour, and I basically told him that our relationship was too serious for me right now, and that I liked a bunch of different people. He was like, crying, and I felt so bad, but I knew that I needed to break up with him. But it wasn't harsh or anything—it wasn't like we are going to be enemies again.

AUGUST 7, 1999

I haven't written in such a long time! I'm sorry.[2] It's a Friday. Stacy and Melanie came over today, and we made another movie. I'm obsessed with making movies—it's so fun! We were dancing around in tube tops and short shorts when the doorbell rang.[3]

1. I'm so glad my mom forced me to be a decent person in this situation.

2. I forgive you.

3. Most of the movies I made with Stacy and Melanie involved dancing around in tube tops and short shorts to our favorite songs. We would put my dad's handheld camcorder on a flat surface to set up the shot; editing involved rewinding the tape to the perfect spot and rerecording over old footage.

It was Scott and James, and Scott had my yearbook, which he forgot to return to me after he accidentally picked it up with his own on the last day of school. We all went on a walk to Dunkin' Donuts, which is about a mile away. After we got some Coolattas, we hung out behind the pizza place.[1] There is a parking lot there and a stone wall that separates it from the cemetery behind it.[2]

We sat on the stone wall and talked for about an hour. Scott told me some interesting information. It turns out that Michelle had a party, but she has no impact on my life anymore. She is the type of person who no one really likes, but she invites popular people to her parties because maybe she sits next to them in Math and they asked to borrow a pencil once, and she thought it was a big deal, and the other person doesn't even care, but she thinks they are great friends, so she invites them to parties.

I wasn't invited, but Tyler, Scott, and Zach were.[3] The party was last Friday night, a week ago. I talked to Tyler on Sunday night and he said this: "Jacob, Louis, Steven, and I were at Jacob's house and we were hungry. Jacob had no food so I was like, 'Well, I was invited to Michelle's party—maybe there will be food there.' So we walked to her house, ate her Cheetos, and left."[4] So then Scott told me this while we were sitting on the stone wall: "Michelle has this hot friend, Casey, from London. Zach asked her out at the party and on Tuesday, they went to third base." Hmm… sounds like he's on the rebound. I feel stupid now though because he has someone and I don't.

1. We really loved our Coolattas!

2. That stone wall was a common meeting spot. It was private and tucked away, but not hard to find. James, Jacob, and their group of friends had been meeting there to play cops-and-robbers-type games for years. Once my girlfriends and I discovered it, we would go there with the purpose of seeking out the boys and then would act surprised when we found them—at which point we'd decide to stay and hang out for a while.

3. So *that* explains my disparaging description of Michelle's social standing: she had invited all the boys I liked to her party, but had left me out. This certainly wouldn't have been the only time something like that happened, or the only time I tried to convince myself it didn't hurt.

4. *I* wouldn't have gone to a party just for the Cheetos. I always found them kind of gross.

I probably could have someone, I guess. But having a boyfriend is way too much of a hassle. I guess I just don't want Zach to feel all cool about himself around me. I know I should be happy for him that he's moved on, but I am a selfish bitch who needs everyone to worship her.[1] I know how guys see me: they only care about my big boobs and that I am pretty. It probably helps that I'm friendly, too, because there are other girls who have big boobs, but no one likes to be around them. Like Steph, who is the fucking town doorknob, and Jenna, whose eighth-grade boyfriend just dumped her because she stupidly cheated on him with Chris Walker, who is a jerk and a retard. People used to respect Jenna, until she did that.[2]

AUGUST 12, 1999

Last night, James called at about 8 p.m.[3] I thought it would be sort of awkward, since I haven't been talking too much with him, but it turned out we still have everything in common. He is a great listener and very open-minded. He's one of the only guys I can talk to about anything. He is maybe my only friend who is not using me at all. All the other guys I hang out with seem to have the idea that if they're nice to me, I'll put out.

Things with Tyler are definitely weird right now. We both changed our passwords, so we couldn't go online as each other anymore.[4] But a few days ago, we told each other the new ones.[5] It seems that his password for IM is the same as for e-mail. Meaning, I can check his e-mail whenever I want. He is aware of this, so he made me tell him my

1. Yeesh. That's a pretty harsh judgment of myself.

2. I was echoing a joke I'd overheard in a televised stand-up routine, in which a woman was referred to as "the town doorknob" because "everyone gets a turn." I'm disturbed that "slut" shaming came so easily to me, especially given my own experience with Chris Walker. I hope I never called Steph "the town doorknob" anywhere but here in my diary.

3. I spent a lot of time on the phone, even with people I hardly knew. AOL Instant Messenger was our other mode of remote communication, since we didn't have text messaging or social media.

4. Oh, phew.

5. Noo! Why?!

e-mail password, just to be fair, even though we both agreed not to check the other's e-mail. Well, being nosy, I went ahead and looked at his old e-mails. There are a lot from a girl he met at Louis's summer house.

Her e-mails say things like, "I'm so glad we're going out," and "Why have we only gone to 1st base?" and a lot of "I love you sooo much!" Hmm. So he is going out with this girl. That would explain why he's been acting so distant lately and not reminding me how much he wants to hook up with me.

Now about Stacy. I love her to death. She's away at camp, and the letters she's sending me imply that she's having a hell of a time: "All the guys here love me! I have a boyfriend and we're always making out!" But instead of being happy for my best friend, I am annoyed. Not jealous, because I know she is probably exaggerating. Plus, I'm not having a bad summer, myself. But I'm annoyed because she's having fun without me. I guess finding out that she doesn't need me makes me insecure.[1]

I'm very worried about Jenna. Ever since her eighth-grade boyfriend dumped her for cheating on him, she hasn't been her usual, crazy self. She's been acting very depressed; it is obvious she hates herself. So she has been hanging out and hooking up with the trashiest group of guys in the ninth grade. These guys always hang out with younger girls (Jenna) with low self-esteem (Jenna) who aren't thinking straight (Jenna). I try to tell her they are trouble, but she doesn't listen.[2]

1. I wanted Stacy to be a supporting character in my life, not the protagonist in her own life. And I have to admit, I'm proud of myself for having such a self-aware moment! I was using my diary as a therapist, talking through my feelings until I reached a conclusion I was comfortable with.

2. There was cause to be legitimately worried about Jenna's mental health. I never spoke to her mother or the guidance counselors at our school about my concerns, so I'm not sure if an adult ever reached out to her about it. She wasn't even confiding much in me, not that that would have provided enough support for her. I really did worry a lot about Jenna, but I suspect I was also using her as a proxy for fears I harbored about myself. I, too, spent time hanging out with those older guys. Sometimes it felt like the depression Jenna displayed publicly was a reflection of what I felt but kept secret.

AUGUST 13, 1999

Today is Friday the 13th! Oooh! Melanie came over and Scott called. He had Jacob, James, and Steven over and asked if I wanted to do something. I said sure, that we would meet them in town.[1] Now, our downtown is nothing big, but it is spread out over about a mile and a half. I figured we could probably find the guys behind the pizza place. When they weren't there, we decided to cut through the cemetery and come out beside the church.[2]

Well, we walked a while into the cemetery and then we saw four guys sitting on the side of the walkway. I thought it was probably Chris Walker and his friends. I tensed up immediately—I didn't want to deal with them and what they might say or do, but we couldn't very well turn around after they had already seen us and probably recognized us. I started feeling like I couldn't breathe well.

Luckily, Jacob called my name from back the way we came, so we had an excuse to turn around and head that way, away from Chris. We sat and talked for about twenty minutes and decided we were bored. So the boys led Melanie and me up behind the school, into the woods. I had never been in there and had certainly never known that they were a shortcut to Starbucks, which they are.[3]

We sat down in the woods and the guys started reminiscing about fights that had taken place there. It seemed like the type of place where you could just sit, smoke a cigarette, and think.[4] We sat there for a while, talking, and then walked to Starbucks. Starbucks has air-conditioning, which was awesome after sitting outside in the 85-degree weather.

1. During the summer, I had much more freedom than during the school year. There was no homework to be done and since the weather was nice, my parents let me go on walks as long as I told them where I was going. Our town was a quiet, safe place, and they probably figured I would get into more trouble if I were bored indoors.

2. Sounds like a good idea on Friday the 13th.

3. Isn't everything a shortcut to Starbucks?

4. For the record, I have never been a smoker. I just had this romantic, poetic idea about what it would mean to be the type of person who needed to smoke a cigarette in order to think clearly.

James, Scott, and Steven were supposed to be at football practice, but they decided it was stupid and they didn't want to go. It was optional, anyway. Jacob had to drop his bike off at his house, so we decided to just go there to hang out. On the way, James and I lagged behind the others, talking.

I said, "I can't wait for the first day of school! I have this whole outfit picked out and I'm going to look so cute."

He smiled and said, "How does it feel to know that... when you walk in a room, all heads turn to look at you?"

I was so flattered by that comment, and I had to fish for more. "I don't think that's true..."

"Oh, come on," he said. "You could just strut in, being like, 'I own the world.'"

"Do you think I think that?"

"No. But you could, and it would be justified. Whenever you enter a room, everyone stares at you. You didn't notice that?"

I said, "Oh. I thought there was something wrong with me. Because people whisper about me."

He sighed. "They're whispering about how hot you are. And some of them are probably calling you a slut."[1]

In my letter to Stacy, I lied and said I had hooked up with James. He knows I did that, so if she asks, he'll lie, too. I don't know why I did that. He said, "Well, I don't want to have to lie... so why don't we really hook up?"

I laughed and said, "James, you're making me uncomfortable." So he stopped talking about it. But I don't know. I don't really like him as anything more than a friend.[2]

1. Awesome...? Without knowing it, James was exhibiting proto-pickup-artist behavior; nowadays, subtly insulting a woman to undermine her self-confidence with the goal of eventually seducing her is called "negging" and it is absolutely revolting.

2. Keep in mind that, just the day before, I had written: "[James] is maybe my only friend who is not using me at all. All the other guys I hang out with seem to have the idea that if they're nice to me, I'll put out." Now here he was, asking me to hook up with him. This is an example of a time I *know* I wasn't being completely honest with my diary, because this was more than a small disappointment. It was evidence that *every* boy in my life—even James, whom I had trusted to care for me as a friend—saw me as nothing more than a "slut." This was devastating. But admitting that to my diary would mean admitting that to myself, and I must have known deep down that I wouldn't be able to cope with that.

AUGUST 14, 1999

Stacy got home from camp today, and she is sleeping over. Right now, she is writing a letter to a friend from camp, crying hard because she misses them. I can understand that she's depressed, but I do think she's overdoing it a bit.

I called James tonight and found out that he's going out with Amanda Collins. I don't have a problem with it, but honestly... she's a big skank-face.[1] He probably doesn't like her, but they've already gone to second base. So... whatever.[2]

I was telling him how I wanted to hook up with Jacob, and he said, "I have no doubt in my mind that Jacob will hook up with you. I guarantee it." That made me feel so good. But then he said, "I'm just not sure YOU would ever hook up with HIM."

"What are you talking about?" I asked.

He said, "I don't know... I think you're a tease."

"What the hell is a tease?"

He sighed. "It's a girl who is really hot and she lets on like she'll hook up with guys, but then she doesn't." James got a call on the other line and it was Amanda Collins, so he had to go. But he said, "Check your e-mail." This is what I found. It was from Jacob:

Hey,

Emily I'm writing to you after a conversation me, Scott, and James just had. We think you're real cool and hot... But I guess we as a group are telling you that you are a tease... A tease as in you're really, really hot and umm... Well, you can take it from there... I know none of us have ever really told you to your face that you're hot but you are.

1. Ooh, "skank-face"! I had heard my mom use "skanky" interchangeably with "raunchy" to describe things she believed were sexually inappropriate. She proclaimed, for instance, that certain movies were "rated R for 'raunch'!" and that therefore, I would not be allowed to see them. "Skanky" could imply lewdness or even straight-up grime; my mom would use it to describe the smell of my Adidas Sambas, which I wore without socks almost every day. And of course adding "-face" to the end of just about any noun made it hilarious to me. By this time, my classmates and I had graduated from "butt-face," "loser-face," and "poop-face" to "skank-face" or, in the case of Tyler's AOL password, "bonerface."

2. "Whatever" translation: I care so, so, so much but I TOTALLY DON'T CARE, OKAY?

And you kind of have to accept that… It's not your fault or anything. We still all like you as a friend and have nothing against you but I don't know… We just want you to be aware of it, I guess. —Jacob, Scott, and James

I don't even know what to think now. Hmm. Maybe I am a tease. But I know I would hook up with Jacob. Also, I guess I just assumed those guys wanted to hang out with me anyway, whether or not we hooked up. I didn't think I was leading them on, I just thought we were friends.[1]

AUGUST 25, 1999

Today I got my schedule for my classes in the mail. Everyone called to see which classes we have together. After that, I was in a really depressed mood. It was pretty random, actually.

I guess I just realized that I am an extremely fake person. I find out what people want me to be, and then I be that for them. I don't even know who I really am. I was so upset that I started crying really hard.

Then I went into the bathroom and slit my left wrist with the razor I use to shave my legs.[2] It hurt a ton, and so I finally stopped. It wasn't bleeding too badly, so I put a couple of Band-Aids over it and went back to my room where I contemplated my fake life.

After dinner, I went online and confided in Tyler about it. I don't know why I told him— I probably just wanted the attention. That's the only reason I do anything, anyway. Here is a bit of the conversation we had:[3]

1. It strikes me how apologetic the e-mail was. I, like most girls at this age who start to recognize their sexuality, was in a lose-lose situation. When I acted on my sexual curiosity, I was labeled a "slut." When I held back for fear of the "slut" label, I was accused of being a "tease." Given the way my body happened to look, those were my only two options. It also strikes me how deeply upsetting the realization must have been that, contrary to what I had believed, even my so-called friends were only spending time with me in the hopes that I might hook up with them.

2. I wish I had written about *why* I decided to cut myself This type of self-harm is pretty common among girls, and I'm a bit disappointed that I didn't sort through all the emotions behind it here in my diary. Maybe the absence of any explanation is revelatory, though: it's likely I didn't exactly understand why I was doing it at the time. It seems more like an impulsive, physical reaction to the sadness I was feeling in that moment than something I planned out.

3. In my diary, the conversation is printed out and pasted here. I did that with most of the conversations I had online with the boys I had crushes on. Sometimes I even highlighted them for later reference.

Tyler: why did you do it?

Me: because I am very fake

Tyler: holy shit emily. you aren't.

Me: You wouldn't know, because I'm fake around you.

Tyler: how do you mean?

Me: I find out what people want me to be, and then I act that way for them.

Tyler: Like, how do I want you to be then?

Me: You want me to be sexy. And you want to be smarter than me.[1]

Tyler: first of all, I don't WANT to be smarter than you... I AM smarter than you :)

Me: lol

Tyler: yeah I knew I could get you to laugh. so what stopped you?

Me: the blood was kind of disgusting

Tyler: holy shit. never do that again. because i was thinking how friggin sad i would be if you weren't like alive

Me: well I don't want to DIE.

Tyler: well you're like my best girl friend. I would be extremely sad.[2]

AUGUST 26, 1999

Today was a good day. At about 1:30, Scott called. He was at Hollywood Video with Jacob, and could they come over? I said sure. I was supposed to go over to Melanie's house at 3 p.m., so they could stay at my house until then. We went on a walk around my neighborhood, eating freeze pops.[3] I mentioned that I am going to go on a liquid diet and eat only freeze pops.

1. The truth in these two sentences ran deeper than I realized at the time. They could be applied to *many* of my future interactions with men and, I imagine, those of almost every other woman.

2. Poor Tyler. It seems like he really wanted to help, but he lacked the vocabulary or the emotional means to empathize in the way I needed him to. It's possible I found some comfort in his response, though. At least he seemed to care.

3. I don't care who you are—you hate the green ones, right?

Jacob said, "Why? You are so thin."

I laughed. "Are you kidding?!"

"No," he said seriously. "You don't have any gut." He lifted his shirt, revealing where his gut would be, if he had one. "See?" He said, "I have a gut. Now lift up your shirt." Scott laughed. Jacob glared at him. "I didn't mean all the way, you loser." I lifted my shirt to show my stomach. Jacob was satisfied. "See?" He said, poking my stomach. "You're perfect."

But I hardly ever feel perfect.

At 3 p.m., my mom gave me a ride to Melanie's house, and we walked over to Shauna's to jump on her trampoline. We jumped for a while and then got tired and lay down.

After we went back to her house, I showed Melanie my wrist and told her what happened. She looked at me seriously and said, "Emily, what's wrong with you? Don't ever do that again." I don't know what's wrong with me. It doesn't make any sense.

Tonight, I sliced my left wrist again, after everyone was asleep. I cut it in the same places where scabs were starting to form, so they opened up again. I don't know why I did it. I don't think I want to die.[1]

AUGUST 30, 1999

Today, Jenna, Gina, Scott, Daniel, and I were all sitting beside the pond. Jenna was explaining how guys in our grade don't know how to kiss. Scott said, "Emily could teach me how."

I said, "Okay, sure." He just stood there, looking uncomfortable. He hadn't expected me to agree.

Daniel rolled his eyes. "Scott, you retard, it's not

1. I still can't put into words why I did it. I think it was a mixture of wanting to believe my life was a struggle and wanting other people to see me as a kind of tortured soul. But it also likely had to do with all the feelings I wasn't writing about in my diary, because writing them down would have made them somehow more solid and *true*. I've heard people in my adult life describe cutting as "a cry for attention," and although I don't necessarily disagree with that characterization, I don't believe that makes cutting any less tragic. If we just dismiss girls whose self-harming actions seem driven by a need for attention, at what point do we start taking them seriously?

that hard. Go like this." And all of a sudden, Daniel was sitting on top of me facing me, so he was straddling me and holding onto my shoulders. He leaned in as if to kiss me, but I freaked out and pushed him away.

Scott insisted, "Come on, Emily, teach me how to kiss!" Daniel wandered over to the water, obviously removing himself from the situation.

I sighed and looked up at Scott. "Okay." He leaned over, and it was actually a pretty good kiss. It was different. My upper lip was touching his upper lip, and my bottom lip was touching his bottom lip, so our mouths weren't really fit together. He reached up and put his hand on my boob, outside my shirt, and I shoved him off me.

Afterward I couldn't believe I had kissed Scott. I decided not to tell anyone. When Scott and Daniel had to go, we all gave them hugs. Daniel again leaned in to kiss me, but I turned my face and pushed him away.[1]

I am honestly such a tease. I don't want to be like that, though. I have no clue why I am. There must be something WRONG with me.[2]

1. Daniel really wouldn't take getting pushed away for an answer.

2. I hate that I wrote this. There was nothing wrong with me, nor was there anything wrong with the way my male friends felt about me. There *was* something wrong with the way they refused to take getting pushed away again and again as the equivalent of a forceful "no." As soon as I pushed Daniel away the first time, they should have shut the whole thing down and changed the subject. But we hadn't been taught how to communicate about our sexuality, and the result was this type of awkward, nonconsensual interaction.

...tes every day, and talk on...

ry night. We talk about we...

...we were afraid of as kids, ...

...lentines. Two nights ago, we ...

...crazy relatives. He said, "Onc...

...her came to stay with us, and ...

...fume. For the whole summer, y...

...perfume, and I smelled of perf...

...knew I loved him. He could ha...

...e," but instead he said, "smelled o...

...so perfect to me. Last night, for ...

...d to call him. I had a weird ...

...want to talk to me. I was ...

...that he would call me, becaus...

...to him. And then he did. I ...

...nent, and my sister called to ...

...hat I had a phone call. I re...

...was him, but I knew it woul...

...want to get my hopes up. Bu...

...he top of the stairs, my sist...

...d "It's him," as she handed ...

...ad! I am so ...

EIGHTH GRADE

SEPTEMBER 6, 1999

School is all right, I guess. Today is Labor Day so we got it off, even though we just got back. The major thing in my life right now is this: Scott told everyone that I let him feel my boobs. This is technically true, but… it was outside the shirt and I pushed him away as soon as he did it. So I decided to tell everyone that it was definitely not true.[1]

I was talking to Jacob online a few nights ago and he asked me about it. I denied it, but I could tell that he didn't believe me. About an hour later, I checked Tyler's e-mail, the messages he'd already read.[2] There was a message entitled "Convo with Emily" from Jacob. It was a copy of the conversation I had just had with him, and at the bottom, Jacob had written: "Don't believe her. She's lying. Emily's cool, but… she is a SLUT… I don't care how big her boobs are, don't believe her lol. —Jacob"[3]

This made me want to cry, but seeing as I wasn't supposed to be checking Tyler's e-mail, I couldn't very well confront either of them about it. James called right then and, not thinking clearly, I told him what I had just read in Tyler's e-mail. That was a big mistake. Here is a section of the conversation I had immediately afterward with Jacob online:

Jacob: emily…

Me: what?

Jacob: someone told me you were mad at me over an e-mail

Me: the one about how I am a tease?

Jacob: no a different one. an e-mail that wasn't to you

1. Well, it's not even *technically* true that I "let" him do anything. I hadn't consented to this kind of touching, even though Scott, as well as the other boys, seemed to assume that my reputation as a "slut" was the equivalent of ongoing consent.

2. Gah! Snooping!

3. Everyone knows it's much easier to believe someone who has big boobs.

Me: stop it. just tell me what you are talking about

Jacob: I'm talking about the e-mail that I wrote to Tyler that you told James about

Me: that never happened

Jacob: I know it happened

Me: Talk to you later, okay? I have to go

1. Er... I don't know if "technique" is the right word. The behavior I thought was so clever and manipulative is so transparent now.

I tried to use an evasive technique.[1] But the problem is, it didn't work on Jacob. I know he can see right through me.

SEPTEMBER 26, 1999

Wow, I haven't written in twenty days! Well, I've been busy. Here's what's happened so far, in the first month of school: Stacy got it into her head that since she was a slut at camp, she should be a slut at home, too.[2] But she is just about as far from a slut as you can get. She just has a prudish air about her. I guess if you try really hard though, no reputation is unachievable, especially a slutty one. She started wearing halter tops to school without a bra and spreading the word that she would hook up with any and every guy who wanted to.

2. This was likely based on conversations in which Stacy had confided in me, since she considered me a good friend. I doubt she would have used the word "slut" to describe herself, but it's clear she had discovered at camp that she liked getting sexual attention and that she wanted that attention to continue. I'm not sure when exactly it happened, but I had discovered something similar, and it was already complicating my understanding of my own reputation. By calling Stacy a "slut," I was dismissing her as inferior rather than admitting that I was uncomfortable about the competition for sexual attention.

3. *Literally* threw herself? Ow!

Having sense, I have realized that if I do hook up with all the guys who want to, they will get sick of me within a week or so and then I will be forgotten, a past phase. Stacy, however, came to no such realization. She literally threw herself at Jacob.[3] She told all his friends that she wanted to hook up with him, so they obviously told him.

About a week ago, I was talking with Jacob about it. I asked him, "Do you like Stacy?"

He shook his head. "Not as anything more than a friend."

"Yet you say you would hook up with her..." I wasn't understanding.

He said, "Well, yeah. Emily, I'm a thirteen-year-old boy, with a girl throwing herself at me. What do you want me to do?"[1]

I, of course, told Stacy about this conversation, hoping it would convince her not to hook up with him. But she giggled, "So, he'll hook up with me?"

Now, I don't know about anyone else, but if I found out the guy I liked was only using me to get some, I would be quite pissed off. And the last thing I would do would be to hook up with him! But Stacy actually liked it. It was so frustrating! She just wouldn't listen to me. She thinks being a slut is glamorous. She said she wants a new Stacy, that she's sick of being a nobody. She even said to me, "I'd rather be known as a slut than not known at all."[2]

Well. On Tuesday—today is Sunday, so five days ago—Stacy, James, Jacob, Tyler, Daniel, and I went to the cemetery after school. You have to climb a steep slope to get there, and then there's a field between the Dunkin' Donuts parking lot and the cemetery. There is also a pile of empty Coolatta containers.[3] Daniel picked up a branch that looked like antlers and yelled, "I am a horny reindeer! Emily, I'm going to rape you with my antlers!" and he proceeded to chase me around the cemetery until he got tired of holding up the branch over his head.[4]

Stacy and some of the boys left to get Coolattas so I grilled Jacob. He told me that he didn't want to hook up with Stacy for these reasons: 1) He didn't

1. The old "I'm male, so I have no self-control" defense! It's even more sinister when grown men use it, and it's unacceptable at any age.

2. Stacy's situation adds another layer to the lose-lose dilemma of either being a "slut" if you do and a "tease" if you don't. The other option, as we understood it at the time, was to be a "nobody," and that idea was unbearable.

3. All those Coolattas!

4. We never talked about consent in a formal setting at our school, so rape mostly came up in "joking" interactions like this one.

want to hurt her reputation, 2) he didn't want her to think that he liked her, and 3) he didn't want everyone else to think that he liked her. Okay, so that was okay. But when Stacy got back, James said, "Jacob, I dare you to go into the woods with Stacy." And he looked at Jacob and raised his eyebrows. Jacob glared at him, but Stacy was already on her feet. And he couldn't very well turn down a dare.[1]

So they left to go into the woods. Then Emma and Kaylee walked by. They stopped to chat and we told them where Stacy and Jacob were. They immediately set off to sabotage the hookup because they said Stacy was not popular enough to hook up with Jacob. The rest of us followed behind. When we found them, they were standing awkwardly, and Stacy later informed me that they only made out.

But that was enough to ruin their friendship. Jacob no longer talks to Stacy, and James always tells me how annoying he thinks she is. They don't mean to be cruel, but it's just natural—they got sick of her poser-slut act, and now it's just annoying. I told her it would happen.[2]

OCTOBER 14, 1999

I just had an hour-long phone conversation with James. He predicted that Tyler and I will go out sometime in the future. He said, "You like him."

"No, I don't," I said, not knowing whether or not that was true.

"Well, yes you do. You just don't know it yet. And soon, he's going to realize how he feels about you and tell you. And then you'll realize, too."

I don't find that too far-fetched. Tyler and I are

1. Heaven *forbid* he turn down a dare. So much of what we did was because we were dared, in a sense, by classmates pressuring us to kiss, to break up, to start a fight, or anything else we wouldn't have felt comfortable initiating on our own.

2. How disturbing that I removed all the blame from the boys, even using the word "natural" to describe what happened.

constantly teasing each other in a flirtatious way. I know I do like him, but I'm not sure how much. He's been writing me e-mails saying we never talk anymore, which we don't, really.

Yesterday, I was hanging out at the playground with Erin, Stacy, Shauna, Gina, Maggie, James, Jacob, Daniel, and Tyler. Erin and Stacy were all over Jacob, and Maggie was upset because she likes him, too. So does half the grade. It should be a religion or something, Jacobism: the worship of Jacob.[1] Anyway, Stacy was wearing a padded bra and everyone knew it because her boobs had gone from like, barely an A cup to a B overnight. So the guys were all making fun of her. Stacy is so stupid lately. She's all into talking about how all the guys want her—which they don't—and when they make fun of her, she thinks they're flirting. At first, I felt bad for her, but now it's just really funny.[2]

Zach got some people tickets to his Catholic school dance. Catherine told me that Zach hates me. Why, with him, does it always have to be either we're going out or we hate each other? Why can't we just be friends, which is what I want? He is so frustrating.

Anyway, hardly anyone in the grade is "going out" anymore. In fifth, sixth, and seventh grade, we only went out with people for the sake of going out with someone. It made us feel secure, like confident that someone liked us. But now we can feel secure without someone to cling to. I think that is a sign of maturity.[3]

OCTOBER 21, 1999

I've started slicing my left wrist again. It's not because I want to die. I definitely don't, anymore.[4]

1. Well, *Jacobitism* was already a thing and I guess it went okay, depending on whom you ask. I wouldn't learn about it until we got to the unit on the Stuarts of Great Britain in Honors Modern European History sophomore year of high school though.

2. I'm sure Stacy found it hilarious. I had started a rivalry with Stacy, but as far as I know, she hadn't noticed yet.

3. Maturity... yeah, that's probably it.

4. That's usually true for people who cut their wrists like this: it's not a suicide attempt, but rather a tactic of using physical pain to distract the mind from emotional pain. According to the UK's Mental Health Foundation, self-harm is also used as a way to "wake up" in situations of emotional numbness.

It just makes me feel better… I can't explain it. I'm not using a razor anymore. You know those nail clipper things that like, fold out? Well, I use the sharp thing that pushes back your cuticles. I just run it back and forth over my skin, pressing down hard, and it draws blood. I can't understand why this is calming to me, but it is.

About ten minutes ago, I got off the phone with Tyler. I had already told him about it, but talking about it out loud was hard for me. He said, "I don't want you to get hurt. You need help. Tell your parents, please."[1] Fat chance of that. But he seemed genuinely worried. He said, "Next time you think of hurting yourself, think of me instead." Then the subject switched to something else, and we talked for about an hour before my mom told me I had to go. "Hold on," he said before we got off the phone. "Next time you feel depressed, like you're gonna… do that crap, think of my laugh." Tyler has the gayest laugh. He usually changes it so it's normal, but sometimes if you catch him off guard with something really funny, he accidentally laughs in this high-pitched giggle.

"Okay, Tyler," I said, laughing.

"'Cause that will make you laugh, instead," he said. "Think of me and how I don't want you to do it anymore."

I said, "Thank you, Tyler," and I smiled, but he couldn't see it, obviously.

OCTOBER 30, 1999

I just got off the phone with James. We talked for three hours! And the weird thing is, we didn't even

1. Good for Tyler for encouraging me to reach out to my parents. It's not that I didn't confide in my parents about *anything*, but I remember feeling particularly embarrassed about cutting my wrists. I wanted my parents to think I had it together. I also knew they might take drastic measures, like admitting me for inpatient care at a mental hospital, and I didn't want it to become a *huge* thing that all our relatives and family friends gossiped about.

really talk about anything, just random thoughts. It's fun. Tonight was the first time he'd called me in over a week.

Anyway, there was a dance last night and it was so fun! You got free candy if you dressed up, so Erin, Maggie, Melanie, and I wore flannel pants and white tank tops and said we were "pajama princesses."[1]

I didn't dance with anyone on the first slow song, but Stacy was dancing with Tyler and I wanted to rip her head off. The guys were all attempting to break-dance and it was funny, because none of them can at all. Stacy and I started doing "the worm," which is when you go into a handstand and then lower your body to the ground, chest first. When your toes hit the floor, you use your arms to push your chest up again. Well... whatever, it looks cool.[2] Anyway, Mark came up to me when "Da Dip" by Freak Nasty came on. He stood behind me with his hands on my hips, and then pushed downward on my hips in kind of a rolling motion.[3]

On all the fast songs, I danced really hard. Soon, I was totally wiped out and went out into the hall to get some water. There were tables set up there, where people could sit and eat. As I was walking back into the gym, someone called, "Emily." I looked, and it was Tyler. I became immediately aware that my bangs were matted to my forehead with sweat and that my eyeliner was hopelessly smudged. Now that I was out of the dark cafeteria, these things would be noticeable. He said, "Come over and talk."

"No, I'm gonna go... dance," I said, looking at him like he was the one with bangs matted to his forehead and smudged eyeliner.

1. I'm just going to go out on a limb and say that's the least inspired costume idea ever.

2. "The worm" *does* look cool, and I still pull it out as a party trick.

3. We learned about new dance moves from MTV, mostly, or from people's older siblings who told us they got into dance clubs with fake IDs. Dancing was a way for us to perform overt sexuality without having to take responsibility for it; if someone had scolded me for rolling my hips when "Da Dip" came on, for instance, I could use the excuse that I was "just doing what they do in the music video!"

On the last song, Mark came up to me and I was disappointed because I didn't want to dance the last song with MARK. Plus, I saw Tyler wandering around and I'd rather dance with him. So I said to Mark, "Oh, slow dancing is no fun!" and gently pushed him away. But he rolled his eyes and held onto me. I looked around and saw Tyler, dancing with Emma. So whatever, I stayed dancing with Mark.

We were really close. I don't think I've ever danced that close with someone in my life. Our legs were between the other person's legs, and his face was buried in my neck. At first, it felt kind of good. Then I became aware that he was slowly tracing his fingers around the top of my butt, kind of squeezing every so often. I whispered, "Hey." He didn't respond and moved his fingers farther down, around my butt so they were almost between my legs. My thigh came up between his legs and I could feel his boner. I squeezed my eyes tightly shut, thinking about how to move away. But then the song ended, the lights came on, and the dance was over.[1]

NOVEMBER 15, 1999

I haven't written in a long time. I just haven't been in the mood. I'm not really in the mood now, either, but it's been like two weeks and I need to get caught up. First of all, Halloween. It was a TON of fun! All the girls met at Stacy's house and then went out to meet the boys. Actually, we didn't really have a plan to meet them, they just attacked us with eggs and shaving cream and then stayed with us.[2]

Matt and most of his friends were there, hang-

1. I wonder why I felt compelled to go along with what Mark wanted to do—why was it even necessary to think about "how to move away" rather than just *moving away*?

2. The boys often used quasi-violence as a way to initiate interactions with us, whether it was shooting spitballs, throwing snowballs, or attacking us with shaving cream on Halloween. I resent the old adage that boys pick on girls when they have a crush on them—it excuses and even reinforces aggressive behavior—but these boys were definitely exemplifying it.

ing out with guys I'm more comfortable with, like Jacob. Stacy is like, still in love with Jacob, and they made out again. But then Matt somehow became the mediator between the two of them, screwing everything up and making a whole big shenanigan that I don't know the details of.[1] All I know is what happened afterward, because Stacy was so upset.

Actually, I'm not sure what started it. What really set me off was that she called me a "manic-depressive bitch." And then she screamed so everyone heard, "Don't be mad at me! It's not my fault you fucking slit your wrists!" After she said that, I wasn't aware of any noise or movement from anyone. It was just SPACE. I felt like everyone was looking at me, like they weren't sure I was really Emily. I could feel tears in my eyes but I didn't want to cry, because silly girls always cry for attention and I didn't want people to think I was like that.

I managed to control myself and just said through my teeth, "I didn't want anyone to know that, Stacy." I knew if I stood there looking at her stupid face for one more millisecond I would strangle her, so I turned and walked away. Nobody mentioned or asked whether what Stacy said was true. Erin came over and gave me a long hug and told me she loved me, and I appreciated that.[2]

But then Zach was there in front of me. He looked at me like it was weird for him that I should be crying, and then he said, "This has got to stop. You and Stacy both have to just admit that you are partly wrong. And do it fast, because this is damn near ruining my Halloween."[3]

1. Sounds about right for Matt.

2. The problem with attracting attention is that it gets out of your control pretty quickly. I wanted my peers to be interested in my life, but I wanted to get to decide what they knew and what was private. Unfortunately, it's impossible to maintain that control. That's even truer today, when a sexy photo shared with a small group can be made public with the touch of a button.

3. Who *talks* like that? Who talks like that in *eighth grade*? I feel like Zach might have been watching a little too much *Dawson's Creek.*

I said, "Well, I don't want to ruin your Halloween, Zach." I was annoyed at him for assuming he knew what was going on, when he doesn't even go to our school anymore and doesn't know Stacy as a person. I don't think he even knows me anymore.

Stacy had a birthday party two days ago, on Saturday, and I couldn't go because I was grounded![1] That made me angry because even though I can't stand Stacy—she thinks we made up from our fight though—lots of people I like were there. But everyone who went said it was the most retarded party ever. All they did was sit on the couch and be bored. And Matt and Stacy hooked up. Matt thinks she has really nice legs or something. They went out for about two hours, but then he dumped her because he realized what a retard she is. And now she has Emma, Lisa, Catherine, and Steph all ready to kick her ass.

Unlike Stacy, I can predict the obvious future. She will obsess over Matt, he will decide to hate her, and then she will get her ass kicked. LOL. Oh, I'm being mean. I just really can't stand that girl.[2]

NOVEMBER 16, 1999

I think Tyler likes me again! Yesterday and today we were both online at the same time and we had conversations. And they weren't boring conversations, they were like how they used to be in the summer. He brought up inside jokes from a while ago subtly, like not on purpose—but it probably was on purpose.[3] He even asked me to hook up with him a few times. In the summer when he did that, it was like oh, haha. But now, if he's serious, I'm all for it.[4]

1. I don't remember what I was grounded for this time, but I spent a solid portion of my preteen years being grounded either from leaving the house or from using the phone, and sometimes from both. It was my parents' go-to punishment when I spoke disrespectfully, disobeyed them, or when they discovered I had lied to them about where I had been or what I had been doing. Grounding me must have given them some peace of mind, since they knew I couldn't get into trouble if I was up in my room sulking about being grounded.

2. My feelings toward Stacy soured so quickly once she started asserting herself sexually. I really wanted her to remain a supporting character in *my* life, and she was insisting upon becoming the protagonist in her own story.

3. Yeah, it definitely was on purpose.

4. Even though I trusted Tyler more than most boys, I was still paranoid that his whole friendship with me was an elaborate scheme to humiliate me.

Today is Monday. Next Wednesday, we get out of school early. Jenna is coming over that day. Maybe we'll walk into town with the guys. Jenna is not into hooking up with guys in our grade. She had sex with one of Aaron's friends from Catholic school and then didn't get her period for two months. I was so worried she was pregnant! But then she got it last night and she told me today. That would be awful if she were pregnant. She's only thirteen! She shouldn't even be having sex. She has the lousiest reputation right now.[1]

Once, about a week ago, I was at the playground after school. Tyler and Jacob were having a contest to see who could hold himself up on the monkey bars longer. Jacob kept losing and Tyler said, "Wow, Jacob, you suck! This is easier than Jenna!" Everyone laughed, but I felt bad. Jenna is easy, but I still feel bad. She needs to stop being a slut. Otherwise, next time she will get pregnant.[2]

DECEMBER 6, 1999

Today is Monday. On Friday, we had a dance.[3] It was fun, and I danced with Tyler three times. I didn't dance with Jacob—I didn't really feel the urge to. I guess I like him more as a friend. Anyway, everyone was saying that Tyler was going to ask me out.

The DJ announced that it was the last song, and I looked around for Tyler, but I couldn't see him. Then all of a sudden, Mark was right next to me, just sort of looking at me.[4] He had been watching me all night, but had not yet asked me to dance. So he just looked at me, and it was becoming kind

1. It's quite possible Jenna was making up this pregnancy scare. Teen pregnancies were very rare in our town. Jenna's mother was the only person I knew of who had accidentally gotten pregnant in high school, and that had been thirteen years earlier, obviously. There was one girl in my sister's class who would leave to have a baby her senior year before coming back to graduate. I remember my sister's friends making fun of her because she wrote, "being a mom" as one of her favorite memories in the yearbook.

2. No mention of birth control here, whether or not she was using it, which seems like an obvious miss on my part. But I guess we hadn't really learned about birth control yet, since our sex education was limited to what happens to your body during puberty.

3. I am amazed at how many dances I attended. Maybe it just seems that way because I felt the need to write about every single one of them in such detail.

4. Creepy.

of awkward, so I said, "What is it, Mark?"[1]

He said, "I want to dance with you," as if it were the most obvious thing in the world, and I was a dummy for not realizing it. So we started to dance, and I wished he were Tyler. Then I noticed Tyler come into the gym from the hall, where I guess he had been getting a drink.[2] He looked around for a minute, and I saw his eyes coming toward me, so I looked away. I knew he saw me dancing with Mark, though. He just kind of stood there dejectedly, and I was seriously considering saying to Mark, "Sorry, I have to go dance with Tyler." But I decided against it because that would have been rude to Mark.

After the dance, Gina was like, "Tyler, you have to ask Emily out!" But I did not send her over to do that! I was mad at her for saying that to him, because I don't want him to get annoyed with me.

2. There was usually a table with water and juice set up in the hallway during dances, or you could pay for a soda from the vending machine. I tried to avoid the hallway, since it was well lit and I didn't want anyone to see how sweaty my bangs were after all that dancing.

DECEMBER 9, 1999

Okay, I'm going out with Tyler! Yesterday in Science, I could hear him and James whispering again, and once or twice I heard the words "write," "note," and "Emily." I kind of got the idea that they were writing me a note. I turned around quickly to see what they were doing, and James was leaning over Tyler's shoulder, helping him write it. Then after class, James handed me the note and said, "This is from Tyler…" and he had this sly grin on his face. I tried to be nonchalant, like I really didn't care what the note said, but I opened it. It said:

3. NMH = "nothing much here." Not exactly true, in this case.

Hey Emily, what's up? NMH[3] I think you know why I'm writing this. I was gonna ask you out but I was too afraid…

I'm too scared to ask you to your face, so I'm writing you a note. Will you go out with me? —Tyler

I totally flipped out when I read that note. I was so giddy, I would have been disgusted with myself if I were anyone else.

I told James to tell Tyler, "Yes," so that we were going out! After school I went over James's house with Melanie, Louis, and Tyler. Tyler and I were goofing around, just like we always do, and it was fun. He's going to England on the 16th—that's where he's from, originally—and I'm going to miss him so much! I have to hook up with him at Michelle's party—I must![1]

1. It's important to set goals.

DECEMBER 11, 1999

It is 10:30 a.m. and I just woke up—it's Saturday! Last night was Michelle's party and it was really fun.[2] It was supposed to be a surprise party for Gina, but Gina found out about it. Tyler was there, but we weren't really talking and it was kind of stupid and awkward.

2. I often began diary entries with prescriptive declarations of how "fun" something had been. I *wanted* it to have been fun, and writing about it that way allowed me to reshape my interpretation of the event.

Steph was there, too. At one point, she stood up and said, "Excuse me! I have an announcement to make."

The only response she got was that one guy yelled out, "Take off your shirt!" And everyone laughed.[3]

But at least that got everyone's attention, and she could continue. "Everyone form a circle. We're going to play Truth or Dare." There were a few groans but everyone obeyed, and soon we were sitting in a circle of chairs with some people on the floor.

Jenna jumped up and said, "I'll start!" And she

3. Why is it that whenever a woman stands up in a social setting to make an announcement, some asshole will shout out, "Take off your shirt!" or "Show us your tits!" Many of the people at this party had not yet hit puberty, but whichever eighth-grade boy had yelled out had already learned that behavior.

spun around in a circle with her eyes closed for effect before pointing her finger at me. "Emily," she said in this suspicious way that made me nervous. "Truth or Dare?"

While I was thinking about it,[1] Louis cried, "I dare you to go bang Tyler!"

1. What's there to think about? Always pick truth!

"Truth!" I shouted. Everyone groaned and the game kind of broke up for a moment while everyone discussed whether or not they thought Tyler and I should go hook up. It was so embarrassing.[2]

2. Embarrassing, yes, but I also found the attention delicious. The whole point of Truth or Dare was to have an excuse either to act on a secret desire or to force someone else to, after all. Jenna was doing me a favor by choosing me, and we both knew it.

Then Daniel came over and said, "Tyler needs to talk to you… in private."

"Does he, really?" I said sarcastically, because of course he didn't, really. Tyler came over and took my hand and led me to this little storage room off the main part of the basement. I know it must have been hard for him to work up the guts to do that. When we got there, he let go of my hand and turned to face me. We just kind of stood there for a second. He looked extremely uncomfortable, and I felt the same way.

"Oh, this is so embarrassing!" I said, and he just kind of nodded. Then I started babbling on about something, and neither of us was really paying attention to what I was saying. Louis ran by screaming something ridiculous, and we both turned to look at him. I was seriously contemplating just running away from this situation, but I knew I would hate myself later if I did that.[3] So I turned back to Tyler and said, "Are we going to hook up?"

3. Running away is always a valid choice.

"Yes," he said, and that was that. I reached up and put my hands around his neck and he put his hands around my waist. I hadn't realized we were standing that close to each other. I closed my eyes and our lips met, and it was the most beautiful kiss I've ever experienced.

It was not a head-swallowing, let's-see-who-can-move-their-tongue-the-fastest kiss.[1] It was like a movie kiss. There was a little tongue, but there were lips, too. I just completely lost myself in the kiss.[2]

That is, until Stacy looked in and shrieked, "Oh my god!" totally breaking the mood. We gently stopped kissing and I put my head on his shoulder. He's the perfect height for that. After that kiss, we didn't actually talk much for the rest of the party. I hate it how now that we're going out, it's all weirdness. I wish I could talk to him like we did when we were friends. Maybe I should talk to him about that.

Anyway, the rest of the party was a blast. Jenna taught me and Louis how to pole dance—don't ask me how she knew![3] I tried to teach Melanie how to do the worm, but she couldn't. The girls who knew the dance to "Boom, Boom, Boom, Boom!!" by the Vengaboys did it when that song came on, and Louis and Daniel stood behind me for the part where we kind of stick out our butts. Ew.[4]

DECEMBER 15, 1999

I will not see Tyler again for almost three weeks! He is leaving for England tomorrow morning at like, 6 a.m., and he won't be back until January 2nd.

Anyways, today, Stacy, Gina, and I went over Maggie's house. We're really interested in witchcraft and the Wicca religion, and we've decided to be a coven.[5] We all sat up in Maggie's room, casting a circle and calling the quarters: North, South, East,

1. Sorry—*head-swallowing*?! Yikes.

2. Kisses were one thing I always wrote about with stark honesty. I had romanticized almost every other aspect of Zach's and my relationship, for example, but the way I described our kisses revealed how weird the whole thing had been. In contrast, this kiss with Tyler actually seems like it was enjoyable, if only because it was markedly less aggressive than what I was used to.

3. This was before pole dancing classes became a popular way to work out, so I still have no idea how Jenna had learned. It's possible she had no idea what she was doing, but we trusted her because we thought of her as the type of person who *would* know how to pole dance.

4. "Ew" is right. Declaring in my diary that the party was "a blast" was my way of convincing myself that it was so. Not being able to dance without getting harassed by the boys I wanted to believe were my friends sounds like the opposite of a blast.

5. I should mention that our knowledge of the "Wicca religion" was limited to what we'd learned from watching *The Craft* and doing a few cursory Internet searches on AskJeeves.com. Our obsession with the idea of being a coven was a way for us to solidify our small group of closest friends; there could only be four participants in each spell, to represent the four elements of Earth, Air, Water, and Fire. If a fifth person happened to be hanging out that day, they were begrudgingly given the element of Spirit. Since our friendships shifted so often—and since none of our spells ever really worked—the Wicca phase lasted only a few months.

and West. We were going to do a binding spell on Jenna, which is when you wrap white ribbon around a picture of her and chant, "I bind you, Jenna, from doing harm. Harm against other people and harm against yourself." The "harm against yourself" part was what we hoped would work, because we care about Jenna. We hoped putting a spell on her would make her stop being a slut.[1]

But we were interrupted by the doorbell. Maggie ran to get it, and came back and said, "James, Tyler, and Louis are here. What should I do?"

"Just tell them to go away," Stacy said.

But I objected. "Guys, this is the last time I'll see Tyler in three weeks. And if the world ends at the turn of the millennium, this will be the last time I ever see him.[2] Let's go outside and talk to them and finish our spell later."

Everyone agreed, so we all went outside. It began to rain, but not that hard, so we just put our hoods up. Well, the guys did. I just let my hair get wet, because I don't think wearing a hood is very flattering to my face.

Pretty soon, people began thinking along the same wavelength: that Tyler and I should hook up. It was pretty embarrassing, because they would be like, "Okay, we'll just go over here..." and when I tried to follow them, they were like, "No, Emily, you should stay here with Tyler." So we were left alone in front of Maggie's house.

Tyler and I looked at each other, and then we wrapped our arms around each other. As we leaned in to kiss, I kept my eyes open until the moment our lips met. I watched his eyes close and his mouth

1. What an interesting inversion of the usual "witch" = "slut" trope. How progressive of us.

2. I wasn't immune to the Y2K panic... More on that later.

open, and I will always remember that image. This kiss was, if possible, even more beautiful than our first. It was unpredictable and exciting, but also calm and relaxing. I wanted it to last forever.[1]

But then I heard James say, loudly, "They've been making out for like, a really long time!" And I felt a bit silly then, knowing that Tyler had heard it, too. If we continued to kiss after that, it would seem like it would only be to impress James by kissing for longer. So I gently ended the kiss and just hugged him. It felt so utterly romantic, standing there, holding him in the rain. I love him to death, I absolutely love him. I hope to God that the world doesn't end in the next two weeks like it's supposed to, so I can see him again![2] And I hope all the computers don't get messed up that run the airplanes and stuff, or he'll have to stay in England for longer!

DECEMBER 24, 1999

It's Christmas Eve, but I just woke up so I'm not quite in the spirit yet. Today is a Friday. Yesterday was our last day of school before Christmas break, and last night Shauna had a party. It was a bit of a disaster but also a blast![3] After school, before the party, we all hung out at Michelle's house. Jacob and I were having MAJOR bonding time. I feel almost completely comfortable around him now. He always refers to me as his "twin," and it became a very big inside joke for us.

I guess the first hint that it might become a problem was when Daniel pushed me into Jacob saying, "Emily, what are you doing?! You have a boyfriend!" At the time no one cared, but at the party, it was

1. Nowhere is my love for age-inappropriate romance novels more obvious than in my intricate descriptions of kisses.

2. I wasn't sure exactly how the world would end on Y2K, but in my imagination it involved some combination of dark clouds, volcanic ash, and being grounded.

3. This is another example of self-deception through writing. It's not that parties weren't a big deal to me—attending them was of *utmost* social importance—but I experienced most of them in a state of anxiety. I wanted my life to be a string of exciting adventures, and writing about it that way was almost like making it so.

blown out of proportion.

I had a piano lesson at 5 p.m. and then arrived at Shauna's party at 7:30 p.m. Most people were already there. As soon as I walked in, Matt came over with his mouth literally hanging open. "Oh my god," he said.

"What?" I asked. I became very aware of what I was wearing: tight black flares and a low-cut shirt. The way Matt continued to stare at me made me a bit uncomfortable.

Hunter walked in and whistled. "Wow, Emily," he said. "You have an onion ass."

"What the hell is an onion ass?" I asked.

"So good it makes you cry." And he and Matt slapped high five.

Jacob was wearing a really cool hat—it was like a winter cap, but with a brim. I took it off his head and put it on mine, but he took it back. "Hey!" I said, and pretended to be hurt.

He said, "Oh, Emily, don't cry…" and gave me a hug. I hugged him back, and even though it was a perfectly innocent hug, we got a few suspicious looks.

Then Jenna came over with a mistletoe, hung it over my head, and kissed me on the cheek. We laughed and she goes, "Come on, Emily, let's go in the closet together!"

Jacob said, "I'm coming, too!" and we closed the closet doors behind us. We started making noises like we were all having a threesome![1] It was fun, but I had a feeling it might get screwed up… and then the doors opened.

Matt was standing there, staring straight at me, completely serious. "Emily, get the fuck out of there," he said firmly, not yelling.

1. The idea of "having a threesome" came up often at these parties. It was exciting because it was so taboo, but also because it seemed safer than one-on-one sexual interactions. With Jenna there, for instance, I had a witness to what had gone on inside the closet in case Jacob decided to try to convince everyone I had hooked up with him.

"What?" I asked, confused. "Why?" I did step out of the closet, so I could talk to him.

"Because you don't want to do that. I know you're going to regret it later."

"It was just a joke," I told him.

He shrugged. "Trust me, Emily. You have a boyfriend. You don't want to do that." There was something about the way Matt was saying all this that made me wonder about him.[1]

"Thank you," was the only thing I could think of to say.

A few people came up to me and were like, "Why were you in the closet with Jacob? Did you hook up?"

I said, "No, of course not!" to everyone who asked, but people were still suspicious.

Jenna was dancing on the coffee table and Hunter kicked the leg of it so it snapped in two. The table collapsed, Jenna landed on her butt, and everyone was silent. Shauna came running in and started to cry. I would probably have cried, too, if I were her— her basement was completely trashed.

I went in the other room, where people were dancing. Melanie came up to me and said, "Emily, I need to talk to you." She pulled me over near the stairs and said, "Um, you might want to take the flirting down a notch." She wasn't being mean, but she looked serious.

Jacob popped up next to me and I said, "With him?" She nodded. Jacob didn't know what we were talking about. "But Jacob's my twin!" I said, and hugged him.

Melanie said quietly, "Yeah, that's what I'm talking about." Then she walked away.[2]

1. Yeah, like wonder if he actually had a moral compass. Or if he should mind his own business.

2. Leave it to Melanie to bring up her concerns in a private, reasonable way. She was really ahead of the curve when it came to mature social interactions.

"What was that about?" Jacob asked. "Do people think we're going to hook up?"

"Yeah," I said. Then people started coming down the stairs so we had to move. Shauna was making everyone go outside.

I tried to talk to Stacy, but Hunter came over, too. He is so annoying. He and Stacy are kind of starting to date and everywhere she goes, he goes, too. "Hunter, leave us alone!" I said to him, because he was really starting to get to me, plus I just felt like flipping out on someone.

Stacy got mad at me and ran inside. Fine. It didn't bother me, because she can be a stupid bitch anyway.

Jacob came outside and I went to take his hat off his head. But he put up his hand to stop me: "No," he said. "People are going to start stupid rumors."

"But that's dumb," I said.

"I know." He nodded, "but people are stupid, and they're going to think the wrong thing about how we are twins."

"You're right," I said. And he was right. But does that mean we can't talk anymore? That would suck. I know we are flirting, and I know it's for my own good that we don't anymore, and I know he's only doing this because he cares about me and doesn't want me to screw things up with Tyler, but... it still sucks.[1]

1. It was Christmas Eve, for Pete's sake, and all I wanted to write about was my social life.

DECEMBER 31, 1999

Okay, it's 6:21 p.m. on the last day of the year. And of the decade. And of the century. And of the millennium! We weren't allowed to use our computers today, because people think the switch to year

"00" will screw them up or something.[1] There are fireworks at the high school at 7 p.m., and I'm going with my parents.[2] There's been a lot of talk that the world is going to end tonight, at midnight. I don't think that's true at all, but I'm not really that sure. I think it will be midnight and then keep going, no differently than in years past.

But just in case… I don't know, it's scary to even think about, but just in case the world ends tonight, I want to sum up my life quickly. So far, it's been pretty normal. I am an average thirteen-year-old girl, I'm pretty sure. I've made a lot of mistakes but I've also accomplished a lot.[3] And if every living thing is destroyed at midnight tonight, and then like, a billion years in the future, life re-happens, and somehow this diary survives those billion years and is found by those new life-forms, and they are somehow able to decode it… I hope it gives them a good idea of what life was like.[4]

Wouldn't it be weird if that actually did happen, and the new life forms are reading this and thinking how weird it is? Wow. But I have to go to the fireworks now. If I don't get a chance to write again when I get back, then this is the last time I'll write in my diary in this millennium! How strange! So this is Emily Lindin, signing off.[5]

JANUARY 4, 2000

Okay, obviously nothing happened on New Year's. Like, the world didn't end. We didn't even lose electricity! I was a bit disappointed, because all the hype and build-up had kind of gotten to me, I guess. Well, now it's the New Year and it should be

1. As the year 2000 approached, people were worried about a worldwide computer crash because data storage systems that had been using two-digit representations of years ('98, '99, etc.) wouldn't be able to distinguish between 2000 and 1900. Somehow, this computer glitch—referred to as Y2K—was supposed to result in the entire world ending. It made no sense, but the news media ran with it and otherwise reasonable people started stocking up on guns and food rations in order to survive the impending apocalypse.

2. One of our family traditions was to go see fireworks together every year on New Year's Eve. Sometimes if it was too cold outside, we'd just huddle inside the car and watch them through the sunroof.

3. I got really autobiographical in this entry. I was writing almost with the expectation that strangers would read it someday, so I wanted to be sure they saw me as a trustworthy source. Hence the mention of everything I had "accomplished."

4. This is so typical of my generally self-centered, narrow worldview: I saw my own life as somehow representative of the entire human experience.

5. I remember the feeling of gravity with which I closed my diary after writing this entry. Lucky for us all, this diary will *not* be the only piece of evidence available to future life-forms by which to judge human life. Thank God.

a blank slate, but it's really not. Now that I think of it, each year never is. I'm still friends with the same people, I still dislike the same people, the same people still dislike me, and I'm disappointed.

Tyler is still in England even though he told me he'd be home by now. Louis says Tyler won't be in school until Thursday. It's not as hard to wait now, though, since vacation is over and I have things to occupy my mind with, like schoolwork.

I guess Jacob and I are still friends, because at first I was ignoring him but he noticed so I felt bad and stopped. I also brought doubles of my pictures from Shauna's party into school today to give him, as I had promised. He was so happy to have the doubles that it made me happy, too, even though I had been in a bad mood.[1]

I talked on the phone with James tonight. I like the way my friendship is with him—I can tell him everything I tell my girlfriends. We're not affectionate though, like we never hug. I like that though because it means he hasn't accused me of being a tease in a while.

JANUARY 12, 2000

I AM STILL GROUNDED! And my mom said I will not be un-grounded for another week! But that is right before the dance, thank God. Anyway, Tyler wrote me a note today and I was so happy. I just read it for the third time and I am so dorky—I actually squealed with delight. Then I walked around my room with my hands on my head because I hate being infatuated like this. Well, I love the feeling, but I hate it because I can't think straight and so I no

1. For those readers born into the age of the digital camera: A "double" refers to a second copy of a print photo, which could be ordered by checking a box and paying an extra few dollars when you left your film to be developed at CVS, and which was distributed to the person featured in the photo whom you thought most deserved it or to someone who needed it for the shrine they were building of that person.

longer have the power in the relationship.

If I see Tyler coming down the hall to my locker, it takes skill not to scream and clap my hands like a moron. Oh, and he brought me back my Christmas gift from England. He got me a candy bar that was not made in the US, these funky clay animal figure things—I accidentally broke off the elephant's trunk, but I glued it back on!—and perfume.[1] I love the way the perfume smells and I spray it constantly.[2]

Oh, last night my mom was yelling at me because I went over Laura's house after school. It was the first time I'd gone over Laura's house—we're becoming closer friends.[3] But I was grounded and wasn't supposed to. I started crying and went up to my room, where I changed into my pajamas. I found the nail clippers and cut another gash in my wrist. It hurt like hell. It's the first time I've done it in a while. Then I went to sleep at 5:30 p.m.[4]

JANUARY 19, 2000

My life is going better than usual right now! You know what works really well for me? Being in a good mood. Yesterday I was walking down the hall, and I said hi to everyone I passed. Even if they didn't smile or say hi back, some people did, which put me in an even better mood. People don't like people who sulk around, so even if I'm in a bad mood, I'm going to try my hardest to pretend I'm in a good one.[5]

Tyler has started coming upstairs to my locker after school and walking outside with me and my friends. But my friends usually walk ahead, so I get to talk to Tyler alone. Today, I went to the cafeteria

1. Relative to what I was used to from boys, this was a *lot* of gifts. I still have those clay animal figurines on display in my old bedroom. They're the type of tchotchkes he could have purchased at a tourist-trap booth on the sidewalk, but they look hand-painted and they're really cute.

2. *Constantly.* Like those guys in the perfume section of department stores.

3. Laura had always been on the periphery of my ever-changing friend circle. She struck me as slightly aloof and disengaged from drama, which made her devastatingly cool.

4. It's hard for me to say whether it was actually cutting my wrists that made me feel better briefly, or if it was the act of recording it in my diary. I was constantly trying to paint my life as much more dramatic than it really had to be, and writing about the times I cut my wrists probably gave me the sense that I was struggling to cope with what I wanted to believe were overwhelming problems in my life.

5. There's something to be said for trying to "fake it until you make it" when you're having a bad day. I don't stand by my reasoning here though—the goal should be to turn your mood around for your own sake, rather than for the sake of people who might be annoyed by your bad mood.

for study period, which is where he usually has study period. But as I was walking there, he was walking toward me, as if he were leaving. "What are you doing for study period?" he asked, looking confused, because I was walking in the opposite direction from my usual study period classroom.

I said, "Oh, I'm getting a pass to go to the cafeteria."

"Oh... I have to go to Ms. Walsh's room to take a test." He sounded disappointed. When I made a face, he added, "But I'll take it very quickly so I can get back here and hang out with you!" and he smiled.

I smiled back and said, "Okay, you'd better!"

About halfway through study period, Tyler walked into the cafeteria. He came over to my table, where I was sitting with some of my friends, and said, "That test was hard."[1]

I laughed, because I'd taken the same one earlier in the day. "I know!" He sat down across from me and we had a conversation. Now that he got his braces off, I love it when he smiles!

The high schoolers got out of school early today because of testing, and some of them came to the middle school. After fourth period, I was at my locker and I saw Chris Walker. There were a few other people in the hallway, but it was weird because I could like... sense him getting closer to me. I slammed my locker without getting the books I needed and just went into the nearest classroom. Luckily, he didn't come looking for me and I didn't see him again.

James and Jacob both hate Stacy, who's going out with Hunter officially now. They made a webpage

1. Good thing he rushed through it to get back to the cafeteria.

about how stupid and slutty she is. I think it's pretty funny, but she doesn't. I know I wouldn't like it if I were her.[1] She's been very PMS-y lately and it's annoying, but I try to give her advice. I like her now, for the most part. But she's still annoying when she's around Hunter, and he's annoying when he's around her. Isn't love supposed to bring out the best in people when they're with each other? Hunter says he's going to start something with James if the webpage doesn't come down, but James could easily take him. Plus, all of James's friends would jump in to help him, but none of Hunter's would, because they hate Stacy anyway. They don't think she's popular enough to be dating Hunter.[2]

Meanwhile, I have been thinking a lot about Matt. He is a mystery to me. Well, he probably wouldn't be a mystery anymore if I had a few conversations with him and tapped into his brain, although that might be more difficult to do with him than with other people. The thing about Matt is, I have always hated him because he's just so mean to everyone. But lately, I think I've been seeing through that.

I've been concentrating on reading people. That requires interpreting everything they do and say to figure out how they work.[3] Since I've been observing Matt, I've realized that when he says something mean, all I need to do is smile at him and then he'll smile, too, and say, "Peace." And sometimes, when he is about to say something nice, he'll catch himself and not say it.

One time in Spanish class, we were talking about how we used to hate each other. He said, "Yeah, I used to always make fun of you and stuff, but you'd

1. We had just discovered how to create our own webpages, and we thought of them as semi-private spaces. Yes, we could share things more publicly on a webpage than in a diary, for instance, but we never worried about anyone outside of our peer group discovering or spreading the information we posted there. This was before Google or social media sites, so there was no possibility anything we wrote online could go viral. James and Jacob intended to hurt Stacy and to humiliate her in front of our classmates, but there was a limit to how far this webpage could spread.

2. It blows my mind how James and Jacob, both of whom I remember as kindhearted boys, would cyberbully Stacy in this awful way.

3. It's a scientific system. Don't question it.

just be like, 'Oh, I'm sorry you feel that way,' and smile at me, so eventually I stopped. Plus, now I realize that you're actually pretty... not as annoying as I thought." He caught himself before he could say I was pretty cool.[1]

1. But I'll take it!

JANUARY 25, 2000

This happens nearly every day: I write Tyler a note about nothing during Social Studies, and then he writes a note about nothing back when he is in Social Studies.[2] But today the notes weren't about nothing. I felt like I opened up to him. Not completely, of course, but just enough to let him know that something's there so he can decide whether he wants to know more. In my note, I told him I do not understand him, which is true. I was just about to write, "which is untrue," but then I realized that it is true. For some reason, I was under the impression that I had him figured out. I don't know why. I guess I need more practice in understanding everything. Because I know I have the ability to understand things in me, I just need to learn how to use it more effectively.

2. Social Studies was not the most engaging class, obviously. We wouldn't be separated into different achievement-level classes until high school. To avoid boredom, I wrote notes.

I was talking to James in Social Studies today and he told me, "Tyler bet me that you two would still be going out by like... the summer. He also wanted me to switch lockers with him so his could be closer to yours." That is so cute!

Tyler called tonight at 5:50 p.m. We talked until 6:30, when I had to go eat dinner, and there were no awkward silences! Believe it or not, that was the first time we've ever held a real conversation on the phone. Before he went to England, we would only talk if we had James on three-way. I guess we felt more comfortable that way. As soon as he got back from England, I was grounded from the phone, so we couldn't talk then. So we really talked tonight, not about anything deep, really, but he was being very talkative. We talked about Stacy and Hunter and how annoying they are when they're around each other, and also about our crazy cousins, and also about our classes and why they're cool or not— fluffy stuff, but it was cool how we floated from topic to topic without any random spaces where we just said, "So, anyways…" I don't think I said that once in our entire conversation. Oh yeah, we also talked about how he never takes the Lord's name in vain.[1]

Poor James. He got dumped by Laura yesterday, and then after CCD last night, he got beat up by two freshmen.[2] I think his self-esteem is extremely low, so I want to be there for him. I just had a horrible premonition of him committing suicide! I want to call him to make sure he's all right, but it's too late. I'll see him tomorrow.[3]

JANUARY 29, 2000

Yesterday was absolutely horrible. A bunch of freshmen and sophomores have been bugging and threatening James for the past couple of weeks, including Chris Walker. Last night, Maggie and I were going to the football banquet that was being held at the high school. There was going to be a varsity basketball game going on at the same time in the gym. When we got there, we met Jenna, Shauna, and Erin. James was there because he plays football and had to get his trophy.[4]

1. Oh my god. Tyler's family was Catholic, like my family, and I believe we usually attended the same church. But as is typical of Catholic churches in New England, there wasn't necessarily a thriving church community outside of attending Mass on Sundays.

2. A reminder: CCD stands for Confraternity of Christian Doctrine, and it's been the Catholic version of Sunday school since 1562. All of the Catholic kids in my town used it as an excuse to socialize and, I guess, beat each other up.

3. If I had really been concerned he was going to commit suicide, I would have called him regardless of the late hour. It's more likely I was just projecting my own preoccupation with suicide onto James.

4. Getting a trophy used to feel so good, even if everyone else on the whole team got one, too.

My friends and I went into the gym first to watch the basketball game for a minute. Lots of people were there, including Chris Walker. So we went back to the banquet, which was in the cafeteria, to tell James that Chris was there, but Andrew was already talking to him. Andrew said, "He wants to fight you, man."

Then Chris came into the cafeteria and came right up to us. "James." He said. "Let's go."

"I need to get my trophy," James said nervously.

"No. Come on, you pussy." And Chris left, expecting James to follow. And James did.

"James, don't!" I said and tried to stop him, but he shook his head and kept walking. He thought he could take Chris, and he was going to get him to leave him alone once and for all. When I got out to the hallway, James and Chris were talking heatedly, surrounded by a bunch of random high schoolers.

James said, "All right, we're gonna fight in the lobby back there. Come in whenever you're ready." And he turned to walk into the lobby.

"Chris," I said, and reached out to touch his arm. "Why are you doing this? You don't need to."

"Shut up, bitch!" he said, and swung his fist into my eye. I wasn't so much hurt as just shocked that he would hit me like that. I stepped back and watched as three of his friends went into the lobby.[1] And then James, followed by our friends, went in too, for some reason. I had a bad feeling about the whole thing[2] but I knew James was strong and I tried to have confidence in him.

When we were all in there, Chris and James threw a few punches. James was on the floor almost

1. This wasn't a straight-up punch in the face; I was standing nearly behind him, so he made a fist and swung the back of his hand up to hit me. This kind of behavior was shocking in the context of what usually went on in our town, but it was less shocking coming from Chris Walker. Many people threatened to get into fights, but Chris Walker was probably the only person who actually followed through with any regularity, and we all knew this about him.

2. Probably because I'd just gotten hit in the face...

immediately, but I told myself that was okay, because he would get back up. And he started to, but Chris kicked him in the face. Out of everything everyone was shouting, I picked out the words "steel-toed boots." As Chris kicked James in the face again, I saw that yes, his boots had steel plates on the toes. I wanted to do something so badly, but I felt like I was going to throw up. Chris got James's limp body in a headlock and wouldn't let go. James wasn't even trying to get out—he wasn't moving at all. His face was turning from red to purple, and Chris just held him tighter. Finally, a high schooler got Chris off of him. Chris put his arms up in the air and whooped, "Yeah!" All his friends were like, "Yeah, man, you kicked his ass!"

James lay in a heap on the floor. Blood was bubbling out of his mouth and the whole left side of his face was a mess. I went into the corner and threw up my dinner. When I came back, someone had carried James into the snack bar room, where he was sitting on a chair. The door was closed, but I could see him through the open snack bar window, and it made me cry. His mouth didn't even look like a mouth. It was covered in blood, and his face was all bashed in. The police had arrived, and they closed the window. But every so often the door opened to let in a paramedic or an officer, and I could hear James crying. His parents arrived from the banquet and disappeared inside the room.[1]

I sat outside the snack bar room with Louis and Scott. They were both crying and not even pretending not to cry, and I felt hysterical. James's mother came out after a while to inform us that James had

1. Witnessing James in this state was one of the most intense moments of my life up to that point. It was just so real, in contrast to all the imagined drama I was always cooking up surrounding everyday situations. The image of James with a bloodied face through the snack bar window was ingrained in my mind for so long that I can even conjure it up now.

a concussion and didn't know where he was or what had happened. Then a cop came out and said, "All right, everyone just move over there." But we didn't, because we wanted to see what he didn't want us to see. James was rolled out on a stretcher, covered with a white sheet except for his face, which was purple and bandaged and at least not so bloody anymore. His eyes were shut, and he looked dead. I wanted to run to him and hold him and put my hands on his face, but he was wheeled away down the hall.

When I got home, the first thing I did was call Melanie and tell her what happened. She started crying, which made me start crying all over again. I went online and everyone was talking about it. Louis told me I was brave to try to stop it, but I didn't feel brave. I felt guilty, because really I just stood there and watched. There was probably nothing I could have done, but I don't know. I went to bed crying, wondering if James was okay.

Today, I went over James's house to see how he was doing. He had Tyler and Louis over, too. When I got there, he answered the door. His lips were all cut up and the left side of his face was horribly bruised and his eye was swollen shut. But he was acting like himself and talking and laughing with us. He, Tyler, and Louis were pissed that Chris had hit me, because now I have a black eye, too.

My dad made me go to the police station today to tell the cops the story, since I was a witness. There weren't that many witnesses, and most of them hadn't seen the whole thing. I showed the officer my black eye and he took pictures and told me that he would keep in touch with me about how I could help.[1]

1. This was my only interaction with the police, other than the D.A.R.E. officers who came to our school to tell us not to take drugs. I wrote about the whole experience rather nonchalantly not because it wasn't a big deal, but probably just to downplay it to myself so I could wrap my head around it without panicking.

JANUARY 31, 2000

I guess the whole fight thing is an extremely big deal. Chris Walker is being charged with assault and battery with a deadly weapon: the steel-toed boots he was wearing. A police officer called my house today and I had to go down to the station. They took more photographs of my eye, which is still fairly swollen, and had me tell them exactly what happened. They said I was a victim, like James, and that I should file a complaint or something against Chris, to add to the charges against him.

My parents really want me to do that, but I don't really want to get more involved than I already am. I am willing to serve as a witness to what happened to James, but I don't want to make a big thing out of how Chris hit me. I told my mom to tell the officer that, because he told us to talk about what we wanted to do, and she said she'd think about it.[1]

Today in school was very retarded. At the beginning of the day, everyone was like, "Oh, Emily, your eye!" But then, people started to spread rumors, like they always do.

There were so many going around: "Emily's father did that to her, and she's just saying it was Chris to cover it up." And, "Emily did that to herself. She cuts her wrists, why not punch herself in the eye?"[2] And, "She's wearing a lot of makeup to make it look like she has a black eye." I was very upset that people who I considered to be so-so friends, like Erin, were saying these things. Why can't people just accept things the way they are? Why do they always have to look for holes in everything, and if they don't find any, just make their own?

1. Suddenly, I had an aversion to attention. It's likely that I just wanted to forget the whole episode and that I didn't want to intertwine my life with Chris Walker's anymore.

2. I'm imagining punching myself in the eye—*okay*, I just tried it—and it's comically ineffectual.

FEBRUARY 3, 2000

Tyler and I have a really good relationship. It is like, fun. I am comfortable around him—I can make fun of him, he can make fun of me, and neither of us is ever serious. We write notes to each other every day and talk on the phone almost every night. We talk about weird things, like what we were afraid of as kids. Two nights ago, we were talking about our crazy relatives. He said, "One summer, my grandmother came to stay with us, and she wore this strong perfume. For the whole summer, the entire house smelled of perfume, and I smelled of perfume." In that instant, I knew I loved him. He could have said, "smelled like perfume," but instead he said, "smelled of perfume." That just made him so perfect to me.[1]

Then last night, for some reason, I was afraid to call him. I had a weird feeling that he didn't want to talk to me. I was really hoping, though, that he would call me, because I wanted to talk to him. I was down in the basement and my sister called to me from upstairs that I had a phone call. I really, really hoped it was him, but I knew it wouldn't be, and I didn't want to get my hopes up. But when I got to the top of the stairs, my sister smiled and whispered, "It's him!" as she handed me the phone. I was so glad!

I am so infatuated by him, I can't even stand it. I remember the first time I saw him, in fifth grade. I was new to the school and Michelle was showing me who everyone was. Tyler was playing basketball, wearing a green and blue plaid parka. Michelle said, "That's Tyler. He's from England." At the time,

1. What can I say? I have very specific taste when it comes to grammatical choices.

I didn't really think twice about him, but for some reason, that memory stuck in my mind.[1]

FEBRUARY 4, 2000

Today in school, I was so upset with Tyler. After Science, he came to my locker. I usually write him notes in Social Studies, which I had next, but I had been thinking that I really needed to start paying better attention in that class, so I said, "I'm not going to write you a note today."[2]

He shrugged and said, "I don't care." Then he walked away.

I was hurt. Did he not care about my notes? I save and treasure all the notes he writes to me, and he doesn't even care. He probably just throws them all away. I told James next period that I was a little hurt, and he told me not to be. His face isn't really swollen that much anymore, and he kind of looks like a person again.[3]

Anyway, next period was Music for me. I asked to go to the bathroom and passed by the computer lab and looked in to see who had Computer this period. There was Tyler, typing at his computer. And there was Kaylee, leaning over his shoulder, whispering in his ear, both of them smiling. I felt hot waves boil up inside my stomach, and I recognized the horrible feeling as intense jealousy. I ran into the bathroom and took a few deep breaths. Then I had to walk back past the computer lab to get back to Music, and I wanted to look in again to make sure Kaylee was back at her own computer. I looked in, and this time I saw that not only had Kaylee not left, but now Catherine was huddled around Tyler also!

1. For someone who was from England, poor Tyler didn't act nearly as exotic as we all wished he would. He didn't even have an accent! His mother always had a strong British accent, so he might have worked to get rid of it in order to fit in—exactly what I did with my strong Boston accent upon arriving in that town.

2. I really don't remember a single thing we learned in Social Studies that year.

3. It seems that James had more important issues to worry about than whether or not Tyler appreciated my notes.

I made a little choking noise by accident, and they all looked up. I kept walking, so it appeared I was just passing by, but Tyler saw me. I leaned against the wall with my hands on my head. I hated this feeling! I wanted to sob loudly, scream, or tear something apart. But I reminded myself how inappropriate that would be and was able to keep my body under control. But my mind was raging. I couldn't think straight. I was literally seeing red.[1] When Music ended, I walked upstairs to my locker. Tyler had French next period, which is right next to my locker. I hurried gathering my stuff for Math, because I didn't want to have to look at him.

As I was walking the few feet from my locker to the classroom, I heard him say, "Hey, Emily." I turned my head and gave him the worst glare I've ever given anyone. I am known for many things, one of them being that I am a slut, and another being my deadly looks. I am very good at expressing myself with my face. This look said, "If you come one step closer, I will personally feed you to rabid goats."[2] All through Math, I couldn't concentrate. The anger was wearing off, and now I just felt hurt. I had this lump in my throat that made it hard for me to talk. I was miserable. When Math ended, I slowly made my way to my locker and started getting my stuff for Spanish. I became aware of Tyler standing next to me, but I did nothing to acknowledge his presence. "Here," he said timidly, and handed out a note for me. I took it, not saying anything, and walked into the Spanish classroom. Here's what the note said:

1. Er... This all seems like a *bit* of an overreaction.

2. What a horribly *specific* fate. But I wasn't exaggerating about the intensity of my facial expressions. They can be alarming.

Hey Emily,

Well I am guessing you're pretty mad at me and I'm sorry for whatever I did. Are you mad at me for not caring about you writing me a note, or because of in Computer class? I'm really sorry about the note thing—I do care about your notes. I have all the notes you ever wrote in the drawer right next to my bed, even the notes on my folders from sixth grade. Well, I hope you're not mad at me because of Kaylee and Catherine. They are just my friends. Besides, both of them have boyfriends. Well, I'm really dumb if that's not what you're mad about, but if it isn't, I'll tell you about it later. What are you doing after school? I'm pretty sure I'm going to Louis's house and I'll call you from there, no matter where you are.[1] You don't have to write back if you don't want to.

<3,

Tyler

1. We didn't have cell phones, so he would have had to find out where I was planning to be after school in order to call me there.

All my anger and hurt washed away and was replaced with a light, floaty feeling in my stomach. In study hall, I was in the cafeteria and Tyler and his friends were sitting at the table behind me. I heard him say to his friends, "I'm gonna go talk to Emily." I tensed up as he sat down next to me, but when he looked at me, I couldn't help a smile from spreading across my face.

"I'm not mad at you anymore," I told him.

He smiled, too. "Good." Then we had a friendly conversation. There's a dance tomorrow night and I can't wait![2]

2. This entry in particular demonstrates just how volatile my emotions were. From "boiling" rage to butterflies in the course of a few hours? How exhausting.

FEBRUARY 12, 2000

Lately, Stacy and Hunter have been stuck together. Like, if you tried to rip them apart, you wouldn't be able to. It's really annoying, because she acts different around Hunter.[1] It is making me have awful urges that I'm able to keep under control for the most part, but sometimes I slip and say something very cruel.

Like during study period yesterday in the cafeteria, I was frustrated with my homework. Stacy giggled and said, "Well, life sucks and then you die."

I looked up. "Only for you, Stacy." She stopped giggling. That had been my goal. Everyone else laughed, though, even Hunter, which made her face go completely hard. I thought, good. I hate it when she giggles.

Monday is Valentine's Day, so Ms. Fontaine was having her classes make valentines in French. Tyler made me one that I am going to keep and cherish forever. It is red, with little hearts in different colors pasted on it. And inside the writing is in orange, so it is very hard to read. Also on the inside, there is glued white paper around the edges with a huge heart cut out of the middle, where the red shows through. There are little hearts drawn in red crayon on the white paper all around the big heart.[2] It says:

> Bonjour Emily,
>
> Bonne fete de Saint Valentin! Tu es si belle.
>
> This is pretty hard to read because of the orange, and because you don't speak French. Je veut a suke ton grande nenes. Hahahaha! I'm writing in orange so nobody can read

1. With slightly spiked, bright blond hair and a cunning smile, Hunter had always been one of the popular boys in our class. That was part of what annoyed me so much about Stacy's relationship with him: it proved that, to some extent, her new "slutty" persona was working.

2. Sounds... beautiful?

this and see how gay I am.[1] Have a happy Valentine's Day. I'm looking forward to tonight. I LOVE YOU! Je t'aime.[2]

Love,

Tyler

Isn't that just too cute? He's so adorable because he's very shy and doesn't really show affection toward me when other people can see, because he's embarrassed. So when he does do something sweet, like spend all period making me a beautiful valentine, it is that much better.

Anyways, the dance was at the all-boys Catholic school and it started at 7 p.m. I arrived with Melanie. When we got in, we didn't know anyone there! But then some of our friends started showing up, so it was fun. There were lots of random guys coming up to me and grinding on me for a second, or grabbing my ass or something. And I'm not saying I didn't provoke it—my pants were kind of tight and the type of dancing my friends and I were doing wasn't exactly prude.[3]

But I was spending all the slow dances with Tyler, and we talk when we dance. He finally agreed to dance with me the way I think is really cute, when you hold each other's hand with one hand and dance cheek-to-cheek. In order for this to be possible, though, I had to stand on my very tiptoes so my cheek could be next to his. That got tiring quickly, so we decided to stick with regular slow dancing.[4]

I taught him to grind, too, which was fun. But he's very uptight, so it's hard for me to get him to move his hips. I actually had to put my hands on his hips and press down to make him roll them. He

1. Right. Because making a valentine for a girl makes you gay. For us, the threat of being labeled "gay" as a boy was almost as prevalent as the threat of being labeled a "slut" was for a girl. We used the word "gay" flippantly, illogically, and ubiquitously to describe anything distasteful to us, but in this case, Tyler was actually worried about being thought of as effeminate for composing a Valentine.

2. I was enrolled in Spanish class instead of French (those were our only two options in middle school), so I didn't speak it or understand it. Reading his valentine now, it doesn't seem like Tyler had that solid of a grasp on the language, either.

3. But wearing pants that are "kind of tight" while dancing does *not* mean I was provoking boys to grab me. In fact, there's nothing I could have done that would have been an excuse for that kind of behavior. I wish I had understood that they were responsible for their actions, plain and simple.

4. Oh, middle school slow dancing. Is there anything more awkward?

eventually got the hang of it, and then we could grind. He's so cute, how he tries so hard to learn just to please me.

By this time, the gym was a sauna. I pulled my hair up in a ponytail off my neck, but my bangs were still matted to my forehead. I would brush by random people dancing and get their sweat all over me. Someone opened a door in the back of the gym, and my friends and I rushed toward it. The cold February air was a momentary relief from the heat of the gym. But soon, we were told to get back inside.

Tyler and I went downstairs, where there was free food, and got Pepsis. I don't like soda, but it was a bit refreshing. Then someone announced that they were playing the last song upstairs in the gym, so Tyler and I walked back up. I wanted him to kiss me, so instead of resting my head on his shoulder like I normally do, I put my face next to his, tilted downward. This way, if he wanted to kiss me, he could without making much of an effort. We danced this way for a while.

Then Tyler said, "Louis says we should make out." I looked over to where Louis was, and he was making obscene gestures and lolling his tongue around. I laughed. Tyler kissed me on the cheek. I turned my head and we began to kiss.

Kissing him is so interesting! He moved his hands down to my butt and I pressed against him to tell him to keep them there. I ran my fingers through his hair, down his back, and up again. Another slow song began, and we kept kissing. I was developing a crick in my neck from turning my face up to kiss him, but I ignored it because I didn't want to stop. This was the first time we had kissed since he got back from England. I opened my eyes for a split second, just to see what he looks like when he kisses me. He looks good.[1] I immediately closed my eyes again so I could become lost in the kiss again.

The song ended, but we continued to kiss until a chaperone said, "All right, guys, it's over." Then we drew apart and I hugged him, opening my eyes. The lights were blinding to me.

Then I was crushed into Tyler by Jacob and Louis, who wrapped their arms around us both and yelled, "We love you guys!" Then Tyler and I walked out of the gym together. Tyler's ride came first, so he hugged me goodbye. Oh, I love him so much. I wonder what he got me for Valentine's Day.[2] I haven't bought his gift yet, but I am going to get him this gorilla I saw that sings the song "What I Like About You" and like, vibrates when it dances. It's ridiculous and I know he'll like it.[3]

FEBRUARY 15, 2000

Yesterday was Valentine's Day and Tyler is so cute! We sit together in Science now, because James has been absent and I'd rather sit next to Tyler than Stacy. He said, "Come down to my locker after class, and I'll give you your present." So after class, I went to my locker first and got my stuff for Social Studies, then went downstairs and put it in the classroom.

Then I walked to Tyler's locker, which is not too far away, and he was there with Louis, who was like, "Oooh! Emily's here for her present!" Tyler reached in his locker and handed me a heart-shaped box of chocolates, the kind with assorted fillings.

1. Phew! Thank goodness.

2. You mean besides the French, orange Valentine?

3. In addition to snacks, CDs, and clothes our parents wouldn't approve of, my classmates and I spent most of our spending money on small gifts for each other. One of the most important markers of being someone's official boyfriend or girlfriend was that you bought them a gift for Valentine's Day, Christmas, their birthday, or any other holiday you felt warranted a display of affection. Since our funds were limited, the gifts usually ended up being something bizarre like a vibrating, dancing, musical stuffed gorilla.

I was like, "Thanks!" and turned to walk away, but he said, "Hold on, I have something else for you." And he reached in his locker again and this time he pulled out a long-stemmed rose. It was in a plastic case, with white confetti all around it and a bow of netting tied around the case. He looked so adorable standing there, holding the rose out to me. I took it and hugged him.

"Thank you!" I said. Then Ms. Fontaine told us to get to class.

The chocolates were in a gift bag, covered with tissue paper. I took them out to eat them during Social Studies, and that's when I saw the note. It was written in orange and folded up, held in place with a paper clip. I unfolded it to find that it was the front and back of three pages! I read it slowly and cherished every sentence. I almost cried out of pure joy.

I swear, I have the best boyfriend in the entire universe! He knows I love it when he writes me notes, and that note made me even happier than the rose—which, by the way, is unusually beautiful and vibrant. My mom took a picture of it! I love the idea that he cares about me enough to spend all that time doing something he dislikes: writing notes. Oh, I love him!

FEBRUARY 18, 2000

Tonight there was a surprise party for Kaylee at Catherine's house. Since I don't really hang out with those girls anymore, my mom had to call Catherine's mom to make sure she'd be there. There was a blizzard outside so not a lot of parents wanted to drive anywhere. I got a ride with Laura's mom because neither of my parents wanted to go out driving. When we got there, there were about ten girls there, mostly from the Abercrombie and Fitch clique.[1] And there were only two guys: Hunter and some random kid Catherine had met at the Catholic school dance. Eventually, about fifteen other people showed up, including Tyler and James.

Tyler and I were talking and hanging out, and he has started touching me more, which gives me shivers, which I like. Emma said, "Come here, you two," and she led us down a hall in Catherine's basement and opened what looked like a closet door. "This is the storage room," she said. It was the part of the basement that wasn't finished. "I know you might not feel like going in there now," she said. "But... later if you do, I'm just letting you know it's here." Then she patted me on the back and walked away. I looked at Tyler and he looked really embarrassed.

James was being a nuisance. He kept bugging me to hook up with Tyler, and although I wanted to, I didn't want to act like I did. James said, "Hey, why don't you two hook up?"

"Where?" Tyler asked. "There are like, a bajillion people around."

James raised his eyebrows and said, "Come down this way." We followed him to the end of the hallway and he said, "Why not right here?"

Suddenly Emma was there, and she said, "Why not in the little room I showed you?"[2] I sighed and went in, and Tyler followed. Someone shut the doors behind us. We started making out right away, and I love kissing him. He placed his hands on the front of my shirt and squeezed my boobs gently. I was sending him mental vibes to reach up my shirt, and

1. Every school had one, right? It's not that no one else wore Abercrombie and Fitch—almost everyone I knew did—it's just that there was something about the Abercrombie and Fitch brand that really resonated with my opinion of that clique, after they decided to ostracize me. The clothes were expensive and kind of preppy, but most importantly they usually had the word "ABERCROMBIE" emblazoned across them. That label was a way for the girls in that group of friends to mark themselves as belonging.

2. Wow, Emma was really excited about getting us in that little room.

1. Way to work, mental vibes!

he cautiously put his hands on my sides, under my shirt.[1] I stood on tiptoe so I could kiss him more efficiently, and hopefully give him the hint that I liked what he was doing and wanted him to continue. He moved his hands up my sides and touched my bra.

Just then, someone opened the door a crack, and Tyler and I stopped kissing. "Oops! Sorry!" the person said, and closed the door.

I reached up and undid my bra for Tyler. He looked grateful as he leaned in to kiss me again and moved his hands back up my shirt. I never thought having someone feel your boobs could feel good or turn you on or anything, but apparently it can! I kissed him harder.[2]

2. It would have been nice if my first sexual interaction had been this consensual and respectful. Aside from the way Emma was pressuring us to go into the storage room, Tyler and I seem quite comfortable with each other. I don't know if I would have admitted to the other people at the party that I was actually enjoying making out with Tyler, for fear of reinforcing my "slut" label, but it's clear from the way I wrote about it that I was completely on board with the whole thing.

Then, once again, someone opened the door, this time on purpose. "Hey, what are you two doing in there?" They laughed and walked away, leaving the door wide open. The mood was ruined, and I went to re-hook my bra.

"That's enough for now?" Tyler asked, and I nodded.

3. It's funny to me that I never wrote about *how* I had experienced the build-up to an orgasm. I had discovered how to masturbate years earlier and returned to it every so often, probably about once a week. I'm not sure why I didn't write about it in my diary, but my suspicion is that I found it embarrassing. Not just because it was shameful according to my religion, but because it seemed kind of... *pathetic* to me: if boys wanted to hook up with me, I shouldn't have to masturbate. Thank goodness I outgrew that faulty logic!

Now that I'm thinking about it, it seems really unromantic being in that storage room, but at the time I felt really... horny. I guess. I have never been that horny. I'm usually never really horny at all! I was thinking about having an orgasm. I've never had one, but I think I've felt the build-up to one.[3] But in a storage room in Catherine's basement doesn't really seem too special, so I decided against going to third base.

Anyway, Tyler started being weird then, like he wasn't talking to me. Actually, I was also being weird, because I felt different around him now. Ever since the summer when we were friends, he would always joke about how he wanted to feel my boobs. It was kind of strange, now that he had felt them, even though it probably shouldn't have been.

I quickly became un-horny, because Stacy was crying because Hunter was being mean to her. I didn't bug her about it. I held her and told her over and over not to cry, that Hunter was a guy and all guys are assholes, even though I didn't really believe that. She was really upset, so Laura and I took her upstairs to the bathroom and dunked her head in cold water.[1] After that, she calmed down enough to go back downstairs.

I was having fun at the party, because it was mostly popular people who don't ever hang out with me anymore.[2] Tyler finally came over and hung out with me. Then Laura came over and she said, "I'm driving James and Tyler home, right?" They nodded. She said to me and Tyler, "Well, then, you guys better hook up now if you're gonna do it, 'cause my dad's upstairs." Then she and James walked away.

Tyler was standing awfully close to me. I said, "Why weren't you talking to me earlier?"

He shrugged. "I think you were avoiding me." I thought that he was right, because I sort of had been. There was a short silence before he said, "Want to go in that little room?" I smiled and nodded and led him back down the hall.

We weren't in there for long before we started kissing again. Mmm, I love kissing him! Before long, he put his hands up my shirt again and started rubbing my boobs outside my bra. I stepped back.

1. Of course. Problem solved! I had seen this in a movie—I forget which one—and I assumed it was a reliable way to shock people out of unhappiness.

2. These were the girls who had been my friends before I was labeled a "slut." Even though I had established new friend-ships, I was still being rejected and outright mocked by the Abercrombie and Fitch clique on a daily basis. I must have seen this party as a step in the right direction toward patching things up with them.

"Do you need me to do this again?" I asked, and unhooked my bra.

He said, "Thank you!" before we kissed again. But then the door opened and it was Laura.

She said, "Sorry to interrupt you guys, but we gotta go." Tyler and I stopped kissing and I rehooked up my bra. He gave me a long hug before he left and told me he'd call me tomorrow. I hope he does!

FEBRUARY 29, 2000

Today was a leap day! Which doesn't really affect anything, but... it was also a Tuesday. Tyler and I are having problems. I don't know exactly how it started, but I was thinking a lot, and probably I was the one who caused it. Yesterday, I was thinking that Tyler and I make out more than we really talk. Like, we talk, but we haven't had a deep conversation in over a week.

So I wrote him a note in Social Studies, saying that I didn't really want to hook up anymore, until we started talking. 'Cause I didn't want our whole relationship to be based on hooking up, you know? I wanted to work on our emotional relationship, too. So he wrote back, and it seemed like he understood. But ever since then, we haven't talked at all! Except once in the hall when he told me how Louis wanted to beat up this poor crippled boy because he had stolen Louis's pencil or something.[1]

Then today, I went online as my new screen name, which is IMAQTpieNUlikeit, to make a new profile.[2] Out of curiosity, I checked Tyler's profile. He had stolen color codes out of my profile![3] That

1. As far as conversations go, this isn't much.

2. This is the one name I haven't changed for the protection of the people in this diary. My screen name was actually IMAQTpieNUlikeit—and it was amazing.

3. Back in the days of AOL Instant Messenger, one of the limited options when it came to personalizing your online presence was to use html code to customize your profile. For instance, you could use one code to make the background pink and another to make the text blue. Jacob was the only one of my friends who actually understood html—the rest of us just copy-and-pasted codes we stole from each other.

meant he must have gone online as me and copied it from the editor! And he didn't even give me credit for it.[1] What's worse is that it used to say, "I WANT EMILY" at the very top, and now it doesn't anymore. I'm not mentioned in the whole profile. There's even a list of all his friends, and I'm not even in that. I started to cry. What is his deal?!

1. Plagiarism!

MARCH 4, 2000

Yesterday, Tyler and I broke up. Technically, he dumped me, and that's what I was feeling last night, but now that I've been thinking about it more I like to say "we broke up." Kaylee likes him, so I'm pretty sure he dumped me for her, which… hurts. Luckily, I was at Shauna's house with Jenna and Maggie when I found out, so I had their shoulders to cry on. Tyler was with Louis and Steven. After he had broken up with me, I talked to Steven about it and he was being really sympathetic. Louis kind of was, too. He said I didn't have to talk to Tyler about it if I didn't want to—I hadn't actually heard it from Tyler yet. He had James call me, which James said he hated doing, and I cried to him for about a half hour.

I decided that I did want to talk to Tyler about it, because it wasn't fair that he could just dump me without an explanation. He got on the phone and said, "Hey."

"Hi." I was trying really hard not to cry.

"How are you doing?" he asked.

"Bad," I answered, "You just broke up with me."

He said, "Well, it wasn't something you did, I just kind of changed." It sounded rehearsed.

"But why was it so random?"

He said, "Well, it wasn't really random. I've been thinking about it for a while. We just weren't getting along after what happened at Catherine's party." He meant when we hooked up in the storage room. At the time, I had to get off the phone with him because I was going to cry.

James said, "He told me that you two just sort of grew apart." Now that I have been thinking about it all last night and today, I guess he's right. We were always getting annoyed with each other and our relationship was kind of falling apart. I just don't get it.[1]

MARCH 6, 2000

Today was my first day in school being single for almost three months. It's a different feeling, like having freedom around every guy. Well, every guy who's not taken. In Science, I was not by any means cold to Tyler, but it's not like we talked or anything. I want to be friends with him, but I don't think I should start on that mission until I can think of him as just another random kid. Well, I guess I could start now. I feel like I'm over him. But I'll start just trying to be acquaintances. We'll build our friendship back eventually, I hope. He and Kaylee aren't going out. In fact, they hardly talked at all today, as far as I observed.

Okay, also, on Saturday night I talked to James on the phone and he told me that Matt likes me and that he talks about me all the time. Matt.[2] I was a little flattered, but Matt had a girlfriend. Well, he dumped her today. In Math, some girls were talking about it and one of them said, "Matt said he wanted

1. It sounds like *I did* get it, at least as far as what had been slowly going wrong. Writing "I just don't get it" was probably a way to neatly move on from the issue without considering how I might have been at fault.

2. Yes, *that* Matt.

to be single because he likes someone else, but he wouldn't say who!"

Emma, who is exceedingly annoying and shallow, piped up, "Oh, I bet it's me! People have been saying he liked me forever." I rolled my eyes, but she didn't notice. I couldn't imagine such a complex soul as Matt ever connecting with an airhead like Emma.

Next block was Spanish, where Matt sits next to me. I asked him about Emma and he made a face. "No!" he said incredulously, "I said I thought she was hot, that's all." I shrugged and we started talking about other stuff. Then I faced forward again to copy some notes off the board. Steven sits right behind me and James sits next to him. I heard them whispering with Matt and I secretly tried to make out what they were saying.

All I heard was Steven say, "Emily?!" Hearing my name, I spun around and looked imploring at them.

James said, "Um... turn around," in the blank voice he uses when he's trying to take control of the situation. I did turn around and they shut up after that, which disappointed me because I had wanted to hear more.

We had a class meeting today, and those are always really boring.[1] I sat right in front of Matt and Hunter in the auditorium. Mr. Bates, the gym teacher at one of the elementary schools, had come in to speak to us about his experience in Vietnam.[2] He was showing us slides he had taken when he was over there for the war in like, 1968 or something. It was really sad—there were all these slides of like, seven-year-old kids, dressed in rags. But most of them were smiling.

1. In order to participate in the eighth-grade class trip to New York City, which we were told would be the highlight of our middle school experience, we needed to attend a class meeting every month. There was no obvious connection between the content of the meetings and the pending trip to New York, though.

2. That seems like heavy stuff for an eighth-grade class meeting.

Mr. Bates said, "See? They're just like you guys. They do the same things, play the same games... Only... maybe not the same games, because they don't have any equipment."

Hunter laughed and said, "So what do they play? Catch the Lizard?"

Everyone giggled and Matt said, "No, they play Don't Get Shot." That cracked the whole class up for a good few minutes, until Mr. Bates reminded us to focus.[1]

When we had calmed down, Matt leaned over so his head was right next to mine and whispered, "Are you still upset about Tyler?"

I shook my head. "No, I got over that on the weekend."

He seemed interested. "How did you do that?"

"Well, I just thought about it a lot, and it was like, for the best that we broke up, you know?" He nodded thoughtfully and sat back in his seat.

After the meeting, Lisa came up to me and said, "Guess who likes you!"

"Who?" I pretended not to be interested.

"Matt." I let my mouth hang open for a really long time to show my shock, which was actually fake. While I was waiting outside for my ride to come, Catherine told me the same thing. Hmm. I wonder...?

MARCH 15, 2000

Well, Matt blew it today, just like I knew he would. He went over to Kaylee's house and he hooked up with her. He called me tonight and confessed and admitted to being wrong. I told him I

1. As sheltered kids who never seriously had to worry about violence in our day-to-day lives, we apparently thought war was *hilarious.*

wouldn't be able to trust him ever again, and he told me he didn't blame me, but that he didn't want me to like, hate him.

I don't hate him. It was cool of him to call me and tell me himself, instead of letting me find out tomorrow in school.[1] But it took him six months of sitting next to me in Spanish to build up a friendship after the way he treated me in sixth and seventh grade, and even then I didn't completely trust him. And now he just threw it all away. I won't ever be able to trust him, and I don't want to! He made me fall for him and then turned around and threw it in my face.[2] I don't even have the words to describe how angry it makes me. I'm not even that angry at him, just at myself for being stupid enough to give him a chance.

MARCH 16, 2000

Today was an extremely weird day. Hunter broke up with Stacy, because yesterday Catherine gave him a blow job while they were both on Valium, and now they're going out.[3] Catherine and Emma are like, obsessed with doing Valium now, which is unnerving to me. They're becoming really bad, and I don't want them to screw up.[4]

Also, the Kaylee and Matt thing. It wasn't such a big deal compared to what happened to Stacy, so I got over it quickly. I'm not mad at Kaylee because she's really shallow and too innocent, mind-wise, to be upset at.[5] Matt and I acted the same way as we always do in Spanish, which I liked. I don't want to be enemies with him, but I couldn't ever trust him at all.

Stacy and I are friends again, which is the one

1. That's true.

2. Spending less than two weeks considering the possibility that he might have a crush on me doesn't exactly constitute "falling for him."

3. I should point out that all of this was hearsay.

4. It must have been the only drug available for them to pilfer from their parents. It wouldn't have been difficult for any of us to get Valium or similar prescription drugs from one of our parents' medicine cabinets. I guess none of us had really thought of it before.

5. Ouch.

good thing that came from this whole mess. I feel so awful for her! Today she was crying in the bathroom, and I had to go to the guidance counselor's office with her. I'm disgusted with Catherine for giving Hunter a blow job—I don't even think I can stand to look at her! But starting a fight with her won't help anything, so I'm not going to.

The other messed up thing that happened today is that everyone found out some interesting news about Emma and Catherine, which is that they ate each other out. I am not sure when—some people said it was yesterday, while they were both on Valium, some people said it was two days ago at Steph's house, and some people said it was some time over the summer. I think that's the nastiest thing I ever heard in my life, and now I'm realizing how I don't really know Emma or Catherine well at all.[1] Oh, well. This weird day is over. I had this conversation with Jacob online a few hours ago:

> **IMAQTpieNUlikeit:** what do you think about today?
>
> **Jacob:** no opinion
>
> **IMAQTpieNUlikeit:** it was the weirdest day ever i think
>
> **IMAQTpieNUlikeit:** i think you were right about matt, which makes me mad. because you're always right and then you don't even gloat, you're just like "yeah, whatever, i'm right AGAIN" only you don't say that, you're just LIKE that. it would be better if you said it.
>
> **Jacob:** thats like self egonistic.
>
> **IMAQTpieNUlikeit:** what is self egonistic?

1. You'd think I would have had some compassion for the subjects of such a vague rumor.

Jacob: as in self centered. big ego. egonistic.[1]

IMAQTpieNUlikeit: oh you mean "egoTIStic." you spelled it wrong.

Jacob: no. egonistic.[2]

IMAQTpieNUlikeit: it doesn't matter.[3]

Jacob: anyway it's the best way to learn from your mistakes. the truth isn't always best.

IMAQTpieNUlikeit: but you were best friends with him and zach for years.

Jacob: i know him inside and out

IMAQTpieNUlikeit: but he told me he doesn't open up to his friends. he said he hardly knows hunter at all.

Jacob: wuts he mean by that? his true self doesn't show? that's pretty corny...

IMAQTpieNUlikeit: i know it is. but the reason i'm mad is cause i feel stupid for trusting him cause it was like... i thought he was this tortured soul who had no one to talk to and i was like, i'll be the one he can talk to. but it turns out he was just a dick, and you knew that but you didn't tell me.

Jacob: i did tell you... kinda. i didn't want to go out and bluntly tell you don't go out with him.

IMAQTpieNUlikeit: why not?

Jacob: me and him are in enough shit.[4] dont want to associate with him or talk about him. if you like him you like him.

1. Oh, egotistic.

2. Eh... it's egotistic.

3. But it's egotistic.

4. I can't remember what Jacob was referring to. Apparently, the boys in my class had some issues keeping friendships strong, just like the girls did.

MARCH 27, 2000

"Scattered Pieces"
Walking down a winding road
Surprised at what you didn't find

And stopping when you come to notice
Scattered pieces, left behind.
Settle down and take your time
Gather all the pieces in
You know you can't go on until
You're done. You might as well begin.
Touch your heart and know it well
Close your eyes to feel the pain.
What once was here is shattered now,
But all its pieces still remain.
Let them fit themselves together.
If you give them time, they may.
And when you're finished, when you've healed
Get up again, and be on your way.

I'm really scared. I'm scared of getting older, of not being this age anymore.[1] I know in the future, I'll read this and go, "Wow!"[2] I am doing a good job at this age, I think, figuring everything and everyone out. I've never stopped to consider what will happen when I'm done figuring things out. Then what is there to do?

Anyways, what's the point? The people and things I try to figure out usually don't need to be figured out—they'd be just as well left alone. It's kind of like a puzzle. Yes, each individual person is a puzzle. Once I have all the pieces, I can see the clear picture. But who cares, you know? No one does puzzles because they want to see the picture—if that's all they cared about, they'd just buy the picture and not go through all the trouble of putting it together themselves. People like doing puzzles because it takes skill. Most people have enough skill to put to-

1. That was the silliest fear I've ever had. There are very few things I'm more thankful for now than the fact that I'm not in middle school anymore.

2. Wow! In all seriousness, it would be nice if this could be a two-way conversation. If my thirteen-year-old self were reading this commentary, instead of the other way around, I'd have some advice for her. First of all, stop worrying about manipulating everyone. It's a huge waste of time. And second of all, stop trying to please everyone you're not worried about manipulating. There's no need to be so self-conscious or to feel *on* all the time. Most people are too busy worrying about their own insecurities to notice any of yours. Love, Future Emily.

gether a silly puzzle, but not many people have the skill or the energy to put other people together.

Of course, though, the person is already "together." I just need to reassemble them in my mind.

But back to my point—what does that solve? The whole point of buying a puzzle is so you can put it together. What do you do once you've finished? Pat yourself on the back for being so clever and then start another one? You can't do that with people. I'm really scared. I have this sickening feeling, because I'm always getting older.

MARCH 30, 2000

I realized I kinda liked Steven at Jenna's party. Like, we always flirt, constantly, and... hmmm... we're really good friends. That's why maybe I shouldn't go for him. Plus, he's not gorgeous. Not to say he's ugly or anything! He's far from ugly. And he has five older brothers who all look like movie stars, so when he grows up a little, he'll definitely be hot.[1]

It's just his mouth... There's just something about it. He has braces, and well, so do I, and so do half the people in the eighth grade! There's just something weird about his mouth that I can't put my finger on. So kissing him might not be too desirable. But I'm not sure.

I guess it's just more fun to flirt with him like I do. I like it that way. Maybe I should learn from my experiences with Tyler and not go out with my good friends. But an ideal relationship for me would be to be really good friends, so you can tell each other everything and have complete trust, and to also hook up with them.[2] Anyway, I had this conversation with Tyler about it today:

1. By the way, I was 100% correct in this prediction. He grew up to be the most attractive of all his brothers. With that said, the shallowness of what I considered when deciding whether to date someone is appalling.

2. Still true.

1. OMG Napster. Nothing
sucked more than that moment
when you had downloaded like,
95% of a file from someone,
and then they just canceled it.
That was the worst. In case you
were born after Napster had
died, it was an early file-sharing
program that was used mostly
for downloading free music files
from strangers.

Tyler: why the fuck can't i connect to the napster server?[1]

Me: haha i hate that. give me advice please??

Tyler: advice on what

Me: on steven! seriously, tyler

Tyler: well i've always thought that if you are good friends with a person, you should not go out with them unless you are willing to lose him/her after you break up

Me: have you really ALWAYS thought that?

Tyler: wutever

Tyler: personally after many long tiring discussions with steven i have concluded that he would not go out with you... matt told him you are a slut and he is not into that... but if i persist hard enough he will definitely go out with you... that is if i choose to persist and if you want to go out with him in the first place[2]

Me: no i DONT want to go out with him. because i agree with you about the friends thing.

2. Boys were always reminding
me in sly ways that I was still just
a "slut" in most people's eyes,
as if I might have forgotten it.

APRIL 8, 2000

Not caring. That is definitely the way to go. If you care about anything or anyone too much, you get hurt. It's unavoidable. You can't let anything affect you too deeply, or eventually you'll get that feeling in your stomach, that sickening feeling, as if your guts are getting wrenched around.

I don't know why I'm randomly coming to this realization. Nothing in my life has happened recently to help me discover it, I just thought of it.[3] So that's the way to go: unfeeling. If ever I catch myself

3. Well, chances are I had just
read a book in which the main
character thought of it; books
were always triggering revelations for me.

being extremely happy, I'll have to stop. 'Cause happiness can't go on forever, and as soon as it stops, you begin to plummet toward the opposite extreme. And I hate being depressed so much that I am just not going to take the risk. It's not worth it.[1] And you know what that means. Absolutely never, under any circumstances, must I allow myself to fall in love. That is absolutely out of the question, since infatuation keeps me from thinking as clearly as I normally would.

On another, raunchier note, Hunter has been telling people he wants me to jerk him off. But now he started kind of dating Emma, so thankfully he stopped saying that.[2] Meanwhile, I hate Matt. I hate how he has such disrespect for girls, and how he is so good at pretending to be a nice kid with good intentions. I can't stand it.

APRIL 25, 2000

On May 4–6 is the eighth-grade class trip to New York, which will be beyond fun! Then on June 9 is the semi-formal dance, and my mom is taking me shopping for a dress tomorrow, hopefully. Then we get out of school on June 15! I can't even believe it—this school year has completely flown by. I don't want to go to high school![3] So many things will be different. Jenna is moving away on May 15th, but she's finishing eighth grade here.[4] But she won't be there once we start ninth grade! And James is going to start at Catholic school. I'm going to miss them both so much.

Anyway, this Friday is the last dance before the semi-formal! It is going to be so much fun. Then,

1. I think it's pretty sad that I felt so strongly about this at thirteen years old. I still get nervous about this sometimes, but it's not such an overwhelming anxiety.

2. At the time I had not the faintest idea what this entailed. Someone had told me that "cum" was something that *peeled off of* a boy's penis when it was touched for long enough, so I assumed it had something to do with that. This was before Internet porn was easily accessible. Give me a break.

3. There was never any serious question about where I would be attending high school. My parents had moved to this town, after all, for the purpose of sending me and my siblings to one of the best public high schools in the state. They threatened me with Catholic school every so often, but the only all-girls Catholic school in our area didn't offer as good of an education as the public high school.

4. Jenna had been living with her mom for a while at their new condo in a nearby town, but she also spent the weeknights with her grandparents so she could still attend our school. For high school though, the plan was for her to attend school in her new town.

on Saturday, Daniel is having a party at his house. This is going to be the first party at a boy's house. They never have parties! Well, sometimes on their birthdays they go like, paintballing with a group of friends or something, but they never have big, fun parties.

Today, James pulled me over in the hall to tell me, "Steven's going to ask you out on Friday. I told him to just do it now, but he wants to ask you out then because it's the last dance and it's special or something." I hope he does ask me out at the dance, because I really like him. But before I say yes, I am going to make him promise that no matter what, when we break up we have to stay friends. I feel like I lost one great friendship when Tyler dumped me, and I'm not going to lose another one, ever![1]

The thing I like most about Steven is that he makes me smile. And it's not just a surface smile, like most of my smiles are—it's a genuine smile that starts on the inside and shines its way through to my face.[2]

APRIL 28, 2000

Tonight was the eighth-grade barbecue, which was fun. When all the parents left, we pushed all the tables and chairs up against the back wall and the seventh-graders started arriving for the last dance before the semi-formal. The first slow song was "Where You Are" by Jessica Simpson and Nick Lachey.[3]

Steven came up to me and we started dancing. A little while into the song, he said, "Emily."

"What."

1. Despite my earnest intentions, I've lost other friendships. It happens.

2. Put that on a Hallmark card!

3. Wait. They had a song together?! I had completely forgotten that they both became famous as singers before signing onto the reality show disaster that was *Newlyweds*.

"Will you go out with me." He said it in the same tone he had said, "Emily."

"Yes!" I said, smiling.

"You knew that was coming, didn't you?" He was smiling, too. We talked throughout the rest of the song.

The next slow song was "I Turn to You" by Christina Aguilera. I said, "Can this be our song?"

"Yeah, okay!" he agreed. I love that song. We danced on every slow song after that. On the last song, I wanted so badly for him to kiss me! Our mouths were right next to each other! But we were both too nervous, I guess. Oh, well. Maybe tomorrow!

MAY 1, 2000

Today is Monday. Daniel's party on Saturday night was so fun! Stacy and Daniel started going out, and they hooked up. That is not going to last at all. Once he sees her in a depressed mood, he'll break up with her pretty quickly.[1]

All the guys decided to go out in the front yard and have a "rumble," which is basically just when they all kick each other's ass.[2] Then the girls went out and started getting involved. It's all in fun! I tackled Tyler, but he didn't fall down. Then Steven grabbed me from behind and hooked my arms behind my head in some weird way. I somehow managed to reverse it, and I totally took him out! I was so excited because he's pretty big and strong.

When we were all walking back inside, I noticed that Steven was limping. I asked, "What happened

1. This wasn't general cynicism about relationships. This was foresight given what I knew about how Stacy acted when she was in a bad mood. It was terrifying.

2. I *really* hope they got the idea for a "rumble" from *West Side Story*.

to your foot?"

And he said, "Someone ruined it in the rumble." So Laura and I went upstairs to get some ice for it. We ended up having to listened to Daniel's dad tell every story he could think of in which Steven had been injured, which took a while.[1] When I brought the ice down to Steven, he said he didn't need it, that his foot was fine, even though he was still limping in a major way.

Well, he came to school today on crutches! That's what he gets for not putting ice on it. I tried to convince him that I was the one who sprained his foot when I knocked him over, but he claims that he hurt it playing baseball last week and it just got worse when he was running around so much.

Anyway, James, Daniel, and Stacy started talking about how I had to hook up with Steven. I wanted to, but they were making it stupid, running back and forth between us, carrying messages. Laura came up to me and said, "Okay, Steven's waiting in the bathroom. Go in!" I sighed because I was embarrassed, but I went in.

Steven was leaning against the vanity.[2] I went over and kissed him, but only for a moment before remembering that I needed to lock the door. I went over and did that, and then came back to him. This time, I hopped up on the vanity counter, so that I was facing him with my legs on either side of him. I held his face in my hands as I kissed him so that I could control it. I knew this was his first kiss because James had told me so, but he was a pretty good kisser. A bit sloppy, maybe, but the kiss was enjoyable. We made out for about a half hour, which I'm pretty

1. Steven really was *always* getting injured. I can't decide if he was just being dramatic or if he was exceptionally fragile. He actually walked with a slight limp for his entire childhood after being tackled in an aggressive football game, until finally a sports therapist adjusted his pelvis or something to make his legs the same length again.

2. Oh hey. What's up.

sure is a record for me.

We had to stop for brief intervals so we could both laugh, like when Louis banged on the door and yelled, "Open up! I gotta take a dump!" After we were done laughing, I leaned back so my head was against the mirror, and Steven leaned forward so almost all his weight was on me. We made out like that for a while, but I didn't like it because he has about twenty pounds on me and it was uncomfortable. So I propped myself up on one arm and kept the other one on his lower back.[1]

When we finally came out of the bathroom, all his friends jumped all over him telling him things like, "Good job, man!"[2] Then Louis performed a strip show, which he said was his congratulatory present to Steven. He was actually quite good at it, which is the interesting part. Tyler and Laura hooked up, too. But they decided to stay just friends, because they supposedly don't like each other as anything more, and it was just a "random hookup." Plus, Laura is madly in love with Jacob.

On the bright side, Tyler and I are officially friends again! It really was "official." We didn't just gradually become friends again—we had a nine-page conversation about it online and decided to go back to the way things were before we went out. He now refers to me as his "new old best friend," which I like, and he doesn't have attitude toward me anymore. Like if he says something mean, he'll apologize and say, "just kidding" before I can even react. Good.

1. None of these make-out sessions were especially convenient or comfortable, but we had incredibly limited options for privacy! Not only did we have to be away from parents or teachers but near each other, we also had to find little spaces that would be hidden away from our peers. It was a huge hassle and when we finally figured it out, we were going to *make it happen*.

2. If it seems like everyone was always pressuring other people to hook up and then waiting around for them to finish, it's because that's exactly what was happening.

MAY 2, 2000

Tomorrow is the eighth grade trip to New York City. I'm so excited! I've been looking forward to it all year. I have the best bus—Steven, James, Jacob, Louis, and Tyler are all on it, as well as Laura, Shauna, and Stacy. I was supposed to be on a different bus, but my mom called the school and got them to switch me.

That's because a couple weeks ago, while James was sweeping the hallway, he found a note from Steph. I should explain why he was sweeping the hallway. He had detention for something, I forget what, and that was his punishment: to hang out with the janitor and help him sweep after school. Anyway, he found a folded up piece of paper that was a note from Steph. It's unclear who it was supposed to be written to, but basically it was a "Kill List" and I was on it.

It had like, six or seven names of people with a little description next to them. Most of the people were high schoolers, I think, because I didn't recognize their names. The only ones I recognized were me and Kaylee. Next to my name, it said "fucking slut" and next to Kaylee's name it said, "snob." Anyway, James showed me the note and said he was just going to throw it away, but I took it and gave it to the vice principal, Mr. Jones. After Columbine and everything, I wasn't taking any chances.[1] I mean, Steph is not a social outcast or anything, but she can get pretty freaking scary when she's mad. I don't think Steph knows I was the one who turned the note in because only James knew and he wouldn't say anything, but she got suspended for a week.

1. After the 1999 massacre at Columbine high school in Colorado, everything about school safety culture had changed. In addition to terrifying the nation, it also made everyone suspicious of high school social outcasts since the shooters, Eric Harris and Dylan Klebold, had claimed they were getting revenge for being socially ostracized by their peers.

Anyway, all that is only important because I was supposed to be on Steph's bus for the New York trip.[1] But my mom didn't feel safe with me being in such close proximity to Steph on a bus for so many hours, so she called Mr. Jones and got me switched to a bus with my friends. So it all worked out! I can't wait![2]

MAY 4, 2000

It's exactly midnight and I'm sitting in bed at the Ramada Inn in New Jersey. Jenna is in the shower, Laura is playing with her video camera, which she brought to document the class trip, and Melanie is just getting in bed. Today was the first day of the eighth-grade trip to New York City.

I woke up at three in the morning because the bus was leaving at five and I wanted to get there early to get a good seat. On the bus ride, we watched the movies *10 Things I Hate About You* and *Scream*.[3] I sat with Steven and Laura at different times throughout the ride, but Steven and I didn't hook up.

When we got to New York, the first thing we did was take the ferry to the Statue of Liberty. I climbed it with Tyler and Louis, so I had semi-bonding time with them. But we didn't climb all the way to the top, because we got bored. Then we all took the ferry to Ellis Island. On Ellis Island, I really had bonding time with Steven. We walked around the whole island together with our arms around each other. I liked being so close to him a lot! And I have like, a billion pictures of the two of us together.[4]

At night, we went to the World Trade Center. We all took the elevator up to the 107th floor, where

1. Right. Let's get back to what is really important here: bus assignments. Even though my mom didn't feel safe, I don't think I ever actually believed Steph would act on what she had written in that note. I was more just hurt to be listed on it as a "fucking slut."

2. If such a "Kill List" had surfaced at a middle school today, I feel fairly certain the consequences would have been worse for Steph. At the very least, she wouldn't have been allowed to go on the class trip.

3. Is it just me, or does the latter seems like a particularly terrifying choice for an eighth-grade class trip? The students must have been given some power in deciding which films would be shown on the four tiny TVs hanging from the bus ceiling.

4. Okay, more like seven pictures.

there's a whole exhibit on New York City—also an awesome view.[1] There is a little picture booth there, and Steven and I went in and got our picture taken together. It came out very cutely!

Then things happened. Also at the top of the tower, there was a little movie thing about the city in this little theater. All the seats in the theater were on a platform that moved with the movie, but only slightly. I watched it once and it was really boring.[2] As I was walking out of the theater, Hunter, who was also walking out, pulled me aside and said, "Want to go back in? And like, jump up and down to make the platform stop and they'll have to start the movie over again?"

"Yeah, okay," I said when I realized I had nothing better to do. So I went back in with Hunter and a few of his friends and we sat in the very back. I was next to Hunter and a couple of them sat on the other side of me, and also in front of us. Matt was on the other side of Hunter.

The movie started and Hunter said, "Emily, will you play with my balls?"

I was pretty sure he was joking, so I laughed and said, "Sure, Hunter."

"Okay!" he said, and he seemed surprised that I had agreed to it.

I said, "No, I was just kidding." But he was undoing his belt. I was sitting with my feet up on the back of the seat in front of me. Hunter put his hand that was closest to me on my inner thigh.

Matt reached across Hunter's lap and said, "Emily, let me read your palm." I held out my left hand, palm up, but Matt didn't even look at it. He

1. It's chilling to think that a little over a year later, this tower and the one standing next to it would no longer exist. This detail points to a larger truth about the world my classmates and I inhabited: "Al-Qaeda" and "Bin Laden" meant nothing to us, and "terrorism" wasn't something we'd ever heard about with relation to our country. As soon-to-be-labeled millennials with no perception of any real danger threatening us, we tried to emulate the "slacker" mindset and aversion to authority that Generation X teenagers before us had made cool.

2. Bo-ring! Just like the Statue of Liberty.

just gripped it and put it down Hunter's boxers. My fingers touched Hunter's dick, and Matt didn't even let go. It wasn't hard or anything, it just felt like a lot of blobby skin. Then some of the boys started jumping up and down to stop the platform, and the lights came on and the movie stopped. I jumped away from Hunter and got up to leave the theater.

As we were leaving, I said, "Hunter, please don't tell anyone." He said he wouldn't. But Matt knows, too. The only two people I told are Laura and Melanie. I am not going to tell anyone else! I cheated on Steven, and I feel so horrible.[1]

On the bus ride to the hotel from the World Trade Center, I was getting annoyed with him, but maybe that was just because of my guilt. I hope, hope, HOPE he never finds out, but I think that might mean I can't go out with him anymore, if there's always going to be that lie between us. I don't even know why I didn't stop Matt and Hunter. Maybe I wanted to prove to myself that I'm not a prude. I don't know.[2]

MAY 6, 2000

It's about 8 a.m. on Saturday morning, and we're on the bus going home. Okay, so now to write about yesterday, one of the weirdest, worst days of my entire life. First off, the main point is that Steven found out about what I did with Hunter. After we toured the United Nations headquarters, we had to go on a three-hour tour around the harbor on a big ferry. At the beginning of the ferry ride, Laura, Shauna, Jacob, Tyler, Steven, and I were sitting on the top deck getting tans. I hadn't really been talk-

1. What had happened in the theater was absolutely not cheating. It's so backward that my first impulse was to beg Hunter not to tell anyone what had happened; what I should have been doing was running to tell a teacher myself.

2. I hate how I blamed myself for this. It's as if my reputation as a "slut" was all I had, and I went along with Matt and Hunter for fear of losing that identity. Or maybe I believed that I truly was a "slut" on such a deep level that it didn't seem possible to make sexual decisions for myself. I don't believe either of them intended to hurt me; rather, I think they assumed that because of my reputation, I had given ongoing, indiscriminate consent to all sexual advances.

ing to Steven too much all day. I told James what happened, and he advised me to wait until after the New York trip to confess to Steven, so it wouldn't ruin the trip for him.

But Lisa came over and said, "Steven, I need to talk to you." As they walked away, she threw me a look like she thought I was just about the most disgusting thing she'd ever seen, and I knew that she knew. I also knew that she was going to tell Steven. Laura nudged me and looked worried. After about ten minutes, Steven came back and sat down again. He didn't say anything, and for a second I had a surge of hope that maybe he didn't know. But he whispered something to Tyler, and then got up and left with his face all twisted up like he was trying not to cry. I felt tears welling up in my own eyes, and asked Laura to come to the bathroom with me.

When we got to the bathroom, Melanie was there, and she said, "Emily, everyone knows. Including Steven." All the girls who had been in the bathroom left immediately because I was there, and they obviously didn't want to be anywhere near me. I started to cry because I felt like such a horrible bitch.[1] All I could think about was how crushed Steven must be.

Emma came down to the bathroom and said, "I was just talking to Steven. He's very upset, Emily. He hates you now, and so do we." By "we" she meant like, all the girls in the grade.

I started to say, "But it wasn't my fault," or something along those lines, but she put up a hand and said, "Enough, Emily." Then she started to walk away, but I said, "Wait! Can I talk to him?"

1. Our assumption that I was somehow to blame for what had happened in the theater demonstrates just how deeply my female classmates and I had internalized the culture's misogyny. Even having been there, having experienced it, and *knowing* that I hadn't initiated or consented to it, I still blamed myself for letting it happen.

She said, "Whatever," and ran up the stairs. I put on sunglasses so nobody else could see that I was crying. A few minutes later, Steven came down. He put his hand on my back and led me over to somewhere where we could talk in private.

The first thing I said was, "I am so sorry."

He shrugged. "I guess I'm just disappointed," he said.

"The last thing I want to do is hurt you at all," I told him, and then continued to explain that it was the biggest mistake I've ever made and that if he hated me forever, I wouldn't blame him one bit.

He was silent for a moment and then he said, "I don't hate you, Emily. Everyone makes mistakes. I mean, I like you so much—I just can't forget about those feelings."[1] Hearing him say that made me start crying again, and I could see that he was already crying, too. I wanted to wipe away the tears from his face, but I was afraid that he wouldn't want me to touch him.

We sat there for the rest of the ferry ride talking. Hunter came by and apologized to both of us. He said he hadn't really known what was happening in the theater, and that Matt had taken my hand without his permission. Steven and I decided to stay going out, and have him try to regain trust in me. I couldn't believe he was being so good about it. I felt so horrible for putting him through that.

We ate dinner in the All-Star Cafe in Times Square, which is really cool inside. I sat with Melanie and Laura because none of the other girls would speak to me. But Steven came over and said, "Emily, will you sit with me at *Beauty and the Beast*?" I smiled

1. I am really impressed by Steven's ability to prioritize our entire history over a single act of perceived infidelity. This is something a lot of adults can't manage to do. With that said, I shouldn't have needed his forgiveness in the first place.

and said yes. We went to see *Beauty and the Beast* on Broadway, and it was the best show I've ever seen![1] Steven and I sat next to each other. During the second act, he had his elbow on the armrest between us, and I pushed it off with my elbow. Instead of pushing it back, he put his arm around my shoulders. I snuggled against him and held his hand. When it was time to applaud, I took his hand and used it to clap with my other hand.

On the bus ride back to the hotel, I fell asleep on his shoulder. When I woke up, I was bothered by something. So I said, "Steven? Do you forgive me?"[2] I said it softly, because it was very dark on the bus and everyone was sleeping and I felt like talking louder would ruin the calm.

"Yes," he answered.

"Do you promise?" I asked, even softer this time.

"Yes, I promise. It was a stupid mistake, and you deserve a second chance."[3] I loved him so much right then, and I knew that he must love me, too, otherwise he wouldn't put up with me. I will never make such a stupid mistake again, I promise myself.

MAY 8, 2000

It's Monday, and I forgot to write about the rest of the bus ride home from the class trip! Steven and I hooked up. He was sitting next to me with his back to the window, and I was lying in his arms. We were both listening to "Against All Odds" by Mariah Carey on the same Discman on repeat.[4] I liked that, because it made me feel like we were in our own little world, since we couldn't hear anything going on around us. We weren't making out at first, we

1. It really was magnificent. I still remember the spectacle of amazingness that was "Be Our Guest." Come to think of it, I'm not entirely sure how the school managed to pay for 150 student tickets to a show like this. Our parents must have signed off on it as they signed checks to fund the rest of the trip. At any rate, it's a relief to know that I was able to enjoy part of the trip to New York, despite everything. I was already interested in musical theater, and seeing that production of *Beauty and the Beast* solidified my love for it.

2. ...Even though there's absolutely nothing to forgive?

3. Mmkay, thanks, but I didn't need a "second chance" since there was nothing to forgive.

4. Discmans were the worst way to listen to music, but they were ubiquitous at this time. Whatever CD you were trying to listen to would inevitably skip every time you shifted in your seat—forget about trying to take a Discman on a run.

were just lying there with our eyes closed. His face was nuzzled in my neck, and I wanted to kiss him. So I wrapped the arm closest to him around his neck backwards, and he tilted his face upward and kissed me. We must have made out for ten minutes or more. We were in our own little world—I didn't even care that everyone could see us if they wanted to. Nobody has been speaking to me except Steven, James, Laura, and Melanie.

Then Emma bumped into my legs hard. I looked up and saw that it was a good thing, because Mr. Jones was coming back to collect trash. We stopped making out, but I think he had already seen us. He didn't say anything, though.

We stopped for dinner when we were about an hour from home. It was then that I found out that Daniel had broken up with Stacy. I should feel at least a little bad for her. But I don't, at all. Today in English class, she randomly started crying... and not just crying, like bawling. Then she stormed out and didn't come back. What a weirdo. She's such a head case—I don't even attempt to be her friend anymore. It's too much of an unnecessary hassle.[1]

MAY 10, 2000

"Your Life"

Your life is passing by so fast
You wish to catch it, hold it still
But time does not stop at your will.
When you are young, you wish to grow
When you are old, you've grown too far
You're never happy with what you are.
You're always building memories

1. I'm embarrassed about how little empathy I had for Stacy. It wasn't that I couldn't relate to her struggles—I certainly could—as much as that I didn't respect this kind of public emotional display. Making sure to cry in private was on my list of rules to live by—more on that list later—and I expected my friends to show some self control, even if I didn't always adhere to that rule myself.

But think about it this way, too:

Your memories are building you.

You'll never figure out who you are

Though most people spend their whole lives trying

We're all the same—we are all dying.

MAY 18, 2000

I can't even believe that school is over in less than a month! We get out this year on June 15th. There is a dance tomorrow night, and it is the last dance ever aside from the semi-formal, which is on the 9th.[1] Anyways, I love how me and Steven are! He is so adorable—he really, truly cares about me and wants me to be happy. We act like very, very good friends in that we always fool around and sneak up on each other and try to beat each other up all the time. He calls me every night at about 8 o'clock, and we talk until my parents make me get off the phone.

An interesting thing about Steven is that he is the youngest of six boys in his family. The oldest three are in college, but one of them was my camp counselor two summers ago. One of them is a high school senior this year, and one is a junior. They are all very hot. So my point is that Steven is going to be very hot when he gets older. Not that he isn't already.

Oh yeah and one more thing, completely unrelated. I am in the school play in a week. Right now, it's very sucky, but I get to sing a pretty solo. So even if the play blows, at least I get to sing.[2]

1. The last dance. EVER.

2. I had always known I enjoyed singing and I'd been participating in community musical theater since I was five years old. At the beginning of middle school, a teacher had encouraged me to audition for the children's chorus at the New England Conservatory Preparatory School and it was always a welcome escape to spend Saturday mornings surrounded by kids from other schools who had no idea about my reputation. Around this time, I started to realize that I wanted to learn how to be a *solo* singer; a few months after I wrote this diary entry, my parents would enroll me in classical voice lessons, also at NEC Prep. That cultivation of singing as a skill made me proud of myself and was a huge catalyst in helping me redefine myself as something other than a "slut" when I got to high school.

MAY 21, 2000

Today is Sunday. The last dance was on Friday, and it was such a blast! Steven's older brother was chaperoning and everyone was going crazy over how gorgeous he is. He is beautiful, but he seems like a bit of a conceited asshole, because he was making fun of Steven right in front of me. It really embarrassed Steven, I could tell.

Speaking of Steven, he and I are so cool! I absolutely love our relationship. It's not just like we are going out, it's like we're really good friends, too. We fool around so much: at the dance, a bunch of guys had on these jumpsuits that gas station workers wear.[1] They got hot in them so they took them off and dared Steven to wear one. He did, and then convinced me to wear one, too.

I felt like such a dork, but in a good way, because Steven and I started to tango.[2] But Laura told me that Emma and some other girls said that my suit was an "easy access" outfit, since it zipped all the way down the front.

Anyways, almost at the end of the dance, they played "Graduation" by Vitamin C. It made me think. I don't really want to leave eighth grade. A lot of my friends are going to different high schools or moving, and it just seems like way too much is ending way too fast. I want to cling onto what's left of being the way I am now, since I know I'll change, too.

MAY 23, 2000

Tonight I talked on the phone with Steven and Jacob, on Jacob's three-way. It was the first time I'd talked on the phone with Jacob in a while. Well, I mean

1. Of course. Didn't you ever wear a jumpsuit like this to a school dance? No?

2. And by "tango," I mean "prance around with a serious look on our faces." Because we definitely had no idea what the tango actually was. It was just a fun excuse to play around at dancing that wasn't hypersexualized grinding.

besides the times we've called each other to like, organize trips to the movies or something. This was also the first time I've had a long conversation with him and not started liking him romantically. I realize now that I couldn't ever feel that way again—that thing I loved about him that I couldn't identify is gone, now.[1]

And that is definitely a good thing. Laura likes him SO much, and when I see the way he teases her heart it nearly makes me sick. Laura is under the impression that he likes her, and she has reason. He flirts with her constantly, and he told some people last week that he did like her.

But tonight he told me and Steven that he definitely didn't, and that he had KINDA liked her about a week ago, but then changed his mind. That does not seem the least bit fair to Laura.[2] He led her on in a major way and he knew that she had feelings for him! I told him that he needs to be straightforward with her, but he acted as if he didn't want to talk about it. So I don't know what's up with that, but I hope for Laura's sake that it gets figured out.

On another note, school gets out on June 15th! It's only sixteen school days, because we get Memorial Day off. All that's left now is the play, a nature field trip thing, and the semi.[3] We have to go on this nature field trip to a nearby reserve where we can do kayaking or ropes courses, and then we have orientation for high school where they tell us about all the different sports and clubs we can do. They divide the class into two parts for the field trip. While one half is on the nature field trip, the other half is watching *Schindler's List*. It's 'cause we're starting a unit on the Holocaust.

1. What a tragic way to word that.

2. Actually, it seems supremely fair to Laura. Why should he continue to lead her on after realizing he didn't like her romantically? Especially given my history of drawing things out for a long time with Jacob, I should have seen this as an indication that he had grown up a bit.

3. "Semi" is short for "semi-formal dance," and I cannot stress enough how important the semi was. Despite the attire prescribed in the event's very name, we treated it as if it were a formal prom.

And then the semi! That will be the ultimate. I have a hair appointment and I am making Steven buy me a corsage. I know the summer will be fun, but I'm so scared of getting older. I don't want to be in high school.

MAY 24, 2000

Rules to Live By:

- Never be mean to someone who doesn't deserve it, or is never mean to you.
- If someone you're in a relationship with makes you cry more than you would otherwise, stick to otherwise.[1]
- Always keep a diary, so you can look back and see how you've changed.
- Don't reminisce too much, or you'll be depressed.
- Try to look people in the eye when you talk with them.[2]
- Don't cry in front of a lot of people, because they'll think you just want attention. Crying alone or with a friend is more therapeutic.[3]
- Never buy junk.
- Don't complain about things that can be fixed—fix them.
- Always expect the worst, in order to jinx it into not happening.[4]
- Don't boast, because then people will expect too much from you and will be disappointed.[5]
- Although looks are not everything, they are a first impression.
- Don't eat out of boredom.[6]
- Laugh at yourself.

1. I was really proud of that clever phrasing.

2. This one came from my parents. I was always distracted and trying to multitask while they gave me instructions or asked me important questions. I've taken this rule to heart, and still try to live by it whenever the person I'm talking with cooperates.

3. Well this explains why I was so impatient with Stacy's public displays of emotion.

4. This can't *possibly* work.

5. Also just don't boast. It's obnoxious.

6. For example... what I'm doing right now.

MAY 25, 2000

Tonight was the opening night of the play I'm in that the school is putting on. I get to sing a song all by myself! I know the song REALLY well, and it is such a pretty song, but the whole class was there and I was so nervous! But everything went beautifully. When I finished singing, the clapping went on forever. Steven stood up and pointed to the stage and yelled, "That's my girlfriend!" I felt so happy that he was proud of me. After the show, literally a million people I didn't even know came up to me to tell me how great I was.[1]

A random sophomore that I've never had a conversation with came up to me and said, "I just want you to know that you were what made this show worth coming to. The rest was pretty boring, but you were so good!" I wish I could have done more than just smile and say thank you.

Another sophomore, Alex, came up to me and gave me a huge kiss on the cheek. "You were AMAZING," he gushed. "Just wonderful." I love that kid so much. He is openly gay and his brother, who is in my grade, is ashamed of him. But I think he is the coolest person.[2] Gina bought me flowers, which was awesome of her. I am on such a happy cloud right now. Nothing could ruin this night for me.

MAY 30, 2000

I was supposed to go to Melanie's family's summerhouse for Memorial Day weekend, but it was rainy so they decided not to go down. On Friday night, there was the other performance of the school play

1. Rounding up to a million. (Way up.)

2. Alex was the first openly gay person I knew, and I'm glad I met him when I did. Meeting him and, soon after, other openly gay people around my own age directly correlated with a sharp drop-off in my use of "gay" as a substitute for anything bad in my everyday language.

and it went well again. I wasn't nervous because no one I knew was there.

On Saturday, Jenna came over and we walked into town and bought Coolattas at Dunkin' Donuts, which reminded me that summer will be here in no time and I can count on filling it up with trips into town and low-fat hazelnut coffee Coolattas, just like last year.

On Saturday night, I went to the movies with Laura, Melanie, Shauna, and Erin. Louis, Tyler, and Steven were at Louis's family's summerhouse, so our usual guy posse was MIA.[1] On Sunday, Jenna came over again.

Oh, wait—I forgot that I slept over Laura's on Saturday night. That was fun, because we had major bonding time. Laura's one of my best friends, which is coolness[2] because I've known her for less than a year. But she's so like me that I trust her with everything. Anyways, when I was at her house, we finished watching the movie that she made of the New York trip, which is really coolness! And a wonderful memory. When Jenna was over on Sunday, we watched it again, and I made a copy of it for myself so that I can have it to keep.

Anyways! On Monday, there was an adorable message from Steven on my answering machine. He had promised he'd call, and I guess I wasn't home, so he left a message. What a sweetie! I love him to pieces!

1. Oh, right. This is around the time I started actively adopting lingo from *Seventeen* magazine like "posse" and "MIA."

2. Another term I kept trying to make happen: "coolness."

JUNE 7, 2000

Today is Wednesday and the semi is on Friday! I'm so beyond excited and psyched for it! We're all going over Maggie's house at 5:30 to get ready and put on makeup and such, and then we're meeting the guys at the school at 7:30 when the dance starts. I absolutely can't wait!

Today, Steven did the cutest thing. I saw him before seventh period in front of the Social Studies room, where he was headed. I was going downstairs to Language Arts, and I stopped to talk with him for a moment. I need to explain something quickly before I continue though, okay?[1] Steven's friends like Tyler, Jacob, Louis, and James all tease him and call him "Emily's Bitch" because he usually does nice things for me if I ask him the right way.[2] But I know he's not my "bitch"—he's just a really nice boy and he wants to make me happy. Anyways, in front of the Social Studies room, Steven took my Language Arts binder and assignment notebook and put them on top of his Social Studies stuff.

He said, "If I walk into Social Studies with all these books, people will think I'm really smart!"

We both laughed and I said, "You want to hold my books? You like it?"

"No!" He laughed, and tried to give them back to me.

But I touched his arm and looked into his eyes with my most wide-eyed, puppy-dog look. "Please? Walk me to my next class."

He sighed, giving in, and laughed. "That always works for you... that look." And he carried my books down the stairs.[3]

1. Okay.

2. This is some multilayered sexism! Why would doing something nice with the purpose of serving someone else make someone a "bitch"—a derogatory word for a woman? The misogyny here worked against Steven, even as a boy.

3. For the record, "that look" only works if you're trying to get someone to carry your books down the stairs to Language Arts class and not in many other situations.

On the way, we passed James, who said, "No way, Steven. Stop it!" But Steven just laughed.

We also saw Emma, who smiled and said nastily, "Steven, Emily's got you wrapped around her finger."

Doing what I do to him to anyone else could probably be considered manipulation. But he is completely aware of what I pull off, and we joke about how he can't resist my looks, when I bat my eyelashes and say, "Please?" He tries it on me sometimes, too, as a joke. Anyways, when we got to the bottom of the stairs I took my books from him and had the sudden urge to kiss him on the cheek, so I did. And so what if I have him "wrapped around my finger," as Emma put it? He has me wrapped around his finger, too. I would do absolutely anything for Steven, I love him so much. I feel so close to him—he's one of my best friends as well as my boyfriend. I hope we go out for a very long time! I don't want to lose such an amazing person.

JUNE 9, 2000

It's 3:30 p.m. I just got home from school, and in fifteen minutes I'm going to get my hair done for the semi. I'm SO excited about it! Today was high school orientation day, and the eighth grade went up to visit the high school. From what I saw, it seemed much more laid-back than the middle school. I'm looking forward to going there next year, but I'm also kind of scared. The sophomores, juniors, and seniors will just be so HUGE! And I'll feel like a loser freshman. So many of them already know me as a slut, and I'm scared to actually have to face them every day.[1]

1. I'd had enough interactions with older kids whose names I didn't know yelling things at me out their car windows or pretending to try to hit on me that it *felt* like everyone at the high school cared about my "slut" label.

Anyway, Steven and I were hanging out all day. He's just so cool to be with! I feel like he's my great friend along with my boyfriend. All the upperclassmen at the high school know him because of his older brothers, and they were like, "Hey, Steven, SHE is your girlfriend?" He didn't care. I felt like he was proud of me, and I liked that feeling.[1]

Then after school today, I gave him a hug and he said, "I'll see you at 7:30."

I said, "Don't forget to tell me how beautiful I look!" and we both laughed.

He said, "I won't, don't worry. You always look beautiful." The things he says just make me want to cry, he's so adorable!

I gave him another hug and said, "I love you to pieces!" And he gave me a kiss on the cheek. Oooh! I can't wait for tonight! But now I gotta go get my hair done.

JUNE 11, 2000

Today is Sunday. The semi-formal on Friday could easily be called the most magical night of my life. It's not that any specific event or events made it that way, it was just the whole atmosphere about it. My hair was done in a mass of perfectly shaped, bobby-pinned, and hair-sprayed curls on the back/top of my head, with tiny twists of hair leading into it around my whole head, topped with a gorgeous tiara. All of my friends got their hair done similarly, but none with a tiara. With my lavender, ballroom-style prom dress, I felt like Cinderella.[2]

The decorations at the dance were spectacular. The theme was Hollywood 2000 and the walls were

1. It seems so strange that these high school students knew about my reputation and, apparently, cared about it.

2. Did I mention I had a tiara?

covered with creative representations of famous movies all throughout the past century, like *The Wizard of Oz* and even *South Park*! There was also an entire corner devoted to snacks, complete with a fake popcorn machine.[1]

Steven looked adorable in his suit and tie, as did all the other guys. I was with Steven almost the whole night, and he got me a rose! I felt like a princess dancing in his arms, especially when he lifted me around the waist so my toes were just above the ground and danced with me like that for a whole song, so we could really be "cheek to cheek." All in all, the evening was amazing. I'll put a picture in here when I get them developed.

JUNE 15, 2000

Well, today was the last day of school. There was a graduation ceremony for the eighth-graders in the new gym from 8:30 to 10:30 a.m. Then we signed yearbooks from 10:30 to 12:15, when we went to lunch. At 12:45, we went back into the new gym for more ceremonious stuff, which lasted until school ended at 2:15.

At the graduation ceremony, each teacher gave out awards to their students who did the best. I received a Certificate of Excellence from the music, theater, science, and algebra teachers, the Middle School Language Arts Award for writing, and a Certificado de Mérito from the Spanish teacher "por su excelente trabajo en español."[2] And then everyone received a "Certificate of Award" from the principal for "Completion of Studies."

Anyways, I'm very sad that school's over, but I'm

1. This is truly shocking. Why was it *fake*? How disappointing for people who like popcorn.

2. Man, I *cleaned up* at that middle school graduation awards ceremony. Being recognized for my schoolwork in that way really boosted my self-esteem. I didn't realize it was happening at the time, but academic encouragement from my parents and certain teachers helped me redefine myself when I got to high school.

also excited for the summer. The yearbook is cool, because the eighth-graders got to write a little "bio" next to their picture. But we wrote them in February, so they're a little outdated now. Mine says:

Emily Lindin
Quote: "Right... do your thing."[1]
Memories: parties, summer99, vids, gr7spn, VSS, LinsCasa, SB, s7[2]

All in all, I got sixty-nine signatures. Last year I got seventy, which is counting stupid ones that just say, "Have a good summer" and nothing personal. I hate those,'cause where's the memory there? In sixth grade, I only got twenty-nine signatures because everyone hated me.[3]

High school seems so scary! And there will be so much more responsibility, and... I don't know. I can't do anything except deal with it. Oh, well.

1. I guess I wanted people to think I said this a lot.

2. Parties, summer99, okay... and you lost me. Here are my guesses at what the other references mean: "vids" likely referred to the home movies I sometimes filmed with Stacy, Melanie, and whichever other people happened to be around. Gr7spn has got to be "Grade 7 Spanish," which was apparently a monumental class for me. Oh! I do remember what "VSS" was. It was an acronym for Very Secret Society, which is what I had named a group of friends including Laura, Shauna, Melanie, and Stacy, I think. But LinsCasa, SB, and s7 are indecipherable to me.

3. I'm not sure how well I did on yearbook signatures relative to the other students in my class. There was always pressure to get as many personal notes as possible, if only to prove to yourself that people cared whether you had a good summer.

egs were still hanging over th
e couch. My body was kind of
got up, picked up my feet, put
e couch, and then lay back do
e. I put my hands on the ba
, and he nuzzled his face into
y neck. But we didn't kiss for
, because of me and my stupi
as really scared and nervous,
making dumb excuses like, "Bu
th smells like ████████" (we had al
shots ████ earlier). But finally
d. It was different than the
It was better physically, but
e was...nothing. It ended, and I
████████ was sitting on a really
h his feet on the top rung, eat
etzals and watching us inten
"Wanna go ████ to second?" I n
e started to stick his fingers

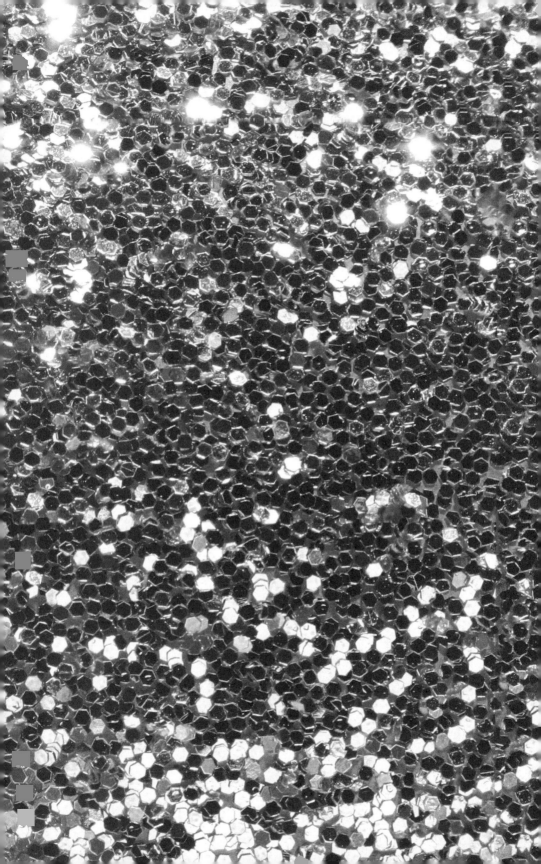

AFTERWORD

BY EMILY LINDIN

High school was scary at first. My reputation had followed me, and for the first few months as a freshman, I continued to be regarded as a "slut" by older boys and by girls my own age. But soon, my reputation dissipated, and by the time I graduated in 2004, I was known more for my involvement in musical theater and my heated, passionate debating in conversations during my honors classes than for my sexual behavior. I dated Steven all through high school as well, so people soon lost interest in my newly monogamous love life. I still love writing, though now it's mostly academic in nature. I am currently completing a PhD in music history. Those passions that helped me work through sexual bullying in middle school—writing and singing—have turned into a fulfilling career path for me.

But now that we've gotten through my diary together, let's take a step back and assess what just happened. I'm talking about not only what happened back when I was in middle school, but also about what happened while I was creating this book with the knowledge and intent that you would read it. I can say with near certainty that while my experience of being labeled a "slut" was by no means rare, the experience of reading through my detailed diary from middle school, posting it online for the world to comment upon, and then revisiting it and re-commenting upon it myself during this process of turning it into a book probably is unique. And it has been a bizarre learning experience for me. I am not yet sure of all the things I'll end up having learned from it, but what I can say is that it has taught me just how important it is to forgive myself—my past self and my present self. Let me explain.

We make each decision in life with very limited information: only what we've gleaned from our experiences up to that point. Later, new experiences—including whatever the result of our decision turned out to be—inform our perspective and might make us wish we had done things differently. And we always have the knowledge that this process of reflection will occur sometime in the future: "What if I choose the wrong thing now and regret this later?" It can cause us a lot of anxiety and even cripple us when the decisions we're faced with seem monumental. Like, for instance, the decision to publish your middle school diaries in all their angst-ridden, self-absorbed messiness.

So back in 2013, as I was reading through my old diary entries, I began to forgive myself for what I couldn't possibly have known fifteen years earlier. When I decided to drink vodka at Matt's house on that afternoon in 1998, everything I had experienced socially so far had taught me that in order to be happy, I needed certain "popular" people to like me, and in order for those people to like me, I needed to emulate their behavior. When I acted like a flat-out ridiculous person for the sake of my love for Zach, I hadn't yet learned that real romantic love doesn't make you constantly question whether you're good enough—it brings out the best in you and makes you love yourself more. When I seriously considered taking my own life, I didn't yet understand how permanent, how final, that decision would be. I have forgiven myself for these things, and that's how I can find humor—or at least poignancy—in what might seem from the outside like a tragedy.

But perhaps more importantly, when I chose to post those diaries online and eventually to create this book, I made a decision on behalf of my future self. I decided that Future Emily would have to forgive my current self for whatever the outcome turned out to be. This is an ongoing process, obviously, since I'm technically always becoming Future Emily. I didn't know then that my middle school diary would strike such a chord with so many readers. I was terrified that it would just make people angry and that they would harass or even physically harm my parents (who still live in the town I grew up in) or me. But all the information I had in the spring of 2013 compelled me to move forward with The UnSlut Project.

By the beginning of 2015, The UnSlut Project was making a lot of progress. "'Slut' shaming" was on its way to becoming a household term, and I began booking lectures and workshops around North America to start conversations within schools and communities. Stories of personal experiences were being submitted daily from women who had survived sexual bullying. For the most part, I was no longer afraid of the backlash from people who didn't believe in stopping "slut" shaming or who personally attacked me for speaking out. Any anger or harassment directed at me for trying to change this part of our culture was, I figured, just further evidence that there was indeed a problem. But there were times I was grateful to be using a pseudonym for a reason I hadn't anticipated: my own physical safety. Any woman using an online platform to write or otherwise share her voice publicly will tell you that the Internet is a deeply misogynist place. Even women covering topics that have nothing to do with sex are the targets of gendered harassment. Since my activism focused on "slut" shaming, I was the recipient of many sexist e-mails, tweets, and messages from people who just wanted me to shut up and stop trying to change things. With that said, the response was still overwhelmingly positive, and the project began receiving a lot of international media attention and publicity opportunities. Some of those opportunities came from media sources with huge followings. That was fantastic, on the one hand, because it meant a ton of people would learn about The UnSlut Project; but on the other hand, it also made it quite likely that people who knew me from middle school would stumble across The UnSlut Project and realize who Emily Lindin really was.

I didn't know what would happen then. I tried to imagine how I would react if I found out that some random person I hadn't thought about since middle school had made her diaries from that time public. Maybe I would vaguely recall that she had been known as the "school slut," but I wouldn't be able to remember all the details of the rumors that had been spread about her. Had I been one of the people who bullied her? Had she mentioned me in her diary?

I was especially worried about Steph. She had been terrible to me in middle school, yes, but nearly two decades had passed since then and, based on her Facebook posts, it looked like she had grown into a strong, kind woman. I imagined we might even be friends in real life today. I didn't want her to think that I had any resentment left toward her, or that I was trying to hurt her by making my diaries public. As it turned out, I was right about the woman she had become. When she heard about The UnSlut Project, she messaged me: "I'm sorry for hurting you when we were younger. I was young and stupid and wanted to be like everyone else. You were my best friend and I should not have turned my back on you." In the brief messages we exchanged after that, it became clear that talking about what we had been through, what we had done to each other, and how we had worked through it could be healing for both of us.

Soon after, I received a message from the woman whose name I had changed to "Jenna." We had faded out of each other's lives in high school, though we remained on good terms. In her message, Jenna wrote that she felt very sad to learn about what I had gone through, that she didn't remember any of it happening to me, but that she was happy I was turning it into something positive. I was shocked. How could Jenna not remember?! More than anyone else, she had been the person who went through all the sexual bullying right there with me. It seemed absurd that she could have just blocked out all those memories. But when I attempted to put myself in her position, I realized that it actually wasn't that strange for her to have forgotten. After all, if I hadn't had my diaries as a primary source, chances are good that I wouldn't have remembered with any real clarity the types of things Jenna had been through either, or the experiences of anyone else I had known back then, for that matter. That's not only because we were so self-absorbed at the time—although we were, certainly— but because after nearly two decades, memories fade. Details get lost. We remember most people from our adolescence in terms of how they shaped our own lives, rather than hold onto any perception of what they might have been going through on their own.

Well, once Jenna started reading my diaries, it was a different story. Almost immediately after she began reading, she messaged me asking, "Am I Jenna?????" I confirmed that she was, in fact, Jenna. I wondered how knowing that would change her reading experience. She continued to send me messages throughout the day as she read, reflecting upon what she remembered and what she had completely forgotten, guessing who different "characters" actually were in real life, and declaring how thankful she was that we hadn't had social media back then. Even though it dredged up a lot of memories she had been happy to forget, reading about our middle school years from my perspective seemed to be, overall, a positive experience for her.

The next day, I got another message. This one was from the man whose name I had changed to Tyler. Since my diary had been up on Wattpad, some of the readers had chosen "teams" based on the different boys my middle school self had been involved with. Team Tyler was one of the most popular among readers, since Tyler had almost always been kind to me, if a little creepy sometimes. I remembered Tyler as being hilarious in an understated way, and his message confirmed that he hadn't changed much in that regard. It said simply: "#TeamTyler." I assumed Jenna had filled him in about The UnSlut Project, but he told me that "Louis" had sent him a link to it months earlier! It made me feel a little silly to learn that they had known about The UnSlut Project for a while, but mostly I felt relieved that they had respected my privacy and that they were, apparently, on board with the project's goals. I'm sure that with the publication of this book, there will be many more messages from the "characters" in it as they recognize themselves and others. Some of them might disagree with the mission of The UnSlut Project, or perhaps they will just think I'm weird for being comfortable with sharing my middle school diaries with the world. But I feel bolstered by the acceptance, support, and mutual healing that have come, so far, from my newfound connections with people from that time in my life.

It is my hope that *UnSlut: A Diary and a Memoir* and The UnSlut Project's ongoing work will contribute to an incredibly important shift in the cultural attitude surrounding female sexuality here in North America and, of course, in countries around the world. By recognizing and confronting our own prejudices, by starting conversations with compassion and confidence, and by refusing to enforce harmful norms and myths, we can all work toward change within our own communities and on a larger, societal level. Soon, if all goes well, the word "slut" won't even make sense as an insult.

RESOURCES

SELF-HARM OR SELF-INJURY

KIDSHEALTH.ORG

http://m.kidshealth.org/teen/your_mind/mental_health/cutting.
html

Provides extensive information on cutting as self-harm and what it is, and offers helpful resources for getting help and staying healthy.

ADOLESCENT SELF INJURY FOUNDATION

http://www.adolescentselfinjuryfoundation.com

Informs on adolescent self-injury and focuses on recovery, with step-by-step guides on ways to help friends, yourself, and others.

SEXUAL HEALTH

SCARLETEEN

http://www.scarleteen.com

A "sex ed for the real world," Scarleteen provides teens with straightforward information, nonjudgmental support, and advice on anything from sexual identity and gender to relationships to sex and sexual health. There's also a section on abuse and assault, and there are pages where other teens share their stories and ask questions.

SEX, ETC.

http://sexetc.org

A comprehensive sex-ed website written by teens, for teens, with articles and stories to promote a healthy sexual attitude.

SEXPLANATIONS

https://www.youtube.com/user/sexplanations

Hosted by clinical sexologist Dr. Lindsey Doe, this web show aims to inform on sex education and promote sex positivity with real, accurate facts.

TEENSOURCE

http://www.teensource.org

Originally developed by the California Family Health Council, this website provides sexual and reproductive health information and resources.

CRISIS HELP FOR BULLYING

CRISIS HOTLINE AND HELP CENTERS BY STATE

http://www.suicidepreventionlifeline.org/getinvolved/locator

CRISIS CALL CENTER

800-273-8255 or text ANSWER to 839863

http://crisiscallcenter.org/crisisservices.html

A GIRL'S GUIDE TO END BULLYING

http://girlsguidetoendbullying.org/

A campaign devoted to ending all bullying, with sections focusing specifically on physical bullying, verbal bullying, sexual bullying, relational bullying, and cyberbullying.

SUICIDE PREVENTION

TO WRITE LOVE ON HER ARMS

http://twloha.com/

A nonprofit organization devoted to helping those struggling with addiction, depression, self-injury, and suicidal thoughts. The movie *To Write Love On Her Arms* was produced to bring awareness to the organization and tell the story of how TWLOHA got started.

THE TREVOR PROJECT

866-4-U-TREVOR (488-7386)

http://www.thetrevorproject.org

A leading national organization in crisis intervention and suicide prevention services to LGBTQ youth. They have trained counselors on call 24/7.

NATIONAL SUICIDE PREVENTION LIFELINE

1-800-273-TALK

http://www.suicidepreventionlifeline.org/

This lifeline is open twenty-four hours a day, seven days a week, and will connect you with a trained counselor operating at a crisis center in your area.

FEMINIST SUPPORT

EVERYDAY FEMINISM

http://everydayfeminism.com/

An online magazine advocating for equality for all people, with articles on sexual consent, "slut" shaming, sexism, and much more.

MS.

http://www.msmagazine.com/

Launched in the 1970s, *Ms.* is still today a leading national magazine in women's rights and journalism.

FEMINISTING

http://feministing.com/

Celebrating women and "feministing" the Internet to inspire a feminist world. This site has lots of fun articles on pop culture, thoughtful pieces on politics, and op-eds in support of feminism and equal rights.

BITCH

http://bitchmagazine.org/blogs

The tag line to the widely known magazine is "Feminist Response to Pop Culture," and that's what it is. *Bitch* opens up a fun and candid dialogue about feminism and activism in the familiar context of movies, TV shows, books, and current events.

ith me so bad! It was so cute. But
gym he didn't really talk to me at a
cept to inform me, "█████ did it, he said
"I wasn't really that surprised
at █████ started ██ the rumors. The
n't really bother me. But they certa
ther █████. He called me today to te
e: "I don't know what to do." "Abou
hat?" "Everything." "I was like, oh......k
continued, "█████ is so pissed off—" "W
es she care?" "I don't know." "Becc
e likes you, that's why." ████ "She's
ways making fun of you." "Why? I do
n know her!" He said, "You have to
front her." "What good will that do
ne." "Well, if you don't..... you know. J
st gonna have to listen to her." "Oh,
ell, I can only take like, a week more
bashing you."
ranslated: If I don't confront ████
s going to dump me. I hate it when
does this!!!
 said, "The only reason she bashes m
ecause she likes you!" He said, "Okay

EDITOR'S NOTE

The process by which we selected and edited the diary entries included here was surprisingly straightforward. After Emily had transcribed the entirety of her middle school diaries and changed the names of people and places (more information about which you can find in Emily's introduction), we only had to correct some handwritten typos and provide a handful of basic edits for clarity and consistency. We thought it was important to maintain Emily's middle-school syntax and thus avoided any further alterations except in cases where clarity was compromised—and in those situations we tried to choose the simplest solution as the best one. That done, her entries were basically ready to print. (She was clearly an excellent writer, even at eleven.)

Emily's diary is poignant both in what it says and in what it fails to say—as her new comments make so clear—and her silences, in particular, would have been less meaningful if surrounded by any amount of extraneous material. The ideal case would have been the simple reprinting of her original, handwritten account. But after protecting the privacy of the people (in most cases the children) involved, I hope that we have been able, in a sense, to keep it all.

Feb. 18, 1998

I was talking to ▓▓▓▓ on the phone today, and she said that she thought everyone was born with a soulmate. Someone you were meant to be with. She said "My soulmate is probably in ▓▓▓▓▓▓ running around with nothing on but a leather thong. But you're so lucky! You and ▓▓▓▓ are definately soulmates. You are so perfect for each other!" I think we are, too. I can't think of anyone I'd be happier with. I borrowed ▓▓▓▓▓ CD from the movie <u>Romeo and Juliet</u>. It is the CD we were listening to on Halloween. The song that was playing while ▓▓▓▓ and I kissed is called <u>You and Me Song</u>. It is by the Wannadies. The chorus goes:

Turn the page

Feb. 24, 1998

Today in Library Skills, ████ was flirting with me so bad! It was so cute. But in gym he didn't really talk to me at all, except to inform me, "████ did it, he said so." I wasn't really that surprised that ████ started ██ the rumors. They don't really bother me. But they certainly bother ████. He called me today to tell me: "I don't know what to do." "About what?" "Everything." I was like, oh......kay. He continued, "████ is so pissed off—" "Why does she care?!" "I don't know." "Because she likes you, that's why." ████ "She's always making fun of you." "Why? I don't even know her!" He said, "You have to confront her." "What good will that do? None." "Well, if you don't..... you know. I'm just gonna have to listen to her." "Oh, God... "Well, I can only take like, a week more of her bashing you."

Translated: If I don't confront ████ he's going to dump me. I hate it when he does this!!!

I said, "The only reason she bashes me is because she likes you!" He said, "Okay. ██ So there are two possibilities why she hates

It's easy to live with your eyes closed
And not understand what you see.
It's those who are blind that can live in a sky
Of peace and tranquility.

You'd see what is real, and all that brings pain
If you' would just open your eyes
So save yourself from the frightening truth
And hide behind happier lies.

                              —Me 3/13/98

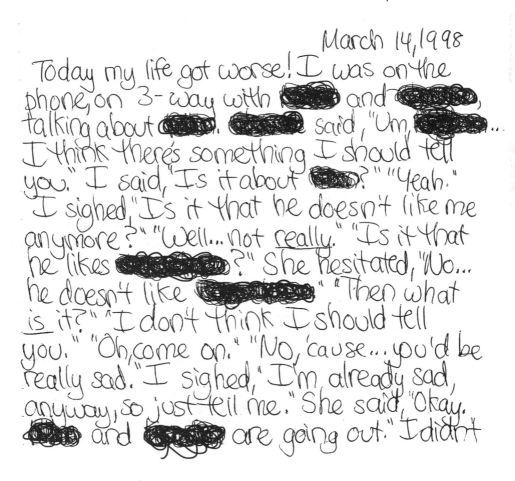

March 14, 1998

Today my life got worse! I was on the phone, on 3-way with ▓▓ and ▓▓, talking about ▓▓. ▓▓ said, "Um, ▓▓... I think there's something I should tell you." I said, "Is it about ▓▓?" "Yeah." I sighed, "Is it that he doesn't like me anymore?" "Well... not really." "Is it that he likes ▓▓?" She hesitated, "No... he doesn't like ▓▓." "Then what is it?" "I don't think I should tell you." "Oh, come on." "No, 'cause... you'd be really sad." I sighed, "I'm already sad, anyway, so just tell me." She said, "Okay. ▓▓ and ▓▓ are going out." I didn't

■■■ and I have a really good relationship. It is like, fun. I am comfortable around him - I can make fun of him, he can make fun of me, and neither of us is ever serious. We write notes every day, and talk on the phone almost every night. We talk about weird things, like what we were afraid of as kids, and homemade valentines. Two nights ago, we were talking about our crazy relatives. He said, "One summer, my grandmother came to stay with us, and she wore this strong perfume. For the whole summer, the entire house smelled of perfume, and I smelled of perfume." In that instant, I knew I loved him. He could have said, "smelled like perfume," but instead he said, "smelled of." That just made him so perfect to me. Last night, for some reason, I was afraid to call him. I had a weird feeling that he didn't want to talk to me. I was really hoping, though, that he would call me, because I wanted to talk to him. And then he did. I was down in the basement, and my sister called to me from upstairs that I had a phone call. I really, really hoped it was him, but I knew it wouldn't be, and I didn't want to get my hopes up. But when I got to the top of the stairs, my sister smiled and whispered, "It's him," as she handed me the phone. I was so glad! I am so infatuated by him I can't ever stand it! ■■■ predicted a long time ago that ■■ and I would go out. He said, "You and ■■■ are so gonna go out. One day, he's gonna realize he likes you, and then you'll realize, too." I remember the first time I saw him, in 5th grade. I was new and ■■■ was showing me who everyone was. ■■■ was playing basketball, wearing a green and blue plaid parka and a baseball cap. ■■■ said, "That's ■■■ the most popular boy in the grade. He's from ■■■." At the time, I